Money and Justice

Money has always represented power. For Aristotle, this power was inseparable from the exercise of justice within a community. This is why issuance of money was the prerogative of the lawful authority (government). Such a view of monetary power was widespread, and includes societies as distant as China. Over the past several centuries, however, private interests increasingly tapped into the exercise of the money power. Through gradual shifts, commercial banks have gained a legally protected right to create money through issuance of debts. The aim of this book is to unravel various layers hiding the real workings of modern money and banking systems and injustices ingrained in them.

By asking what money really is, who controls it, and for what purpose (why), the book provides insight into understanding modern money and banking systems, as well as the causes of growing financialization of economies throughout the world, money manias, and economic instability. The book also increases the awareness of injustices hidden in the workings of modern money and banking systems and the need for moral underpinnings of such systems. Finally, it suggests a money system that could immensely improve human, economic, and ecological conditions.

Leszek Niewdana, a Catholic priest from Poland, teaches mainly business ethics in the College of Management at Fu Jen Catholic University in Taiwan. He holds an MBA degree from the University of Southampton and a PhD in Christian Ethics from Heythrop College, University of London, England. Following the 2007–2009 financial tsunami, his interests have increasingly focused on ethical issues in financial and monetary systems.

Money and Justice

A critique of modern money and banking systems from the perspective of Aristotelian and Scholastic thoughts

Leszek Niewdana

Routledge
Taylor & Francis Group
LONDON AND NEW YORK

First published 2015
by Routledge
2 Park Square, Milton Park, Abingdon, Oxfordshire OX14 4RN

and by Routledge
711 Third Avenue, New York, NY 10017

First issued in paperback 2017

*Routledge is an imprint of the Taylor & Francis Group, an
informa business*

© 2015 Leszek Niewdana

The right of Leszek Niewdana to be identified as author of this
work has been asserted by him in accordance with the Copyright,
Designs and Patent Act 1988.

All rights reserved. No part of this book may be reprinted or
reproduced or utilised in any form or by any electronic,
mechanical, or other means, now known or hereafter invented,
including photocopying and recording, or in any information
storage or retrieval system, without permission in writing from the
publishers.

Trademark notice: Product or corporate names may be trademarks
or registered trademarks, and are used only for identification and
explanation without intent to infringe.

British Library Cataloguing-in-Publication Data
A catalogue record for this book is available from the British Library

Library of Congress Cataloging-in-Publication Data
Niewdana, Leszek.
  Money and justice : a critique of modern money and banking
systems from the perspective of Aristotelian and Scholastic
thoughts / Leszek Niewdana, SVD.
    pages cm
  Includes bibliographical references and index.
  1. Money—Moral and ethical aspects.   2. Money—Philosophy.
3. Banks and banking—Moral and ethical aspects.   4. Banks and
banking—Philosophy.   5. Justice.   6. Aristotle.   7. Scholasticism.
I. Title.
  HG220.3.N54 2015
  174'.4—dc23
  2014018437

ISBN 13: 978-1-138-06687-8 (pbk)
ISBN 13: 978-1-138-78588-5 (hbk)

Typeset in Galliard
by Apex CoVantage, LLC

Quotations from *The End of Money and the Future of Civilization by
Thomas H. Greco,* copyright © 2009, used with permission from
Chelsea Green Publishing Co., White River Junction, Vermont (www.
chelseagreen.com).

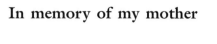

In memory of my mother

Contents

Acknowledgments

I would like to express my heartfelt gratitude to my colleagues at Fu Jen Catholic University for their thoughtful comments and especially for their moral support, so valuable in enabling me to accomplish this project. I am particularly indebted to Fr. Daniel Bauer, SVD for his painstaking proofreading of the text.

My special appreciation also goes also to my publisher, Taylor & Francis, for outstanding professional assistance in numerous ways.

1 Introduction

The economic depression following the 2007–2009 financial collapse is not over yet, and quite likely it will still take some years before the world economy in its present structure gains more stability and growth – if ever.[1] In fact, the expected recovery from the financial meltdown may also need a new definition of the essential indicators of future economic output. Meanwhile, post-collapse depressed economies of many countries continue to take their lot of *human suffering*. While in the immediate aftermath of the collapse much of suffering was caused by bankruptcies and lost jobs and/or properties, now it additionally takes the form of the imposition of austerity programs and budget cuts. What is, however, deeply disturbing about all this suffering is that innocent people have had to shoulder the consequences of greed and the gambling urge of many financial institutions. The financial collapse was not only about wiping out trillions of dollars of so-called wealth. And it was not just a few bad apples that caused the crisis. At the heart of it all was an insatiable desire for money that has now spread its roots from an individual to an institutional level.

One of the upshots of the sudden worsening in the conditions of many people in the aftermath of the financial collapse was an outburst of popular anger, which quickly spread over the media. Perhaps the most visible expression of it were the "Occupy" movements seen in various cities around the world, which turned into a symbol of protest against the gambling of financial institutions at the cost of the public. While some of the money pumped into the banking system has been or will be returned, it is hard to imagine that the suffering caused by the collapse will be acknowledged. Financial institutions did not apologize for their role in the buildup to the crisis and the suffering they caused, and banks did not express gratitude to the public for saving them. On the contrary, banks acted if they were entitled to be saved.

Although the edge of the popular anger has primarily been aimed at the financial industry, governments cannot easily dismiss their "contribution" to the crisis. Over the past few decades, lax oversight of financial institutions and cheap money policies, mingled with big money poured into the lobbying of big power, have become an explosive mixture of "democratic" decision making and crony capitalism.

Undoubtedly, banks as well as politicians would like to put the recent crisis to rest and move on. Yet economic figures, and perhaps more importantly a deep popular dissatisfaction, do not allow the post-collapse dust to settle so easily. And it might turn out to be beneficial for humanity that the dust of the collapse has been kept in the air. The reason is that after such a huge crisis, it is important to continue debating not only about *who* was responsible for the collapse and *how* to repair the present financial system, particularly its oversight, but also to look again at the present economic system in its entirety. Ultimately, the causes of the crisis that began to loom in 2007 were much deeper than mere miscalculations on the part of overseers of financial systems or the misbehavior of some greedy financiers. This does not mean that prior to the crisis there were no voices critical of those ills and problems. Works of Hyman Minsky, Joseph Stiglitz, Charles Kindleberger and Robert Aliber, Michael Rowbotham, or Stephen Zarlenga can serve as noteworthy examples of such a critical stance.[2] Unfortunately, these and similar voices were drowned by the feverish rush to unprecedented riches that had engulfed entire economies.

Amidst the multiplicity of critical perspectives taken in the aftermath of the 2007–2009 financial tsunami, one can also detect a sense of injustice emanating from some discussions addressing the crisis. For example, in *Casino Capitalism*, Hans-Werner Sinn points to the problem of gambling and speculation as providing almost guaranteed profits. According to him, while casinos normally offer games "with a negative mathematical probability to win," the banking system managed to create a business model in which gambling almost guaranteed huge private profits "run at the expense of society."[3] Ellen Hodgson Brown, on the other hand, hints at the problem of injustice ingrained in the debt money system that dominates the modern world and appears to unnecessarily enslave many people.[4] In these and similar works, however, despite the sense of injustice they emanate, the real treatment of the issue of justice remains rather fragmentary.

The aim of this study is to focus primarily on the questions of justice as they affect modern money and banking systems, and to treat the interplay between money and justice in a more systematic way. The main argument driving this work is that lack of justice in the present monetary and banking systems should be considered among the factors affecting instability in modern economies. About three decades ago, Hyman Minsky (1919–1996) posed his by now quite famous hypothesis of financial instability. In plain contrast to the dominant mainstream approach assuming that economies were constantly seeking equilibrium, Minsky claimed that they actually were inherently unstable. The core of his argument was that in euphoric times, banks tend to lend freely, causing a rapid growth of bank credit, but with a sudden change of circumstances, banks can drastically reduce or even freeze lending, leading to economy-wide collapses. According to him, this pattern was at the heart of the instability characterizing modern economies.[5] The main argument of this book builds on Minsky's conviction of inherent instability of modern economies, but focuses on lack of *justice* ingrained in the current money and banking systems as one of the components affecting the instability of world economies.

The method undertaken in this study is twofold. First, the tools to critique the modern monetary and banking systems are the Aristotelian concepts of money and justice. Aristotle (384–332 BC) was among the first, at least in the Western world, to provide a relatively thorough view of money and its social and economic purpose. Yet while his tripartite function of money as means of exchange, unit of account, and store of value has become a standard in discussions on money, what is often forgotten is that his primary concern was how money could facilitate just exchanges among people. For him, justice was at the heart of the money issue. By revisiting Aristotle's concept of money, the main question this study poses is whether the modern money system meets the demands of justice. The medieval scholastics, many of whom anchored their views in Aristotle, are also included in the subtitle of this work because they made a unique contribution to the debate on money and justice, particularly with regard to usury.

One possible objection to taking the Aristotelian perspective in the critique of the present money and banking systems is that modern societies, including their diverse institutions, are far more complex than at the time of Aristotle. Admittedly, some aspects of the ways modern societies function, particularly their institutional aspects, have become very complex (and perhaps have even reached a peak of complexity). From the perspective of mainstream economics, one may argue, for example, that "there was no economics for Aristotle because there was no economy – no distinct social sphere with its autonomous laws of motion."[6] Nevertheless, it also has to be recognized that ancient Greek societies (and many others) had their complexities. What, however, becomes far more important to ask is: has *human nature* changed so much? Have human longings for justice, a good life, and happiness changed much? Are not systems and institutions we create meant to satisfy these longings?

Among the crucial concerns in the thought of Aristotle is how a human person can lead a good life, and thus acquire happiness. This teleological (from the Greek *telos* – an end, goal, or final cause) aspiration permeates both Aristotle's ethical and political deliberations. Alasdair MacIntyre, who contributed immensely to the revival of Aristotelian thought in the twentieth century, described Aristotle's teleological view of human nature as "a threefold scheme in which human-nature-as-it-happens-to-be (human nature in its untutored state) is initially discrepant and discordant with the precepts of ethics and needs to be transformed by the instruction of practical reason and experience into human-nature-as-it-could-be-if-it-realized-its-*telos*." Put simply, the model proposed by Aristotle departs from the "untutored" condition and presents how, by following the precepts of rational ethics (cultivating virtues), the ultimate aim of a good life can be achieved. In fact, this threefold scheme is reflected in many traditional ethical frameworks and in diverse cultural contexts, in which some form of *telos* serves as an important factor providing sense of direction in life.[7] In such a model, ethical considerations are all-encompassing, permeating all known strata of life.

The Enlightenment movement, by setting itself in opposition not only to the medieval but also the Aristotelian worldview, created a new model, in which freedom and rights of the self-interested individual and the equality between such individuals became the core values. In other words, the Enlightenment model practically removed the objectively set *telos* (anchored in the conviction that the good life could not be achieved without due consideration given to the common good), and ultimately turned self-realization of the dissociated individual into a new individualized *telos*. What restricts personal freedom and rights, treated as almost absolute values, are only requirements of the so-called social contract, now basically reduced to legal pronouncements. In this new model, "the self-interested pursuit of wealth" gradually became the "master motive" that "subsumed all others."[8] Classical virtues and the good life *telos* had no place in it. Moral minimalism based on the obligation to respect freedom and rights of others and the requirements of the social contract (the expanding number of laws) became the new standards of moral philosophy.

Despite the great contributions of the Enlightenment to human progress, particularly in terms of bringing to the fore the values of human freedom, rights, and equality between individuals, by overemphasizing these aspects of human reality the new model increasingly idealized an impoverished, dissociated concept of the human person. This was particularly true with the rise of neoclassical economics. As a result, while the early Enlightenment thinkers and classical economists, such as Adam Smith, still saw the need of keeping self-interested actions of individuals in balance with the common good, this began to change in the second half of the nineteenth century. Gradually the Enlightenment model captured public imagination and began to expand in ever-widening circles.

Yet over the past few decades, a growing number of thinkers are rediscovering the value of Aristotelian thought and the ideal of the good life. Through his work of comparing the thought of Aristotle with post-Enlightenment moral philosophies, Alasdair MacIntyre has reached the conclusion that Aristotelian concepts could serve as the vehicle for understanding "what the predicament of moral modernity is and why the culture of moral modernity lacks the resources to proceed further with its own moral enquiries, so that sterility and frustration are bound to afflict those unable to extricate themselves from those predicaments."[9] This is why he has argued that the threefold model – stressing the importance of an objectively set *telos*, and the cultivation of virtues, as the means to transcend the present human condition – was not just some kind of nostalgia for the past and idealizing of the past, but immensely relevant to the needs of modern societies.

In a similar vein, Skidelsky and Skidelsky point out that the conviction that human longings require some form of objectively set *telos* has been reflected in many civilizations. They remark:

> Aristotle's vision of the good life may be parochial, but his assumption that there *is* a good life, and that money is merely a means to its enjoyment, has been shared by every great world civilization except our own.

By articulating this assumption rigorously, Aristotle created an intellectual framework adaptable to widely differing ethical ideals. Followers of Judaism, Christianity and Islam were all able to make use of this framework; parallels to it can even be found in civilizations as radically alien to the West as India and China.[10]

Deeply troubled by the consumerist insatiability of modern individuals and the impact that the capitalist system exerted on quality of life in the form of the spiraling quest for more and more "wealth," the Skidelskys have found that the moral model geared toward the objectively set ideal of good life proposed by Aristotle could serve as a way out of the moral decadence of capitalism.

Also Michael Sandel, in his search for the model of justice suitable for modernity, finds the answer in Aristotle. It became clear to him that advancement of justice cannot be devoid of "cultivating virtue and reasoning about the common good." A discussion of the issue of justice from the perspectives of utilitarianism and the theories anchored in the notion of individual freedom leads Sandel to the following conclusion: "A just society can't be achieved simply by maximizing utility or by securing freedom of choice. To achieve a just society we have to reason together about the meaning of the good life, and to create a public culture hospitable to the disagreements that will inevitably arise."[11]

What these views clearly show is a growing discomfort with the post-Enlightenment focus on human nature as it happens to be, without envisaging how it could be transcended. In contrast, the tripartite Aristotelian model is far more holistic, oriented toward objectively set goals meant to elevate the human condition, and open to the possibility of enhancing a broader spectrum of values. This is why at least some academics attempt to reanimate "philosophical and ethical ideas that have long been out of favor."[12] An increase in the search for new heights and ideals worthy of moral consideration appears to be on its way.

Similarly, although to a smaller extent, the thought of Aristotle is also reflected in the renewed debate on money. In the nineteenth century, those who took the view of money as *nomisma*, or as money created by a lawful authority (government), found strong support in Aristotle.[13] More recently, Zarlenga has revisited the Aristotelian concept of money and found it very relevant to the modern world. Nevertheless, over the past several hundred years, Aristotle's view of money as *nomisma* was marginalized, if not suppressed, by private banking interests, economists, philosophers, and politicians. To Zarlenga, such intentional or unintentional moves away from the *nomisma* concept of money represent "the lost science of money."[14] An aspect revealed by the 2007–2009 financial crisis is a profound need to reevaluate our knowledge of *what* money is, *who* controls its issuance, and *what purpose* it serves. Although these questions seem simple at first glance, this book will show that a lot of misunderstandings about the nature of money remain. Such an outcome, at least to some degree, seems to be intentional. This is how Reed Simpson, himself a banker, puts it:

The process by which money comes into existence is thoroughly misunderstood, and for good reason: it has been the focus of a highly sophisticated and long-term disinformation campaign that permeates academia, media, and publishing. The complexity of the subject has been intentionally exploited to keep its mysteries hidden.[15]

The second aspect of the method undertaken in this study is the importance given to historical shifts. As life makes evident, in order to clean a house, one occasionally has to get dirty and dust different items found there. Such an undertaking, in addition to a cleaner house, may also result in some surprising discoveries. In a similar vein, after the crisis of such proportions as the 2007–2009 financial tsunami, it seems necessary to do some "dusting" of the diverse layers of the monetary and financial structures we have created. Only by making efforts to look back at what led to the crisis will we be better positioned to propose some remedies. Unfortunately, the utilitarian approach to diverse aspects of not only economic but also social, political, and even cultural life tends to marginalize the importance of historical knowledge. Moreover, with ever-growing compartmentalization of knowledge, solutions to some human phenomena often cannot be found in one particular narrowly set discipline. The search for improvements requires a more thorough interdisciplinary investigation. This is why diverse spheres of knowledge, such as philosophical, anthropological, religious, economic, financial, monetary, and so on are integrated in this work.

The underlying conviction of this study, then, is that at times it is worth looking back and listening to the words of wisdom coming even from the distant past. According to MacIntyre, we should "learn from some aspects of the past, by understanding our contemporary selves and our contemporary moral relationships in the light afforded by a tradition that enables us to overcome the constraints on such self-knowledge that modernity, especially advanced modernity, imposes."[16] History is full of twists and turns, some of which are crucial to later developments, while others are not. By looking back we can "unlock" the crucial shifts that brought us to the present stage. In those shifts we actually might find better solutions to our present problems. As such, the focus on historical shifts is not about glorifying the past and criticizing the present, but rather about the search for improving our future condition. This study, then, is not a mere postmortem of the 2007–2009 financial collapse. It is an expression of the concern that by patching up a few holes in the system, the deeper underlying problems will remain, and the institutional insatiability of the financial sector will continue to directly and indirectly victimize not only individuals but entire sections of society. An upshot of this is the argument stressing the need to liberate ourselves from certain ideological assumptions and see how much technological and human potential we possess to create far more just and stable monetary, financial, and eventually economic systems.

Following this Introduction, Chapter 2 revisits the dominant narratives of the causes of the 2007–2009 financial crisis and points to a deeper crisis of modern economies driven by fantasy prosperity based on debt. While manifold causes have been pointed to as enkindling the financial tsunami, such as deregulation and mistaken policies, widespread systemic drive toward financialization of economies, changing norms guiding economic behavior, and free market neoliberal ideology, they in fact were only vehicles driving the expansion of debt. The crisis exposed a deep vulnerability of the modern financial system constructed on growing debt at all levels of the contemporary economic system. As such, the chapter sets the stage for the discussion of the debt virus and its challenge to economic and social stability.

Chapter 3 presents how at a very early stage people in diverse societies began to notice the enslaving potential of debt. At the heart of the problem, they saw the charging of interest on lending, later named usury. Various forms of opposition to usurious lending can be found across legal, philosophical, and religious literature in Greek, Roman, and other cultural contexts. Usury prohibition, aiming to preserve at least a minimum level of justice in moneylending practices, gradually became an important moral standard that for centuries guided financial dealings. Aristotle's condemnation of usury, anchored in his analysis of the nature of money as of itself unable to yield more money, made a particular contribution to ascribing money a social function and to later debates on a morality of lending at interest.

Chapter 4 moves the debate on usury to medieval times and then presents important shifts that influenced later developments. The medieval scholastics, equipped with the accumulated knowledge of the ancient world, looked anew at the ethical aspects of borrowing–lending transactions, and ultimately developed a refined theory of usury. The crucial element in that theory was justification of the compensation to the lender. The developments initiated by the Protestant Reformation led to a direct opposition to Aristotle and the scholastics. As the influence of the Reformation movement spread, particularly in its Calvinist form, gradually the usury principle became blurred and the monetary views of Aristotle became marginalized. An important offshoot of that shift was a progressing money mania.

Chapter 5 takes up the issue of abuse of money power. Already in the Middle Ages, despite the widespread understanding of money in commodity terms issued by kings or princes, there was a gradual shift taking place in both the nature of money and the evaluation of who held power over its issuance. The criticism for an increasing abuse of money power was almost exclusively directed at rulers. What the critics failed to detect, however, was a secretive practice of private banks to create money through debt in the form of bookkeeping entries. This mixing of lending with the creation of money helped banking interests to make steady advances. The monies issued by several North American colonies and later by the government of the United States were among the last government attempts to regain the ancient prerogative of controlling the issuance of money.

Chapter 6 connects the growing power of banks to create money through debt with the issue of usury. Mixing of moneylending with the creation of money and multiplication of money through fractional reserve banking ultimately changed the nature of usury. It became institutionalized and buried in the structures of the very process of issuing "loans." The injustice of usury was no longer exclusively about interest rates. By the end of the seventeenth century, banks were already well entrenched in the money creation process and began to reach for the power to monetize not only the credit of individuals but also of the state itself. Turning debt into "money" allowed banks to shape the new meaning and very nature of money.

The aim of Chapter 7 is to demythologize the view of money as government creation. The core factor of the contemporary money supply is debt. Banks only transform the value of illiquid assets of customers, or whatever can be treated as collateral, into liquid "deposits" on their books. For banks these deposits become additional assets, and for borrowers they become "money" that can be spent. The role of the government treasury in the entire process of money creation is to provide securities (another form of debt), on the basis of which the central bank can increase "base money" (normally a small fraction of all money), which in turn allows the banking system to expand the amount of money in circulation through the issuance of debt. As such, the central bank can control how much base money is issued to the economy, but retain limited control over how much overall money is created through debt by commercial banks.

Chapter 8 discusses confusion over the moral category of indebtedness. For a long time, anthropological literature has argued that the moral force embedded in indebtedness and the principle of reciprocity, depending how it is utilized, can have a positive social function or become a tool of control. With the development of the commercial economy and the expansion of the right to private property, the moral obligation to pay one's debts gradually was also strengthened by legal responsibility toward creditors. Additionally, banks' secretive practice of creating money through issuance of debts in the course of time became their legally protected right. By distinguishing between moral and legal debt, the Aristotelian tradition placed itself right at the heart of the debate on the moral ambiguity of debts and indebtedness. However, the developments that took place after the seventeenth century have increasingly shifted the focus solely to legal debt.

Chapter 9 takes up the issue of injustice in the modern debt-based money system. From the perspective of basic dimensions of justice developed by the Aristotelian tradition, namely legal or contributive justice, commutative or corrective justice, and distributive justice, this study comes to the conclusion that the present debt money system has some strikingly evident injustices inherent in it. Moreover, structural injustices found in the debt money system are now well entrenched in the legal system. The result is that usury, as injustice ingrained in lending/borrowing exchanges, is not at all a thing of the past. It forms the very foundation of the present monetary and banking systems.

The focus of Chapter 10 is on the search for solutions. Different factions tend to propose different solutions to the present debt money system. The argument posed in this study is that democratization of the money system along the lines of the Aristotelian concept of *nomisma* – or truly government-controlled debt-free money – provides not only answers to *what* money really is, *who* controls its issuance, and for what purpose (*why*), but also reconnects monetary and banking systems with justice. At the same time, debt-free money offers enormous opportunities to counterbalance the scarcity aspects of modern economies and forms a basis for economic stability, a boost to local economies, and a far better protection of the environment. As such, the Aristotelian idea of money as *nomisma* makes deep human, economic, and ecological sense.

In Conclusions the emphasis is on the fact that, following the process of democratization of many aspects of the lives of individuals, communities, and nations, it is time now for our money system to break from the current system of plutocratic control and join this process of democratization. Among the challenges to such democratization will be not only the opposition of extremely privileged groups of financiers supported by some politicians, who will attempt at all costs to keep the present system intact, but also our ability to distance ourselves from ideologies, such as the minimal state, the near-sacredness of the free market, and ideology-charged economics that tend to influence our present money system far more than we are willing to admit.

Notes

1 A growing body of research by economic experts as well as energy experts postulates that economic growth, which has nearly become an object of veneration not only in economic and political spheres, but indeed among the public at large, is in the present form unsustainable. Richard Heinberg, for example, contends that the interplay between three crucial factors affecting modern economies – the depletion of important natural resources, the spread of negative environmental impacts, and financial disruptions – is bringing about the end of growth (R. Heinberg, *The End of Growth: Adapting to Our New Economic Reality*, Gabriola Island, BC, Canada: New Society, 2011). See also, e.g., J. Rubin, *The Big Flatline: Oil and the No-Growth Economy*, New York: Palgrave Macmillan, 2012; C. Martenson, *The Crash Course: The Unsustainable Future of Our Economy, Energy, and Environment*, Hoboken, NJ: John Wiley & Sons, 2011.
2 H.P. Minsky, *Can 'It' Happen Again? Essays on Instability and Finance*, Armonk, NY: M.E. Sharpe, 1984; H.P. Minsky, *Stabilizing an Unstable Economy*, New York: McGraw-Hill, 2008[1986]; J.E. Stiglitz, *Globalization and Its Discontents*, London: Penguin Books, 2002; J.E. Stiglitz, *The Roaring Nineties: Why We Are Paying the Price for the Greediest Decade in History*, London: Penguin Books, 2003; C.P. Kindleberger and R.Z. Aliber, *Manias, Panics, and Crashes: A History of Financial Crises*, 5th ed., Hoboken, NJ: John Wiley & Sons, 2005; M. Rowbotham, *The Grip of Death: A Study of Modern Money, Debt Slavery and Destructive Economics*, 4th ed., Charlbury, UK: Jon Carpenter, 2009; S. Zarlenga, *The Lost Science of Money: The Mythology of Money – the Story of Power*, Valatie, NY: American Monetary Institute, 2002.
3 H.W. Sinn, *Casino Capitalism: How the Financial Crisis Came About and What Needs to Be Done Now*, Oxford: Oxford University Press, 2010, pp. 70–71.
4 E.H. Brown, *The Web of Debt: The Shocking Truth about Our Money System and How We Can Break Free*, 3rd ed., Baton Rouge, LA: Third Millennium Press, 2008.

5 Minsky, *Can 'It' Happen Again?*; Minsky, *Stabilizing an Unstable Economy.*
6 R. Skidelsky and E. Skidelsky, *How Much Is Enough: Money and the Good Life*, New York: Other Press, 2012, p. 72.
7 A. MacIntyre, *After Virtue*, 3rd ed., Notre Dame, IN: University of Notre Dame Press, 2008, p. 53. See also, e.g., Skidelsky and Skidelsky, *How Much Is Enough*, p. 78.
8 Skidelsky and Skidelsky, *How Much Is Enough*, p. 51.
9 MacIntyre, *After Virtue*, p. x.
10 Skidelsky and Skidelsky, *How Much Is Enough*, p. 78; italics theirs.
11 Sandel, M., *Justice: What's the Right Thing To Do?*, New York, NY: Farrar, Straus and Giroux, 2009, p. 261.
12 Skidelsky and Skidelsky, *How Much Is Enough*, p. 217.
13 E.g., A. Del Mar, *History of Monetary System*, Honolulu, HI: University Press of the Pacific, 2000[1896].
14 Zarlenga, *The Lost Science of Money.*
15 R. Simpson, 'Foreword', in Brown, *The Web of Debt*, p. xi.
16 MacIntyre, *After Virtue*, p. xi.

2 Crisis of fantasy prosperity based on debt

The world economy had some real reasons to celebrate throughout the 1990s. Perhaps the greatest of them was the collapse of the socialist system in Eastern Europe, symbolized by the fall of the Berlin Wall in 1989, followed by the disintegration of the Soviet Union in 1991. Capitalism was experiencing its glorious moments as even China was opening up her economy to capitalist forces. Also India, after a period of socialist leanings, allowed capitalism to play a bigger part in its economy. Fast growth of these economies provided huge investment and trade opportunities. These, combined with a free market ideology that had been promoted already since the late 1970s, as well as technological advancements, particularly with regard to information technology, helped fill the sails of globalization. The result was that world economies expanded rapidly. In 2000, total world gross domestic product (GDP) was $36 trillion. In just six years, it grew to $70 trillion.[1]

In the atmosphere of feverish optimism, many began to believe that the economic nightmare of the business cycle had become a thing of the past. This is why the crises that hit some South American countries, such as Mexico and Argentina; the Southeast Asian financial crisis of 1997–1998; the burst of the dot-com bubble; and the Japanese economic crisis were seen more as examples of minor setbacks than signals of something happening much deeper in the world economy.

Even when a huge crisis was approaching, those who were supposed to keep economic foundations sound felt a strong sense of assertiveness. In its semiannual World Economic Outlook in April 2007, the International Monetary Fund (IMF) concluded that "risks to the global economy had become extremely low and that, for the moment, there were no great worries."[2] In March 2008, US Treasury Secretary Henry Paulson was even more optimistic: "Our financial institutions are strong. . . . Our banks are strong. They're going to be strong for many, many years."[3] Soon, the world was struck by the economic crisis that almost caused a global financial meltdown. The average world economic growth plunged from 5.2 percent in 2007 to –0.8 percent two years later – a drop of 6 percentage points.[4]

Dominant narratives of the causes of the 2007–2009 crisis

The financial crisis that began to show its first signs at the end of 2007 was the biggest since the Great Depression of the 1930s. Shock and anger that immediately followed the burst of the bubble gradually also intensified reflections and debates on the reasons that led to the crises. The arguments can be grouped around several narratives. Below we explore the most common of these.

Deregulation and mistaken policies

A wave of deregulations, initiated already in the 1970s, is often blamed as the main reason for the recent global economic crisis. Consumer credit in the United States was among the first to become deregulated. The "Marquette decision" of 1978 profoundly affected various types of consumer loans, particularly credit card loans. Before that, usury laws, some form of which every state had had in place since 1886, played a strong restrictive function, making the credit card industry rather unprofitable.[5] The Marquette decision allowed credit card lenders to charge customers from other states whatever rate was legally accepted in the issuer's home state. This, in practical terms, gave major banks enough power to pressure state legislatures to liberalize lending ceilings by threatening to move their operations to states with more relaxed limits on lending and charged interest rates. Gradually, relaxed usury laws allowed lenders to give credit even to the group of consumers with poor credibility and charge them with much higher rates for increased risk of default. In effect, the Marquette decision added significantly to expansion of the credit availability, but at the same time it contributed immensely to the increase of "the average risk profile of borrowers."[6] Quickly the pressure on the part of banks to liberalize the credit market began to spread like fire across the world.

Among the culprits sometimes blamed for loosening lending standards in the United States was the Community Reinvestment Act (CRA). Congress first passed the Act in 1977, and then substantially revised it in 1995, and again in 2005. Its main goal was to strengthen the borrowing power of customers from low-income neighborhoods. The Act in principle stated that "regulated financial institutions" had "continuing and affirmative obligation to help meet the credit needs of the local communities" in which they were chartered, but they were expected to do so without endangering their "safe and sound" operations. In order to enforce the Act, federal regulatory agencies assessed banking institutions' compliance with the statute and took the gathered information into account while evaluating those institutions' applications for new branches or for mergers or acquisitions.[7] For some free-market enthusiasts, the outcome of the Act was that "banks did what government regulators wanted them to do," meaning "to loosen lending standards."[8] Such enthusiasts however tend to marginalize the fact that the financial institutions were still responsible for keeping their operations safe and sound. Moreover, as Aaron Pressman points out, the majority of subprime loans, widely considered as sparking the 2007–2009 financial crisis, were issued by firms that weren't subject to the CRA requirements.[9]

While the Community Reinvestment Act could be viewed as playing a rather insignificant role in the volcano-like credit expansion, there appears to be widespread agreement that the Federal National Mortgage Association (Fannie Mae) and Federal Home Loan Mortgage Corporation (Freddie Mac) contributed immensely to the depth of the 2007–2009 financial crisis. At the time the crisis broke, Fannie Mae and Freddie Mac were private corporations equipped with a very peculiar legal status as their transactions were guaranteed by government. An earlier function of these two mortgage financiers was to buy mortgage loans from banks issuing such loans to consumers, thus allowing banks to remove the sold loans from their books and to issue more mortgage loans. The real change, however, began to take place in the 1980s, when securitization of mortgage loans (the pooling of mortgages into bigger bundles) began to gain acceptance and popularity. By buying mortgages from various mortgage-lending companies, bundling them into securities, and then selling them to other banks, mutual funds, pension funds, and other investors, Fannie Mae and Freddie Mac succeeded in absorbing an even larger amount of debt into the mortgage-lending system. When the financial tsunami struck, enormous debts soon overwhelmed Fannie Mae and Freddie Mac, and in September 2008, Treasury Secretary Henry Paulson put them into conservatorship – a form of bankruptcy – and guaranteed their combined $5.4 trillion in loans.[10]

In the 1990s the deregulation mania hit the US telecommunications and energy industries. Mixed with strong globalizing tendencies, the deregulatory ideology quickly spread throughout the world. For deregulation enthusiasts, however, it was financial liberalization that was the ultimate goal if the expected capitalist paradise was to happen in this world. The underlying economic argument for liberalization of capital markets was that "capital mobility would allow global savings to be allocated more efficiently, channel resources to their more productive uses, and raise economic growth."[11] Because the United States and United Kingdom had better developed financial markets, they expected to benefit immensely from the free flow of capital around the globe. As a result, they became strong supporters of global financial liberalization.

Among the main obstacles to the liberalization of the capital market in the United States was the Banking Act of 1933, often referred to as the Glass-Steagall Act, which separated investment banking from commercial banking and "created important federal rules and regulatory bodies to protect the public from haphazard bank speculation with their money."[12] The Act also declared a 10 percent cap on total income from securities transactions for commercial banks. After that, similar protection measures were introduced around the world. However, beginning already in the 1970s, both the laws and the oversight of regulatory bodies in the United States were "systematically weakened if not actually nullified by corporations, financial institutions and their collusive puppet legislators."[13] In 1996, the 10 percent limit on total income from securities transactions for commercial banks was increased to 25 percent,[14] and in 1999, in an almost unanimous bipartisan vote, the Senate repealed the Glass-Steagall Act.[15] In 2004, the banking regulation was further relaxed by amending the so-called net-capital rule for investment banks, allowing them to raise levels of leverage.

The drive for financial liberalization was not unique to the United States. In the 1980s, the Socialist French government of President François Mitterrand joined the move toward liberalizing capital markets. As one commentator observed, "what a conservative government feared to do . . . a Socialist government accomplished."[16] This was a crucial development, as France became a zealous supporter of free global capital mobility in continental Europe. As a result, by the late 1980s virtually all the major European countries removed capital controls. The region became "the most financially open in the world."[17]

While the repeal of the Glass-Steagall Act was an American way of promoting financial liberalization, what immensely affected the workings of the banking sector in many other countries was the relaxation of the internationally accepted banking rules under the Basel Accord. Prior to the crisis, the Basel rules required banks to hold 8 percent of their capital in reserve as a cushion against losses. Yet, for the banking industry, this was a hindrance limiting the amount it could lend, the level of risk it could take on and, ultimately, its profits. The magic of lobbying combined with the power of free market ideology turned out to be sufficiently persuasive forces to change that requirement. Soon later, the banks were allowed to raise their levels of leverage by lowering the share of common equity in the risk-weighted assets. The result was that banks became further exposed to the danger that if things went wrong, they would not be able to pay their debts.[18]

Of course, free-market enthusiasts disagree with the view that deregulation should be blamed for the crisis. Instead, they insist that mistaken policies of governments and the practice of cheap money pursued by central banks, particularly after the 2001 recession, were to be blamed for the crisis.[19]

However, a growing number of studies actually offer evidence that deregulation is indeed closely intertwined with banking crises. Already in 1996, Caprio and Klingebiel, taking up the issue of banks' insolvency, argued that financial liberalization combined with inadequate regulation and lack of supervision created an enormous potential for an explosion of banking crises.[20] In similar vein, Reinhart and Rogoff, looking at the historical data of many countries, came to the conclusion that "*periods of high international capital mobility,*" normally associated with financial liberalization, "*have repeatedly produced international banking crises, not only famously, as they did in the 1990s, but historically.*"[21] Sinn goes even further and claims that what drove the developments prior to the crisis was "the competition in laxity" anchored in the fear of regulators that in the era of globalization, stricter regulation in their own country would drive banking business elsewhere. For Sinn, this caused "a race to the bottom in regulatory standards."[22]

Financialization of the economy

The second strand of arguments discussing the causes of the 2007–2009 crisis tends to focus on the perspective of developments taking place within the economy. The saying that "you need two to tango" expresses the situation best. Destructive deregulatory competition on the part of governments found a dancing partner in the financial industry.

Already in the second half of the nineteenth century, Karl Marx (1818–1883), looking at the capitalist system of his time, began to point to contradictions intrinsic to the system. In his *Capital,* Marx argues that "the circulation of commodities is the starting point of capital," and that "the simplest form in the circulation of commodities is C-M-C," or Commodities-Money-Commodities. In this circuit money serves as a means to transform the commodities one possesses into those one is in need of. Yet he also points to the existence of a very different circuit, "M-C-M," or Money-Commodities-Money, in which commodities become merely the media of transforming money back again into money.[23] Moreover, in reality, the latter circuit looks for more money to be taken out of circulation at the end than was thrown into it at the start, meaning that the exact form is rather M-C-M′. Marx calls M′ "surplus value."[24] Of course, the C-M-C circuit also encompasses the possibility of an increase in the value between the two Cs, as the possessors of the commodities may take advantage of the differences in values by selling more expensively or buying at more cheaply than the set value. Nevertheless, as Marx argues, "such differences in value are purely accidental," whereas in the M-C-M circuit the "surplus value" is an intrinsic aim of the circulation, and thus M-C-M′ is a normal expected outcome. The M-C-M′ circuit tends to become "the general formula of capital."[25] Because in the M-C-M′ formula of capital there is a much stronger preoccupation with money, it ultimately may turn into an extreme form of M-M′, or money that directly produces more money.[26]

In effect, it appears that based on the intrinsic forces of the capitalist system, especially its tendency to give money an increasing role in capital accumulation, Marx anticipated the possibility of a massive preoccupation with money for its own sake. It took dozens of years before some of the above insights of Marx began to materialize. Apparently in Russia there is now a saying that "Marx was wrong in everything he said about communism, but he was right in everything he wrote about capitalism."[27]

The dangers of finance taking the dominant role in economy that Marx, and later others, warned about began to appear in mature economies in the 1960s. The United States is a striking example of the change taking place in advanced economies. There, in the late 1960s, the percentage of domestic profits coming from manufacturing began a steady decline. Yet it was only in the 1980s that the percentage of domestic profits advanced through the financial sector started to increase rapidly. In effect, while in the 1960s only about 15 percent of all US domestic profits came from financial investments, by 2005, income from financial investments reached almost 40 percent of domestic profits. Manufacturing, which in the 1960s still accounted for 50 percent of domestic profits, saw a drop in the mid-2000s to only 15 percent. Finance also began to show signs of growing importance to the bottom lines of many major nonfinancial corporations.[28]

Securitization became an important vehicle contributing to a widespread financialization of economies. A novel form of packaging loans, called collateralized debt obligations (CDOs), began entering financial markets in the mid-1990s. By that time markets had already known mortgage-backed securities, or financial products that bundled as many as thousands of mortgage loans, assuming, on the basis of the law of averages, an extremely low likelihood that they would all turn into bad debts. CDOs, on the other hand, allowed banks to securitize once again the claims that had already been securitized. Typical CDOs were divided into tranches with varying degrees of risk, thus making these new financial products more attractive to investors such as insurance companies, hedge funds, pension funds, and so forth. The level of risk in each cascade was evaluated by rating agencies, and, of course, payments depended on the level of risk taken by investors. It was only a matter of time before CDOs squared were created out of the existing CDOs. The next step was CDOs cubed.[29] The main purpose, of course, was to absorb as many risky loans as possible and mix them with less risky ones. Yet in effect, the creation of CDOs was "a credit laundering service," which for Wall Street became "a machine that turned lead into gold."[30]

A form of insurance in dealing with much more risk, but providing higher returns, tranches called credit-default swaps (CDSs) further exacerbated the fever of trading debts. For a fee attached to the CDS contract, the risk of default was transferred to another party, because the seller of the CDS was bound to pay the buyer for the losses. As confidence grew that house prices would only rise, at least for the foreseeable future, the trading of CDSs, including very risky ones, also increased. It soon turned out that the confidence in rising home prices was itself a devastatingly risky bet, and the CDS became "graveyard insurance."[31]

What additionally helped to feed the securitization bubble were structured investment vehicles (SIVs). These off-balance-sheet conduits were set up by banks in offshore places such as the British Virgin Islands, the Cayman Islands, Bermuda, or the Bahamas – not only to avoid taxes, but also to stay outside of regulatory terrain. As, so to say, virtual banks, SIVs helped the real banks to look less leveraged, and thus allowed them to free up additional capital for further lending. In effect, by riding the waves of confidence in the housing market, additionally fuelled by very low costs of borrowing (thanks to "cheap money" policy), banks issued more and more credit to borrowers with lower creditworthiness, or the subprime sector. Because subprime mortgages ended up securitized and sold to others, and rising home prices guaranteed that even in the case of default the loan could still be recovered, the appetite for more loans grew.

Yet perhaps the highest level of disconnectedness with the real economy was reached in the market for derivatives, a more complex form of securities. Derivatives are in principle side bets on the price movements of some investment called the underlying, such as commodity, a stock share, a currency, and so forth. As outside bets on how underlying assets will perform, derivatives are inherently driven by gambling.[32] Historically speaking, derivatives have been a long-standing tool of markets for hedging risks involved in contracts. The importance of derivatives to financial markets, however, began to spiral after 1973, when mathematicians Fisher Black and Myron Scholes came up with an equation, later known as the Black-Scholes option-pricing formula, which enabled putting a price on financial derivatives. In effect, this equation opened a new chapter in derivatives trading. It became particularly important to *credit* derivatives, which eventually turned finance into a "rocket science."[33] By December 2007, the "notional value" of derivative trades reached $681 trillion, meaning about 10 times more than the annual output of the entire world economy.[34] This was possible because derivatives can cause the notional values go anywhere market gamblers are willing to take them.

A unique contribution to financialization of economy and the fancy finance that infected financial markets prior to the 2007–2009 crisis was made by a small army of mathematicians, physicists, and engineers, sometimes referred to as "quants." Mark Joshi, himself a famous quant, has described a quant as a person who "designs and implements mathematical models for the pricing of derivatives, assessment of risk, or predicting market movements."[35] For at least a decade, the quants enjoyed sufficient freedom to put their computer models to miraculous work as few, including their own bosses and regulators, understood the models produced by them.

With the quants at the steering wheel, the world of finance was taken up by advanced mathematics, which was applied with the zeal characteristic to religious fundamentalism. Soon the financial world lost touch with common sense,[36] as the quants were squeezing into the system as many risky loans as possible (such as subprime mortgages) without considering a system-wide collapse, which as history and common knowledge tell us occurs not infrequently. In effect, however, they were hiding the real risk by complicating it.[37] Apparently, the mathematical models were good only for the market's good times, and in the end they broke the financial system. But that was no longer a problem for quants. By the time the crisis hit, a number of them had already become millionaires!

Overall, then, finance, particularly in the developed countries, began to increasingly dominate modern economies, and the abstracted "paper wealth" became their powerful inner force. What drove the process was the illusion of security from crises, fuelled with cheap money and encouragement from free market gurus. In fact, this illusion of security gradually became a new reality. Equipped with powerful computers and mathematical formulas, the world of finance moved into a fantasy land of economics. The events that took place in the US financial markets, and also in other countries such as Iceland and Ireland, epitomize the madness that has become an intrinsic part of the modern financial system. Even Marx, in his prophetic analysis of how the capitalist system would rely more and more on the M-M′ (money directly producing more money) form of capital formulation, could not foresee how far the financialization of economy would emblaze entire societies.

Changing norms

The saying "you need two to tango" also expresses well the notion that at the dancing party, when the banks and financial companies first danced with politicians, they soon changed their partners for customers. Underneath the new dancing mode was a profound change in norms, which ultimately are of a moral nature.

Traditionally, debt had a stigma attached to it, as across many cultures indebtedness was associated with inferiority. This, however, began to change radically over the past few decades. The ability to take on more debts to buy a house, or a bigger house, or another house, or a yacht became a sort of greatness. The explosion of consumer debt in the past two to three decades is a manifestation of a tacit and yet important cultural shift.[38] The freedom from stigma associated with being deeply indebted, or in other words a new culture of debt, "helped" many Americans to own houses they could not afford to pay for.[39] Yet the culture of debt has not been characteristic only of American society. It has spread throughout many countries, including those built on more traditional values such as Confucianism and Buddhism.[40]

While the deepening belief in the magic of the "new finance" brought along an increase in reckless lending, the shifting perception toward indebtedness on the part of consumers led to a massive growth of careless borrowing. At the turn of the millennium, the mortgage debts and credit card debts of many customers reached levels that were beyond their ability to continue their payments. At least for some of them, debt enslavement had become a surprising reality.[41]

It is the shift in the perception of greed, however, that is perhaps one of the most obvious aspects of the changing norms. Some critics have attributed the financial tsunami that hit the world at the end of 2007 to greed.[42] Others tend to disagree that greed is to be blamed for the last financial crisis. In the view of White, for example, the mere existence of greed cannot explain why the crisis turned out to be so severe. For him, greed cannot be blamed for the crisis because greed as such is "like gravity" – it is "a constant." This is why, similar to the statement that "an unusually high number" of airplane crashes cannot be blamed on gravity, the "higher than usual" occurrence of "financial crashes" cannot be attributed to greed. Thus, typical of free-market enthusiasts, White takes the stance that the government should be blamed for all "the financial mess" brought by the crisis.[43]

One, however, does not have to be a physicist to see that comparing greed to gravity is grossly simplistic. Undeniably, greed is as old as humanity. But it has always been understood as a human vice, the exercise of which occasionally caused crises and damaged human relations. As such, greed was kept in contempt and was seen as in need of control, either through legal enforcement or moral constraint. Yet over the past few decades, greed has been presented as a positive force contributing not only to individual enrichment, but also to the progress of entire societies. Such perception of greed is occasionally attributed to Gordon Gekko, a fictitious character portrayed by actor Michael Douglas in the 1987 film *Wall Street*, in which he declared: "Greed, for lack of a better word, is good. Greed is right. Greed works. Greed clarifies and cuts through to the essence of the evolutionary spirit." The character reappeared in the 2010 film *Wall Street: Money Never Sleeps*, again played by Michael Douglas.

The "greed is good" view did not remain merely in the sphere of movie entertainment. It began to take much deeper roots. One of the enthusiasts promoting this view was former professor at the London School of Economics Lord Meghnad Desai. "Societies based on greed are in one sense immensely liberating, which societies based on virtue are not," Desai has said. This is so because greed makes people focus on the exchange of goods and profits, which in turn reduces prejudices and discrimination based on "narrow grounds," such as color of skin, gender, race, religion, or social status. For Lord Desai it was only the rise of capitalism that brought humanity a new way of looking at other people, and new levels of tolerance that religions could not provide. According to him, "before capitalism came along, religions were horrible things which went around killing people." So it was only the growth of what he calls "secular materialism" that brought humanity to a higher stage of tolerance.[44]

Despite attempts to present greed as a constructive social force, it is difficult to refute the argument that greed indeed played its role in bringing the entire financial system to its knees.[45] Prior to the crisis, among the most obvious expressions of the destructive impact of greed was a culture of excessive risk-taking. Because taking huge risks was the ultimate reason for giant bonuses, it became particularly strong among the big banks' traders. Such a culture of risk-taking was at least tolerated, if not directly encouraged, by the CEOs, as much of the assumed profits for banks came from trading. Trading loaded with extreme risks "helped" some of the traders to hit the front pages of newspapers. At the time of the crisis, Jérôme Kerviel of Société Générale became perhaps the most famous "rogue trader." His trading caused his bank to lose $7 billion. Although management was quick to depict Kerviel as "a lone operator who spiraled out of control," interviews with employees showed that he was more the product of a corporate culture that welcomed risk-taking, as long as it brought profits for the bank.[46] Kerviel was sentenced to three years in prison.

Sky-high bonuses also show how greed increasingly ate into the banking and, indeed, entire financial industry. Even after the banking foundation began to collapse, Wall Street bankers were still getting high bonuses to – as the claim of the industry puts it – encourage superior performance. As it turned out, the entire reward system encouraged short-term profits gained through taking gambling risks. A stark example of how detached from reality some of the bankers became is the case of Stanley E. O'Neal, the former chief executive of Merrill Lynch. In March 2008, in the midst of the financial tsunami, O'Neal declared: "As a result of the extraordinary growth at Merrill Lynch during my tenure as CEO, the board saw it fit to increase my compensation each year." Of course, he did not have the courage to say that all that growth was just a mirage. If that was not enough, O'Neal became even richer by leaving Merrill Lynch, as the bank granted him an exit package of $161 million on his departure.[47] In fact, at the height of the crisis, about seven hundred Merrill employees received bonuses worth $1 million or more.[48] Only after a huge public outcry, the excesses, so steeped in a spirit of self-congratulation and self-reward, were trimmed down. Even so, only a few bankers returned their bonuses.[49]

As working in finance began to guarantee much higher earnings, university finance departments lured a growing number of students. For example, the number of Harvard graduates who went into finance increased threefold between 1970 and 1990, from 5 to 15 percent. In other traditionally highly valued professions, such as law and medicine, the share of graduates fell substantially.[50] In the climate that presumed greed to be good, a new philosophy among the freshly baked graduates began to take root: make quick bucks and retire before forty.

What also well epitomizes the growing acceptance of greed as a normal factor of social relations is the creation of vast Ponzi schemes. The most famous of these was constructed by Bernard Madoff. In his cleverly orchestrated scheme, at least $50 billion (some estimates say $65 billion) of institutional and personal wealth was lost in the United States, Europe, the Middle East, and Asia. During the roaring 1990s, while AAA-rated corporate bonds yielded 7 to 8 percent interest, Madoff lured customers by offering rates of 10 to 15 percent.[51] By creating the image of smooth high profits, he was able to stir among many wealthy investors the urge to invest their money with his Investment Securities. In 2009, after the scheme collapsed, Madoff was sentenced to 150 years in prison. Looking at the Ponzi scheme he created, one can only wonder what happened to human rationality, for both investors and regulators, that made Madoff's mesmerizing appeal survive for 20 years. Apparently, greed once again showed its blinding effect.[52]

Neoliberal ideology and ideology-charged economics

The music to the two forms of dancing described above came from a peculiar form of ideology propagated by a wide range of educators, businesspeople, and politicians. It only gradually became to be known as neoliberalism. David Harvey defines neoliberalism as "a theory of political economic practices that proposes that human well-being can best be advanced by liberating individual entrepreneurial freedoms and skills within an institutional framework characterized by strong private property rights, free markets and free trade."[53] Free market fundamentalism has been an expression of neoliberalism in the economic sphere. Nevertheless, neoliberalism has had an agenda significantly broader than merely economics. Its goal has been to reshape the entire social space of diverse countries into the form of the market. The preferred method of neoliberalism has been to release competitive forces in all possible spheres of life, including all layers of government and education, and turn them into variables of the market.

The roots of neoliberalism may be traced back to the Mont Pelerin Society, which first met in 1947. It was this society that instigated "the battle for ideas," proclaimed first by its founder, Friedrich von Hayek.[54] Yet it took an entire generation before the neoliberal project began its true implementation phase. Among the main reasons for the neoliberal turn was the economic crisis of the 1970s that hit the United States and Europe. The then taken-for-granted welfare state model began showing signs of weariness, most visibly manifested in rising inflation and unemployment. At the same time, political parties with communist and socialist orientations were gaining ground in various parts of the world. During the postwar period the share of assets held by the top echelons of society, particularly in the United States, also began to drop rapidly. This is why the neoliberal project has sometimes been referred to as a restoration of class power, because in the course of its implementation, the share of total wealth of the richest people began to return to prewar levels.[55] What particularly helped to promote the neoliberal program was the media, owned by the wealthy elite.

The beginning of the implementation of neoliberal ideology is often attributed to US President Ronald Reagan and his British counterpart, Margaret Thatcher. Among the key statements of Reagan's presidency was that the government was the problem, meaning that government was an obstacle to prosperity, and therefore its role needed to be trimmed. Thatcher, a keen follower of Hayek, on the other hand, became famous for the statement: "There is no such thing as society. There are individual men and women, and there are families."[56] This statement turned out to be iconic to the neoliberal ideology, which pushed for setting self-interested actors free from social constraints and thus utilize market forces for their own benefits as much as possible. Quite obviously, many *social* goods that did not match the neoliberal agenda were pushed to the background of this dominant paradigm, resulting in a weakening of the social fabric of many societies. Perhaps this is why Pierre Bourdieu has called neoliberalism "a programme of the methodical destruction of collectives."[57] In just over two decades since Reagan and Thatcher took power, neoliberal ideology was embraced by many governments around the world. Some even view developments in China as neoliberal in nature, only additionally colored with "Chinese characteristics."[58]

Perhaps the most intriguing aspect in the neoliberal project is the role of the state. Theoretically, the state is simply to oversee the basic institutional framework, for example, military, police and legal structures, which are necessary to protect private property and ensure the enforcement of contracts. Yet the developments that took place in the 1990s and early 2000s clearly demonstrate that the state not only protected markets, but also played an active role in creating new ones, or expanding them, even by force if necessary, and provided important assistance in utilizing the competitive potential of the market in diverse public and social spheres. Thus, in fact, neoliberalism has "transformed the state rather than driven it back" and, in effect, the policies of deregulation have actually led to creation of "new forms of regulation with new market-oriented rules and policies to facilitate the development of the 'new' capitalism."[59]

As neoliberal ideology reached ever bigger circles, many economists bought it up and gradually sold to it their profession. This is not to say that all mainstream economists subscribed to the theories of the Chicago School of Economics, the prime agent of free market fundamentalism, and its guru, Milton Friedman. The fact is, however, that, as Dani Rodrik puts it, economists "had become overconfident in their preferred narrative of the moment: markets are efficient, financial innovation transfers risk to those best able to bear it, self-regulation works best, and government intervention is ineffective and harmful."[60] Few, apparently too few, dared to stick out their heads, even if they personally disagreed with the dominant "narrative." Had they tried, their reputation and career would have been jeopardized.[61] As a result, many economists not only lacked professional courage, but actively supported the spread of free market fundamentalism, including financial liberalization.[62]

The humbling effect of the crisis on the economic profession became visible soon after the crisis began gaining momentum. Suddenly a few economists became stringent critics of what had happened. Perhaps among the most important "converts" was Paul Krugman. In one of the surprising statements he made in 2008, he admitted that much of what macroeconomics had been saying over the previous 30 years was "spectacularly useless at best, and positively harmful at worst."[63] Krugman was soon joined by veteran economist Paul Samuelson, who also regretfully admitted: "Many times during seven decades of economics teaching and textbook creation I have been wrong." Looking at the shifts that had taken place in the world prior to the crisis, Samuelson came to the conclusion that "gone forever, one hopes, are the idiocies of Friedman-Hayek libertarian selfishness."[64]

As a matter of fact, already in the 1980s, Amartya Sen pointed out that a serious rupture between economics and ethics was one of the crucial deficiencies in contemporary economic theory.[65] Later, Paul Ormerod came to the conclusion that "conventional economics offers a very misleading view of how the world actually operates, and it needs to be replaced."[66] What followed was an enormous wave of criticism of modern mainstream economics as a discipline that had lost touch with reality.[67] The spread of criticism of modern economics even includes a movement by economics students, later also joined by teachers of economics, termed the Post-Autistic Economics (PAE, or PAECON).[68] It is hard to find another academic discipline that has in recent years undergone an equal amount of criticism from within, from students and professors. Many mainstream economists, nevertheless, have remained faithful to their preferred neoliberal-leaning narratives. Their claim of a growing pluralism of approaches in modern economics[69] is in fact an increasing popularity among mainstream economists to focus their research on those aspects of economic activity where reality deviates from dogmatically set assumptions. As a result, economists are increasingly willing to work on the exceptions, rather than touch the basic assumptions of their field.

To sum up, the narratives discussing the cause of the 2007–2009 crisis point to a range of important shifts that took place over the decades prior to the crisis. Undoubtedly, their combination fuelled the bubble, which needed only time to burst. Yet the crisis also exposed a much deeper aspect of the vulnerability of the modern financial system, which has been far less discussed, namely a monstrous growth of debts. We now turn to this issue.

Debt virus as a growing challenge to the modern world

The statement "man is born free but is everywhere in debt" expresses well the worldwide phenomenon of growing debts.[70] Over the three decades or so prior to the 2007–2009 financial tsunami, most of the world, and especially the developed world, accumulated enormous debts, plunging entire economies into the abyss of debt. Behind a vast array of technological achievements, conveniences, and even what many would consider as necessities of our daily life, as well as glittering towers of corporate and financial institutions, were mountains of debt. A widespread view is that the spark causing the crisis came from subprime mortgages. Some, such as Jeff Rubin, argue that what really instigated the crisis was the spike in oil prices.[71] No matter which side of the argument one takes, underneath the explosion was the ultimate inability to deal with the gigantic amounts of debt.

Although the debt obsession varied from country to country, nevertheless, the overall trend was toward more debt. In the United States, total credit market debt stood at 143 percent of GDP in 1951, but by 2008 it had surged to 350 percent of GDP.[72] Interestingly, after the United States abandoned the pegging of the dollar to gold in 1971, its total debt doubled nearly every decade, reaching almost 53 trillion at the beginning of 2009.[73] A study by the McKinsey Global Institute estimated that the average total debt (of both private and public sectors) in ten mature economies rose from 200 percent of GDP in 1995 to 300 percent in 2008.[74] Among those economies, Japan amassed by far the biggest total debt, which grew from 244 percent of GDP in 1980 to 471 percent in 2009. It was followed by the United Kingdom with total debt of 466 percent in 2009. The total outstanding debt for Spain, which was classified as the country with the third-highest total-debt-to-GDP ratio, reached 366 percent in 2009.[75] What makes Spain rather special, however, is that in 2000 its total debt stood "only" at 193 percent of GDP, which means that it had almost doubled since the launch of the euro in 2000.[76] Yet it was smaller countries like Iceland and Ireland that expanded their debts to astronomical proportions, which in 2008 reached 1,200 percent and 700 percent of GDP, respectively.[77]

Worldwide growth of household debts

In the 1990s, riding the waves of deregulation fever in the financial sector, households around the world began running high debts. This was particularly true of developed economies. In the United Kingdom, for example, such debt rose from 68 percent of GDP in 2000 to 103 percent in 2009.[78] As a matter of fact, average British household debt had crossed the 100 percent level in the late nineties, which means that British consumers already then were spending more than their annual incomes and year after year were making more purchases against their future earnings.[79]

Spanish, Irish, and Greek households were a bit slower in going into huge debt. But that changed radically after they joined the euro, which due to lower interest rates made borrowing much cheaper. In 2000, the average Spanish family ran debts of 69 percent of their disposable income; by 2008 that figure rose to 130 percent – an enormous increase in indebtedness in just eight years.[80] A similar trend was observed among Irish households. By the time the crises hit, the average debt of Irish households reached 166 percent of their disposable income. Irish debt did not rise as dramatically as in Spain, however, because by the time Ireland joined the euro, average Irish families already ran debts equal to about 90 percent of their disposable income. In the case of Greece, which since 2010 became so much the focus of the debt debate in the European Union and beyond, its household debts doubled between 2002 and 2007, rising from 27 to 56 percent. Nevertheless, Greek households were still far from exceeding the levels of disposable incomes.[81]

In booming economies such as China, Brazil, and India, average household debt between 2000 and 2008 grew only from 4 percent of GDP to 12 percent in China, from 6 to 13 percent in Brazil, and from 2 to 10 percent in India.[82] Nevertheless, despite the fact that household indebtedness in those countries reached just fractions of their GDPs by the time the crisis struck, the speed with which household debt grew over the period of only several years was also rather disturbing.

Yet it has to be admitted that there were exceptions to this fever of life on credit. In more frugal Germany, for example, household debt actually fell from 71 percent of GDP in 2000 to 64 percent in 2009. Similarly, household debt in Japan dropped from 74 percent of GDP in 2000 to 69 percent in 2009.[83] The difference, however, was that whereas the German economy was in good shape, and was doing exceptionally well in the export sector, the economy of Japan had been trapped in low growth and deflation since the early 1990s. So it appears that the drop in indebtedness in Germany was for quite different reasons than in Japan.

Mortgages normally are a major component of outstanding household debts in many countries around the world. For years low interest rates, combined with lowered lending standards and rising home prices, became a huge temptation for incurring housing debts. Many people were buying up houses for simple reasons: to wait for the price of the house to go up and then sell it sometime later, even if the house stood empty until then. Earning money on such a deal was guaranteed, so only fools would not try to incur debts when such easy money could be made by such means. At least this was the logic at the time. A census in 2006 in Ireland discovered that the number of empty houses in the country reached 250,000, which was "an extraordinarily high number" when one considers that Ireland has a population of only four million.[84] Undoubtedly, many of those houses were mortgaged for purely speculative purposes.

Rationally speaking, what happened in Japan in the 1980s should have served as a signal of the dangers of the obsession with making easy money in the housing market. At the height of the property bubble, Japanese companies began creating "generational mortgages," even hundred-year mortgages.[85] Because such mortgages went beyond the life expectancy of borrowers, this means that the obligation to pay off the debts was extended to the children, or perhaps even the grandchildren of the borrowers. After Japan's property bubble had burst, home prices plummeted by an average of 80 percent, leaving many individual consumers and financial institutions with huge debts.[86]

As it turns out, in economic activity, people rarely learn from past crises or experiences of others, and the Japanese experience remained merely its own. What followed was a housing boom fuelled by debt, which gradually grew to enormous proportions. In Spain, for example, between 1990 and 2009, property prices rose by 80 percent. In order to make houses still affordable, "50-year mortgages were becoming commonplace, offered with reckless abandon by mainstream Spanish banks."[87] Needless to say, Spain was moving in the direction of the "generational mortgages" offered earlier in Japan.

Credit card debt is most likely to be second largest category of consumer debts worldwide. Availability of such credit was the single most important factor in causing a huge expansion of the credit card market. For example, in the early 1990s, the British were borrowing on average around £2.8 billion a month on credit cards. Their borrowing fever reached its peak in December 2008, when the British borrowed £12.1 billion of "plastic money."[88]

A similar pattern of fast growing credit card debt was observed even in East Asia, traditionally known for having been more frugal and having higher saving rates than most of the countries in the West. At the end of 2005, Huang Tien-lin, a national policy adviser to the president in Taiwan, sounded the alarm about the problems of excessive credit card debt among its citizens. By that time, more than 100,000 Taiwanese – Taiwan has a population of only 23 million – became "card slaves," which caused huge problems "for both banks and the authorities."[89] An even more serious credit card debt crisis took place in South Korea. After the Asian financial crisis of 1997–1998, the country witnessed extraordinary growth in its credit card industry. Eager to boost economic growth, the government pushed for more relaxed regulation of financial markets to increase consumer spending. Allowing consumers to obtain credit cards on easier terms was an important aspect of that strategy.[90] An easier access to plastic credit soon also caused a spike in bad debts. Already in 2003, "nearly ten percent of the entire Korean population (approximately four million individuals) defaulted on their personal credit card debts or loans."[91] In the face of such an escalation in inability to pay off debt, and the fear that it would cause a downward debt spiral similar to the 1997–1998 crisis, the government stepped in and effectively bailed out many credit card debtors.[92]

Ballooning corporate debt

The pattern of incurring increasingly more debt had been particularly strong in the corporate world. Historically speaking, what the period of deregulation prior to the 2007–2009 crisis achieved was to make corporate reporting blur the difference between reality and fantasy. Perception became "far more significant than reality."[93] In the early 2000s, "repaying old debt with new debt" was becoming "an increasingly common practice."[94] In order to be able to take on more debt, companies began to rely more and more on financial engineering, by which debts were securitized and sold to others. Debts became like hot potatoes being tossed around. The crisis struck once the number of such potatoes turned out to be too high for the system to absorb.

A series of deregulations in the second half of the 1990s laid ground for an explosion of debts, and telecommunications became the hottest sector of lending activity at the time. Soon after the Telecommunications Act of 1996 was passed in the United States, many countries around the world (sixty-nine altogether) decided to reduce barriers to access their telecommunications markets. In just a few years, telecommunication companies managed to obtain hundreds of billions of dollars in loans. This, in turn, led to an enormous overcapacity of fiber-optic networks. By the time the crisis struck in 2001, telecommunication companies had already created "over twenty times more capacity than demanded." One estimate speaks of the fiber mileage as enough to circle the globe eleven thousand times.[95] The debt-fuelled mania in that sector led also to some ridiculous takeovers, the most striking example of which occurred in 1999, when Global Crossing, a two-year-old company with about two hundred employees, took over Frontier Communications Corporation, a 100-year-old company with twelve thousand employees. In January 2002, Global Crossing filed for bankruptcy, owing $12.4 billion to its creditors,[96] and became the largest telecommunication company to go bankrupt at the time. Half a year later, WorldCom went far beyond Global Crossing by becoming the biggest bankrupt company in the sector.

A very similar pattern developed in the energy sector, which was deregulated around the same time as the telecommunications industry. Huge amount of loans also began to flow to energy companies. By the late 1990s, some of the companies even managed to mix their trading with financial operations. By inserting this extra component, they increasingly resembled financial trading companies, which, in turn, helped them to easily disguise loans as trade deals and thus take on even more debt. Enron was particularly good at that. Being an aggressive trader and using its image in the market, it was able to obtain US$5 billion in such disguised loans from JPMorgan Chase alone.[97] With the image of a trading star, Enron traded anything it could find trading partners for, from energy to weather to earthquake risk. When the company filed for bankruptcy at the end of 2001, it soon became a symbol of how corrupt some of the corporate world had become. Although the prevailing rhetoric at the time was that the problem was rather with just a few "bad apples," voices of insiders were warning that Enron was "just the tip of the iceberg."[98]

Another sector that became hugely indebted was the automobile industry. In the midst of the hot debt-issuance atmosphere, car companies were particularly keen on expanding their influence in accessing more and cheaper loans. The process caused the car companies to do business with a selected cartel of banks. Their need to raise adequate capital for producing cars and loaning money to car buyers made them extremely dependent on banks. Yet at the same time, banks needed them because they were "high-volume repeat borrowers" who paid "a lot of fees." It was "a classic back-scratching relationship." GM and Ford can serve as an example of how such close relationships led to huge indebtedness. Already in the early 2000s, GM amassed $186 billion and Ford $162 billion in debts. The combined debt of the two companies accounted for 5 percent of all outstanding corporate debt in the United States.[99] As a result, over the past decade, the US car industry has been in particular need of life support.

The deregulation of the banking industry also allowed banks to substantially raise their levels of leverage. Soon, banks' leverage ratios skyrocketed. In the United States the big banks' median leverage ratio reached 35 to 1, meaning that for every $1 in equity capital the banks had equaled $35 of borrowed money or securities (negotiable financial instruments carrying certain values). This, however, was still relatively low compared to some of the big European banks. On June 30, 2008, just before the crisis wave hit many financial institutions, their ratios were: Barclays Bank, 61.3 to 1; Deutsche Bank, 52.5 to 1; ING Group, 48.8 to 1; UBS, 46.9 to 1; Crédit Agricole, 40.5 to 1; BNP Paribas, 36.1 to 1; Lloyds TSB, 34.1 to 1; Credit Suisse, 33.4 to 1; Fortis, 33.3 to 1; HSBC Holdings, 20.1 to 1; RBS, 18.8 to 1. The median leverage ratio in the European Union was about 45 to 1.[100] In reality, the leverage ratio could have been far higher, as banks that engaged in the trading of derivatives were allowed to keep chunks of their assets and liabilities off their balance sheets.

What further exacerbated the debt problem of the corporate world over the last decade or so was the appearance on the stage and fast growth of nonbank financial intermediaries. Unlike banks, such institutions typically borrow short in order to lend long, and therefore it becomes crucial for them to be able to roll over short-term debt. Put simply, from a regulatory point of view they were not banks, but they nevertheless performed banking functions. It was this system that greatly contributed to the acceleration of the debt crisis.[101]

The year 2008 will go down in financial history as the year the world banking system, overwhelmed by the widespread crisis, was on the verge of an abyss. Sinn calls it "a year of bank failures," because in that year well over one hundred banks around the world disappeared due to bankruptcies, acquisitions, or nationalizations.[102] Having reached the point of total collapse, leaders of the banks that were "too big to fail" essentially forced governments to save them. Worldwide bank rescue packages put together reached $7.3 trillion.[103] The bigger difficulty, however, is that nobody knows the real size of the debt hole in the banking system.

Escalation of public debt

The crises that hit economies of various parts of the world in the late 1990s and early 2000s put an enormous pressure on governments to increase the level of public debt. Many governments around the world faced growing debt pressure. For example, following the burst of Japan's property bubble, the Japanese government came up with several stimulus packages, consisting mainly of projects to build roads and bridges, even if they were not so much needed. Of course, much of that was financed with government borrowing, causing a rapid growth in Japan's public debt. In 1991 its government was still running a relatively high surplus of about 2.9 percent of GDP. Five years later it already had annual deficits of 4.3 percent of GDP.[104]

Yet it was the 2007–2009 financial crisis that forced governments around the world to increase sovereign indebtedness to unprecedented levels. In 2009, the total public debt of Japan reached 189 percent of GDP. In the United States and Canada, the sovereign debt expanded to 84 and 83 percent of GDP, respectively. According to the Maastricht Treaty, which laid the foundation for the euro project, the public debt of a member country should not exceed 60 percent.[105] But in 2010, the average government debt of the euro area crossed the line of 85 percent of GDP. By far the highest public debt was in Greece, where it reached 144.9 percent, followed by Italy (118.4 percent), Belgium (96.2 percent), Ireland (94.9 percent), Portugal (93.3 percent), Germany (83.2 percent), and France (82.3 percent). The Maastricht limit was exceeded to a lesser degree by countries like Austria (71.8 percent), Malta (69 percent), Netherlands (62.9 percent), Cyprus (61.5 percent), and Spain (61 percent). Among the EU countries outside of the euro area, high public debt was common in Iceland (92.9 percent), Hungary (81.3 percent), and the United Kingdom (79.9 percent).[106] At the height of the crisis, virtually all EU member countries crossed the Maastricht-set ceiling of 3 percent of annual budget deficit. The rise in some countries like Ireland, the UK, Latvia, and Greece was at least four times higher than this ceiling. In the United States the increase was also over 10 percent.[107] Perhaps most importantly, sovereign debts of many countries continue to grow.

Some argue that a high level of public debt is not a problem, particularly for the economies of developed countries. The stance of this faction is that in a case such as the US government, "there is no operational limit," and therefore "the federal government can, and does, spend what it wants."[108] Yet if history can serve as any indicator, sovereign defaults are becoming more and more frequent. A study by Eduardo Borensztein and Ugo Panizza found out that in the 180 years between 1824 and 2004, there were 257 sovereign defaults, but in the 9 years between 1981 and 1990 there were 74 such defaults.[109] In a similar vein, Reinhart and Rogoff were surprised to find a pattern of "the near universality of default" and that honoring of debt obligations by governments was "far from the norm."[110]

The International Monetary Fund (IMF) and the World Bank, the creatures of the Bretton Woods conference of 1944, have played a rather dubious role in mitigating sovereign debt problems. The main purpose of their establishment was to provide stability to the world economy by assisting in the development of poorer countries through loans (the World Bank) and by helping countries that faced temporary difficulties to keep their payments balanced, again by providing them with loans (the IMF). In the course of time, however, their activities actually began to exacerbate the debt problem. This became particularly striking since the 1990s, when the two organizations turned into ideologically charged instruments of market fundamentalism.[111] By then, the so-called Third World debt and debts of some developing nations already reached enormous proportions.

As it turns out, market liberalization pushed by the IMF increased the instability of developing countries. According to Reinhart and Rogoff, since the creation of the IMF debt problems have exacerbated, leading to "shorter but more frequent episodes of sovereign default." Apparently, the very existence of the institution has made both lenders and borrowers take greater risks, because in the face of trouble countries could always seek subsidies from the IMF, leading to a form of "moral hazard" in international lending.[112] Similarly, the World Bank also miserably failed its mission. In 2010, in its annual report on the forty-nine least developed countries (LDCs), the UN Conference on Trade and Development (UNCTAD) pointed out that "the number of very poor countries has doubled in the last 30 to 40 years, while the number of people living in extreme poverty has also grown two-fold."[113] In the view of Michael Rowbotham, the main problem with the model of development offered by the IMF and the World Bank was that it relied too much on "the loan/export/repayment theory," meaning that the loans should lead to growth of export, which in turn would facilitate repayment of the loans. Yet, in reality, loans of the poor and developing countries only further exacerbated their debt problems.[114]

Aware of the problem caused by indebtedness, particularly for the poorest countries, Pope John Paul II said, in his apostolic letter *Tertio Millennio Adveniente* on preparation for the year 2000: "in the spirit of the Book of Leviticus (25:8–12), Christians will have to raise their voice on behalf of all the poor of the world, proposing the Jubilee as an appropriate time to give thought, among other things, to reducing substantially, if not canceling outright, the international debt which seriously threatens the future of many nations."[115] In the face of growing difficulties for some countries due to unpayable debt burdens, that initiative gained attention also in some economic circles. Zarlenga even called the pope "the best economist."[116] Apparently, at least for some, the call of John Paul II made deep economic sense.

Looking from the postcrisis perspective, it is important to realize that the era of exotic finance is not over. Fancy finance will continue to intoxicate the financial system, because it has become a part of the belief that money producing money is the very nature of money. Finance normally is supposed to support the productive side of any economy. Yet over the past few decades, it gradually became disconnected from the real economy and began a life of its own. The world has shifted into "fantasy economics, creating fantasy prosperity."[117] At the heart of this fantasy economics is the peculiar role of debt. The following several chapters will take a closer look at debt dynamics and its correlation with the growth of fantasy economics.

Notes

1 J. Lanchester, *I.O.U.: Why Everyone Owes Everyone and No One Can Pay*, New York: Simon & Schuster, 2010, pp. 2–3.

2 C.M. Reinhart and K.S. Rogoff, *This Time Is Different: Eight Centuries of Financial Folly*, Princeton, NJ: Princeton University Press, 2009, p. 214.

3 In T.E. Woods, Jr., *Meltdown: A Free-Market Look at Why the Stock Market Collapsed, the Economy Tanked, and Government Bailouts Will Make Things Worse*, Washington, DC: Regnery, 2009, p. 37.

4 H.W. Sinn, *Casino Capitalism: How the Financial Crisis Came About and What Needs to Be Done Now*, Oxford: Oxford University Press, 2010, p. 6.

5 D. Ellis, 'The Effect of Consumer Interest Rate Deregulation on Credit Card Volumes, Charge-Offs, and the Personal Bankruptcy Rate', *FDIC: Bank Trends*, no. 98–05, March 1998. Available at: http://www.fdic.gov/bank/analytical/bank/bt_9805.html (accessed 11 November 2011).

6 Ibid.

7 'Housing and Community Development Act of 1977/Title VIII'. Available at: http://en.wikisource.org/wiki/Housing_and_Community_Development_Act_of_1977/Title_VIII (accessed 25 November 2011), Sections 802 and 804, respectively.

8 Woods, *Meltdown*, p. 18.

9 A. Pressman, 'Community Reinvestment Act Had Nothing to Do with Subprime Crisis', 29 September 2008. Available at: http://www.businessweek.com/investing/insights/blog/archives/2008/09/community_reinv.html (accessed 28 November 2011).

10 E.H. Brown, *The Web of Debt: The Shocking Truth about Our Money System and How We Can Break Free*, 3rd ed., Baton Rouge, LA: Third Millennium Press, 2008, p. 475.

11 D. Rodrik, *The Globalization Paradox: Democracy and the Future of the World Economy*, New York: W.W. Norton, 2011, p. 91.

12 N. Prins, *Other People's Money: The Corporate Mugging of America*, New York: New Press, 2004, p. 4.

13 Ibid.

14 D.P. Stowell, *An Introduction to Investment Banks, Hedge Funds, and Private Equity: The New Paradigm*, Burlington, MA: Academic Press, 2010, p. 32.

15 Prins, *Other People's Money*, p. 4.

16 In Rodrik, *The Globalization Paradox*, p. 103.

17 Ibid.

18 B. Eichengreen, *Exorbitant Privilege: The Rise and Fall of the Dollar and the Future of the International Monetary System*, New York: Oxford University Press, 2011, p. 101.

19 E.g., L.H. White, 'How Did We Get into This Financial Mess?', *Cato Institute Briefing Paper*, no. 110, 18 November 2008. Available at: http://www.cato.org/pubs/bp/bp110.pdf (accessed 17 November 2011); C.W. Calomiris, 'Another Deregulation Myth', American Enterprise Institute, 18 October 2008; J. Sachs, 'The Roots of the US Financial Crisis Lie with the Fed', *Taipei Times*, 27 March 2008, p. 9.

20 In Reinhart and Rogoff, *This Time Is Different*, p. 156.

21 Ibid., p. 155; italics theirs.

22 Sinn, *Casino Capitalism*, pp. 157–161. See also, e.g., Eichengreen, *Exorbitant Privilege*, p. 98.

23 K. Marx, 'Capital', in M. Hutchins (ed.), *Great Books of the Western World, vol. 50: Marx*, Chicago: Encyclopedia Britannica, 1952, p. 69.

24 Ibid., p. 77.

25 Ibid., pp. 71 and 73, respectively.

26 Ibid., p. 78.

27 In R. Heinberg, *The End of Growth: Adapting to Our New Economic Reality*, Gabriola Island, BC, Canada: New Society, 2011, p. 39.

28 J.B. Foster and F. Magdoff, *The Great Financial Crisis: Causes and Consequences*, New York, NY: Monthly Review Press, 2009, pp. 54–55.

29 Eichengreen, *Exorbitant Privilege*, p. 98.

30 M. Lewis, *The Big Short: Inside the Doomsday Machine*, New York, NY: W.W. Norton, 2010, p. 73.

31 Sinn, *Casino Capitalism*, p. 187.

32 Brown, *The Web of Debt*, p. 190.
33 Lanchester, *I.O.U.*, p. 45.
34 Brown, *The Web of Debt*, p. 192.
35 In R.R. Lindsey and B. Schachter, *How I Became a Quant: Insights from 25 of Wall Street's Elite*, Hoboken, NJ: John Wiley & Sons, 2007, p. 1. See also S. Patterson, *The Quants: How a New Breed of Math Whizzes Conquered Wall Street and Nearly Destroyed It*, New York: Crown Business, 2010.
36 E.g., Lanchester, *I.O.U.*, pp. 160–164.
37 Lewis, *The Big Short*, p. 73.
38 D. Brooks, 'America's Culture of Debt', *International Herald Tribune*, 23 July 2008, p. 5.
39 M.A. Dickerson, 'Over-Indebtedness, the Subprime Mortgage Crisis and the Effect on U.S. Cities', *Fordham Urban Law Journal*, 2009, vol. 36:3, 395–425.
40 J. Kim and K. Bhangananda, 'Money for Nothing, Your Crises for Free? A Comparative Analysis of Consumer Credit Policies in Post-1997 South Korea and Thailand', *Pacific Rim Law & Policy Journal*, 2008, vol. 17:1, 1–40.
41 E.g., T.L. Huang, 'Like "Go West," Credit Debt's a Threat', *Taipei Times*, 27 December 2005, p. 8.
42 E.g., N. Lawson, 'Back to Reality', *Time*, 13 October 2008, p. 23; D. Brooks, 'Greed and Stupidity', *International Herald Tribune*, 4–5 April 2009, p. 7.
43 White, 'How Did We Get into This Financial Mess?', p. 2.
44 BBC Radio 4, 'Current Affairs Analysis: The Undeadly Sin', 28 November 2002. Available at: http://news.bbc.co.uk/nol/shared/spl/hi/programmes/analysis/transcripts/02_11_28.txt (accessed 5 January 2012). See also, e.g., D. Kervick, 'An Open Letter to Harvard Economics Students', 10 November 2011. Available at: http://econintersect.com/b2evolution/blog2.php/2011/11/10/an-open-letter-to-harvard-economics-students (accessed 5 January 2012).
45 G. Morgenson and J. Rosner, *Reckless Endangerment: How Outsized Ambition, Greed and Corruption Led to Economic Armageddon*, New York: Times Books, 2011.
46 N.D. Schwartz and K. Bennhold, 'A Suspicion in France "That This Was Inevitable" ', *International Herald Tribune*, 6 February 2008, p. 1. See also the 2011 case of Kweku Abdoli, a UBS trader who cost the bank $2.3 billion in losses (J.B. Stewart, 'UBS Faces More Than Just a "Rogue" ', *International Herald Tribune*, 26 September 2011, p. 21).
47 L. Story, 'As Foundations Crumbled, Bonuses Rose on Wall St.', *International Herald Tribune*, 19 December 2008, pp. 1 and 13, respectively.
48 J. Nocera, 'Bonus Rules Lack Smart Incentives', *International Herald Tribune*, 21–22 February 2009, p. 13.
49 Story, 'As Foundations Crumbled', p. 13.
50 E. Porter, 'On the Origin of Giant Bonuses', *International Herald Tribune*, 10 March 2009, p. 9.
51 Sinn, *Casino Capitalism*, p. 135.
52 Similar to Madoff, Texas banker R. Allen Stanford also managed to orchestrate a large Ponzi scheme for 20 years. In 2012, he was sentenced to 110 years in prison.
53 D. Harvey, *A Brief History of Neoliberalism*, Oxford: Oxford University Press, 2005, p. 2.
54 G. Monbiot, 'Neoliberals Stole the Wealth of Nations', *Guardian Weekly*, 31 August 2007, p. 18.
55 G. Duménil and D. Lévy (D. Jeffers, trans.), *Capital Resurgent: Roots of the Neoliberal Revolution*, Cambridge, MA: Harvard University Press, 2004.
56 S. Clarke, 'The Neoliberal Theory of Society', in A. Saad-Filho and D. Johnston (eds.), *Neoliberalism: A Critical Reader*, London: Pluto Press, 2005, p. 51.

57 P. Bourdieu, 'Utopia of endless exploitation', *Le Monde Diplomatique*, 8 December 1998. Available at: http://mondediplo.com/1998/12/08bourdieu (accessed 18 October 2008).
58 Harvey, *A Brief History of Neoliberalism*, pp. 120–151.
59 R. Munck, 'Neoliberalism and Politics, and the Politics of Neoliberalism', in Saad-Filho and Johnston (eds.), *Neoliberalism*, p. 63.
60 Rodrik, *The Globalization Paradox*, p. xii.
61 For a notable exception to the dominant stance in economics, see the case of Joseph Stiglitz (H.J. Chang, *Joseph Stiglitz and the World Bank: The Rebel Within*, London: Anthem Press, 2001).
62 'Dismal Ethics', *Economist*, 8 January 2011, p. 74.
63 Quoted in 'What Went Wrong with Economics', *Economist*, 18 July 2011, p. 9.
64 P.A. Samuelson, 'Heed the Hopeful Science', *International Herald Tribune*, 24–25 October 2009, p. 6.
65 A. Sen, *On Ethics and Economics*, Oxford: Blackwell, 2004[1987]. See also A. Etzioni, *The Moral Dimension: Toward a New Economics*, New York: Free Press, 1990.
66 Quoted in K. Mofid and M. Braybrooke, *Promoting the Common Good: Bringing Economics and Theology Together Again*, London: Shepheard-Walwyn, 2005, p. 25.
67 Much criticism of modern mainstream economics challenges its most basic assumptions (e.g., E. Fullbrook (ed.), *A Guide to What's Wrong with Economics*, London: Anthem Press, 2005; M.J. Greer, *The Wealth of Nature: Economics as if Survival Mattered*, Gabriola Island, Canada: New Society, 2011). Over the past several years, mainstream economics has also been criticized for a heavy reliance on the assumption of abundant cheap sources of energy (e.g., J.H. Kunstler, *The Long Emergency: Surviving the Converging Catastrophies of the Twenty-First Century*, London: Atlantic Books, 2005; Heinberg, *The End of Growth*; J. Rubin, *The Big Flatline: Oil and the No-Growth Economy*, New York: Palgrave Macmillan, 2012).
68 'The Post-Autistic Economics (PAECON)'. Available at: http://www.paecon.net (accessed 15 January 2012). See also 'Open Letter from Economic Students to Professors and Others Responsible for the Teaching of This Discipline'. Available at: http://www.autisme-economie.org/article142.html (accessed 15 January 2012).
69 E.g., Rodrik, *The Globalization Paradox*, p. xxi.
70 'Repent at Leisure: A Special Report on Debt', *Economist*, 26 June 2010, p. 3.
71 J. Rubin, *Why Your World Is About to Get a Whole Lot Smaller: Oil and the End of Globalization*, New York: Random House, 2009.
72 D. Brooks, 'The Great Unwinding', *International Herald Tribune*, 13–14 June 2009, p. 7.
73 C. Martenson, *The Crash Course: The Unsustainable Future of Our Economy, Energy, and Environment*, Hoboken, NJ: John Wiley & Sons, 2011, p. 68.
74 'Repent at Leisure', *Economist*, pp. 3–4.
75 'Total Debt to GDP'. Available at: http://www.gfmag.com/tools/global-database/economic-data/10403-total-debt-to-gdp.html#axzz1bZ41xQQm (accessed 23 October 2011).
76 M. Lynn, *Bust: Greece, the Euro, and the Sovereign Debt Crisis*, Hoboken, NJ: Bloomberg Press, 2011, pp. 61–62.
77 'Repent at Leisure', *Economist*, pp. 3–4.
78 'Total Debt to GDP'.
79 M. Rowbotham, *The Grip of Death: A Study of Modern Money, Debt Slavery and Destructive Economics*, 4th ed., Charlbury, UK: Jon Carpenter, 2009, p. 64.
80 Lynn, *Bust*, p. 62.

81 'Talking Point: The Euro Debt Crisis – Similarities and Differences', 25 November 2010. Available at: http://www.dws-investments.com/EN/docs/research/euro_debt_crisis_article.pdf (accessed 12 November 2011).
82 'Total Debt to GDP'.
83 Ibid.
84 Lynn, *Bust*, p. 65.
85 Ibid., p. 59.
86 Woods, *Meltdown*, p. 11.
87 Lynn, *Bust*, p. 59.
88 Ibid., p. 98.
89 Huang, 'Like "Go West," Credit Debt's a Threat'.
90 Kim and Bhangananda, 'Money for Nothing', p. 2.
91 Ibid., p. 1.
92 Ibid., p. 40.
93 C.D. Richey, *Whom Shall We Trust?* Baltimore: PublishAmerica, 2004, p. 28.
94 Prins, *Other People's Money*, p. 45.
95 Ibid., p. 134.
96 Ibid., pp. 204 and 208, respectively.
97 Ibid., p. 93.
98 A.L. Elliott and R.J. Schroth, *How Companies Lie: Why Enron Is Just the Tip of the Iceberg*, London: Nicholas Brealey, 2002.
99 Prins, *Other People's Money*, p. 82.
100 Lanchester, *I.O.U.*, p. 36.
101 E.g., P. Krugman, *The Return of Depression Economics and the Crisis of 2008*, New York: W.W. Norton, 2009, esp. pp. 158–162.
102 Sinn, *Casino Capitalism*, p. 47.
103 Ibid., p. 16.
104 Krugman, *The Return of Depression Economics*, pp. 71–72.
105 Sinn, *Casino Capitalism*, pp. 228–229.
106 'Eurostat Table, 2003–2010: General Government Gross Debt'. Available at: http://epp.eurostat.ec.europa.eu/tgm/table.do?tab=table&plugin=0&language=en&pcode=tsieb090 (accessed 16 November 2011).
107 Sinn, *Casino Capitalism*, pp. 228–229.
108 Ibid.
109 'Default Settings', *Economist*, 3 April 2010, p. 72.
110 Reinhart and Rogoff, *This Time Is Different*, pp. xxx and xxxi, respectively.
111 E.g, J.E. Stiglitz, *Globalization and Its Discontents*, London: Penguin Books, 2002; J.E. Stiglitz, *The Roaring Nineties: Why We Are Paying the Price for the Greediest Decade in History*, London: Penguin Books, 2003.
112 Reinhart and Rogoff, *This Time Is Different*, p. 62.
113 UN Conference on Trade and Development (UNCTAD), 'The Least Developed Countries Report 2010: Towards a New International Development Architecture for LDCs', 25 November 2010. Available at: http://www.ldc2010_embargo_en.pdf (accessed 2 November 2011).
114 Rowbotham, *The Grip of Death*, pp. 137 and 131–149, respectively.
115 John Paul II, 'Apostolic Letter *Tertio Millennio Adveniente* (On Preparation for the Jubilee of the Year 2000)', 1994. Available at: http://www.vatican.va/holy_father/john_paul_ii/apost_letters/documents/hf_jp-ii_apl_10111994_tertio-millennio-adveniente_en.html (accessed 20 November 2011), no. 51.
116 S. Zarlenga, *The Lost Science of Money: The Mythology of Money – the Story of Power*, Valatie, NY: American Monetary Institute, 2002, p. 619.
117 Lynn, *Bust*, p. 70.

3 Usury prohibition – an ancient principle of financial dealings

"Usury today is a dead issue, and except by a plainly equivocal use of the term, or save in the mouths of a few inveterate haters of the present order, it is not likely to stir to life."[1] This statement of John Noonan somehow reflects a general trend in modern mainstream finance and monetary circles, and indeed a widespread perception, that charging interest on a loan is a natural result of market forces, and therefore, in principle, there is no ambiguity about it. Charging interest takes on a moral (and legal) meaning only when demanded interests are excessively high. This is why the term "usury" today is normally associated with the lending of money "at an exorbitant interest," or "in excess of the legal rate," or "at an illegally high rate," depending which dictionary one opens. Yet when one looks at historical data, what becomes rather striking is that over a period of at least two millennia, the concept of usury underwent important changes. In this book, it will be argued that, contrary to the claim of Noonan, usury is not at all a thing of the past. We start by looking at the growing awareness in the ancient world of the problems associated with lending at interest and the rise of the condemnation of usury in various cultural contexts.

Legal aspects of charging interest

Lending serves an important economic purpose. In ancient cultures, however, lending often fulfilled also significant social (welfare), moral, and religious functions. This is why, at least in some cultural contexts, at a very early stage particular attention was paid to charging of interest on lending.

Lending at interest and growing awareness of its enslaving potential

In a morally and religiously charged environment, temples quite naturally became centers of life for local communities. It was there that the neediest members of those communities, such as widows, orphans, or the elderly, could seek help. One of the public functions that they gradually assumed was lending. In earlier Sumer and Egypt civilizations, even if interest was charged on loans, "it went back to the temple to fund the community's economic and social programs and to cover losses from bad loans."[2]

Interestingly, also in China, the earliest credit institutions were pawnshops operated by Buddhist monasteries. Because these pawnshops were primarily meant to contribute to local communities, they were strictly regulated by the government, including the rates of interest they could charge and the periods for redeeming debts, but were often exempt from paying taxes. Although gradually other lending entities developed, monastery-run pawnshops remained popular as late as the fourteenth century.[3]

There are even postulates that it was Mesopotamian temples that actually developed money. The main reason for that was to denominate debt, and ultimately, to standardize their accounting practices.[4] Yet apparently after the Indo-European invasions of Mesopotamia in the second millennium BC, the strongly community-oriented lending system of temples was gradually superseded by private lending. In effect, interest on lending was turned into private income.[5]

In earlier agrarian societies, loans predominantly took the form of grains, cattle, or farming tools, and because all these could increase agricultural produce, loans were repaid with interest in the form of the produce. What was loaned possessed the potential for generating more, and interest on loans was a share in what was produced extra. A reflection of such an understanding of interest is the Sumerian term *mas*, which meant both calves and interest, while in Egypt a similar word meant to give birth.[6] The Greek word *tokos* also carried the meaning of offspring as well as interest. In short, in early societies interest was understood primarily in terms of a share in profits, even if fixed in advance. Apparently it was only in Babylon that "inorganic materials" began to be considered "as if they were living organisms with the means of reproduction."[7]

In principle, then, the first important shift in the development of lending mechanisms was its disassociation from lending in an organic sense. In the "natural" lending process, because cattle could breed and grain could produce, it became quite normal that a part of the natural produce had to be shared with those whose lending helped that happen. It was an integral component of the system of reciprocities or in other words, justice. Yet once lending began to be monetized, money, although abstracted from the natural produce, was also expected to be "productive," like cattle or grain. Despite this crucial difference, in the course of time, charging interest on money lent gradually became an assumed part of lending on all actual and potential gains. Private interests began to capitalize on that shift.

Moreover, there is now a growing conviction that the charging of interest in privatized lending in ancient societies often had other objectives attached to loans than merely generating profits from interest. A study by Piotr Steinkeller suggests that very often "the lender's primary objective in advancing loans was to get possession of either the borrower's labor or his land or often both." In some loans, then, "interest was a tool and not an economic end in itself."[8] This is why in ancient, particularly Near Eastern societies, interest charged on lending was often very high. Although not all lending had such an objective, it is hard to deny that the mechanism of charging interest could put some people in a very disadvantaged position. The result was not uncommon debt enslavement, which even led some desperate debtors to abandon their farms and abscond.[9]

Thus people at a very early stage began to see the connection between lending at interest and enslavement. This, in turn, gradually induced attempts to mitigate at least some of the unfavorable outcomes for the debtors. One way of achieving that was through the direct intervention of the rulers. To avoid potential social unrest, rulers of Sumer, Babylon, or Egypt periodically used their powers to reduce or annul outstanding consumer debts.[10] Of course, to minimize fear among creditors, the cancellation of debts by rulers was normally carried out within the confines that reduced the long-term negative effects of such rulings. First, cancellations practically never addressed commercial debts, but only consumer debts, which in ancient societies basically meant agricultural loans. Second, these types of edicts were normally one-time deeds. Third, it was difficult to predict such pronouncements, because they were entirely within the discretion of the ruler.[11]

Additionally, in order to prevent, or at least minimize, tragic outcomes caused by debt, diverse wisdom texts spread among ancient peoples the awareness of the enslaving potential of debt. Such advice can be found in the texts of the Egyptian New Kingdom (1550–1070 BC),[12] as well as the Bible. The Book of Proverbs, for example, warns that "the rich rule over the poor" in the same way "the borrower is the slave of the lender."[13]

The ancient wisdom literature also provides some advice to creditors about how to deal with the debtors who found it difficult to pay their debts. When faced by such circumstances, an Egyptian New Kingdom text suggests that lenders restructure the debt and forgive part of it:

> If you find a large debt against a poor man,
> Make it into three parts
> Forgive two, let one stand
> You will find in it a path of life.[14]

A similar message can also be found in the parable of Jesus pointing to the need of forgiveness in the situation of irredeemable debts.[15]

Interestingly, in the ancient societies, while lending provided by temples became institutionalized at a very early stage, private lending did not take on an institutional form. In practical terms, the conditions for capital formation, and thus the potential for more widespread institutionalization of private lending, did exist. Nevertheless that potential did not materialize. Apparently, among the factors that played an important role in preventing that development was social and moral pressure that effectively ostracized those attempting to expand their wealth through lending at interest. For centuries, including the Greco-Roman periods, some loans were provided by individuals who functioned more "as patrons, not as professional bankers or moneylenders."[16] Nevertheless, historical records show that some individuals did make lending "productive" in the sense of using it as the vehicle to increase their wealth. Apparently for some, ostracism for lending at interest for private gains did not have sufficient constraining force. The Egibi, a powerful family that emerged in Babylon in the sixth century BC, can serve as an example of how some could utilize the process of lending to amass extraordinary wealth and influence.[17] Various examples of "bankers" who prospered and gained influence through lending can also be found in ancient Greece, and to a lesser degree in Rome.[18]

Ancient legal perspectives on lending and interest

In addition to the moral attempts to mitigate the conditions for growing indebtedness and enslavement due to debts, ancient societies also had at their disposal promulgation of adequate laws. The Code of Hammurabi (c. 1780 BC) is an example of an important early attempt to address the problem of growing debts, particularly those caused by natural disasters. For instance, canon 48 states: "If any one owe a debt for a loan, and a storm prostrates the grain, or the harvest fails, or the grain does not grow for lack of water; in that year he need not give his creditor any grain, he washes his debt-tablet in water and pays no rent for this year." Apparently, this does not mean cancellation of the debt, but only postponement. Nevertheless, an obvious form of protection was initiated. For those unfortunates who were unable to pay their debts, and could only offer the labor of members of the household as a form of repayment, canon 117 sets the time limit on such forced labor to three years, and states that "in the fourth year they shall be set free."[19] Unfortunately, despite the fact that the Code considered many diverse forms of compensation, it did not set a clear rate of interest allowed to be charged, which often was at the heart of the problem.

In the Greek context, Lycurgus of Sparta (eighth century BC) is sometimes considered an important early lawgiver. Among various achievements, such as an institutional organization that helped Sparta gain great power, he is also credited for monetary reforms (the introduction of iron discs functioning in principle as a fiat money system) as well as for resolving the debts crisis following an enormous wealth concentration.[20] Solon (c. 639–559 BC), however, is likely to be considered an even more influential Greek reformer. In 594 BC, facing a serious debt crisis in Athens, Solon succeeded in canceling debt contracts, returning land that had been seized, and even in bringing back the farmers who had been sold into slavery abroad. That reform also forbade personal slavery as security for debts.[21] Additionally, Solon reduced the rate of interest, which at that time was apparently as high as 16 percent a year.[22]

Once Rome began to dominate the Mediterranean, it imposed its own legal tradition of lending at interest, and thus also the ways of mitigating the problems caused by debts. In ancient Rome, in principle the laws concerning interest on loans oscillated between *limiting* and *prohibiting* it. When Roman law took the *limiting* stance, the overall tendency was to keep the maximum legal rate of interest within 12 percent per year. Such was for example the case of the Law of the Twelve Tables (451–450 BC). But then the highest legal rate of interest was gradually lowered and in 347 BC it reached just 5 percent. After that, the stance in Roman law shifted to the prohibiting mode. The *Lex Genucia* of 342 BC forbade all interest, but because that prohibition "bound only Roman citizens, it was easily evaded by the use of non-Roman intermediaries."[23] Nevertheless, this law stood until 88 BC when the *Lex Unciaria* brought back the maximum legal rate of 12 percent a year.[24] The Roman Senate in 51 BC decreed this rate as the maximum legal rate in the Roman provinces. Yet the real interest rates gradually turned out to be much lower, with 6 percent as the prevailing rate during peacetime.[25]

There was, however, one type of loan on which interest in ancient Rome (and not only there) was by far higher than in the case of ordinary loans, namely *faenus nauticum,* or bottomry loans to cover sailing ventures. Because of the huge risks of sea transportation, the interest rates charged on such loans could be as high as the parties involved could agree upon. Only the Code of Justinian of AD 533 limited the interest on bottomry loans to 12 percent. That law also set an 8 percent limit on loans to merchants and business enterprisers, 6 percent on those to nonbusiness persons, and 4 percent on loans to "agriculturalists and distinguished personages." It also upheld the Roman Senate decree of 51 BC prohibiting compound interest and limiting to the amount of the initial capital the maximum of accrual of interest that could be demanded.[26]

As far as the enforcement of loan contracts is concerned, there was a difference between the Greek and the Roman societies. The Greek stance was to stress more personal responsibility, meaning that loans were voluntary contracts, and the creditors lent money at their own risk.[27] Moreover, as the reforms of Lycurgus of Sparta and of Solon in Athens suggest, an occasional intervention on the part of the state, mostly in times of crisis, tended to protect debtors. For the Romans, on the other hand, the role of the state was much heavier, and, at least at its earlier stage, it tended to protect creditors whenever necessary. It appears that in the history of Rome there was even a period when law allowed creditors "to divide the body of a defaulting debtor in proportion to the sums he owned them."[28] There is no proof that such execution of the existing law actually took place, but the example, nevertheless, shows a very different approach in resolving debt issues from that of the Greeks.

In the course of time, however, Roman law gradually took on a more humane form. The *Lex Genucia* forbade taking any interest on loans, while the possibility of enslaving the defaulting debtor was stopped by the *Lex Poetelia* in 325 BC. It appears that it was in the context of yet another debt crisis that a law promulgated by Julius Caesar in 49 BC took an even more protective stance toward defaulting debtors, by granting them the right to formally cede their estates and claim a new financial status.[29] Thus, in a way, it was Julius Caesar who laid the foundation for modern bankruptcy laws. Yet when first promulgated, the law of Caesar apparently caused a lot of turmoil.[30]

Roman legal literature also began to make important distinctions in legal concepts, which eventually influenced later debates on usury. With regard to loan transactions, the Romans distinguished between *mutuum* and *commodatum,* where the former meant "the transfer of ownership of consumable goods coupled with an obligation to later return goods of identical type and quantity" and the latter referred to "the lending, for use by the borrower, of a nonconsumable good coupled with an obligation to return the identical good."[31] Lending of money belonged to the former category. What is crucial in this distinction, however, is that while the *commodatum* type of agreement permitted additional charges for use of the goods lent (*locatio conductio rei*), *mutuum* transaction in principle had to be gratuitous. Although with regard to *mutuum* contracts the Roman law gradually did allow the possibility of additional fees promised by the borrower (*stipulatio*), this was perceived as a separate agreement, and "could not be combined into one single contract." As a result, the loan of *mutuum* carried with it *obligatio re* (obligation to fully repay what was borrowed) and the *stipulatio* carried only a verbal promise to pay (*obligatio verbis*), which Roman law maintained to be "unenforceable."[32] These distinctions became important to the Medieval scholastics when they were working out their theory of usury.

In short, legal restrictions did possess the potential to curb abuses of lending at interest. Nevertheless, because laws tended to change and/or were easily evaded, it appears that there were other forces at work that had a more lasting impact on the issue of charging interest on loans. As it turns out, these forces were of a moral character.

Moral condemnation of usury in the ancient world

One of the moral forces challenging the practice of charging interest on lending was the strong criticism raised by some outstanding ancient Greek and Roman philosophers. Another force was the prohibitive stance on usury taken by Judaism, Christianity, and later by Islam.

Ancient Greek and Roman philosophers condemning usury

Among Greek philosophers, both Plato and Aristotle condemned usury, which they understood as the practice of lending money at interest. Yet at the same time both appear to provide different reasoning why lending money at interest should be opposed.

From the perspective of political philosophy, Plato (427–347 BC) was an idealist. Dissatisfied with the deteriorating state of the Athenian democracy, in the *Republic* Plato presents the need for an ideal state, in which true happiness for all citizens can be achieved. An important force driving the process toward such an ideal is harmonious relationships anchored in justice. For Plato, justice is possible under the condition "that each one must practice one of the functions in the city, that one for which his nature made him naturally most fit."[33] But such fulfillment of what could be called the social aspect of justice cannot be achieved in separation from the individual aspect of justice, or justice understood as a human virtue, which for Plato seems to be harmony of the soul.[34]

For Plato, the political system that could best facilitate the realization of the true (perfect) justice at both the social and personal levels and, ultimately, citizens' happiness, was an aristocratic republic.[35] In such an ideal state, the governing role was assigned to philosophers, because only they were thought to have the wisdom and reasoning ability to rule. Enforcement of the order initiated by the ruling class of philosophers was the task of the auxiliaries made up of soldiers. The lowest class in such a state were the commoners. Because the upper two classes were not allowed to own property, the task of the commoners was to support them as the commoners were the only class that could own property and produce goods.

Undoubtedly, Plato was an idealist in the sense of the conclusions he reached while searching for solutions to the degenerating conditions in Athens. His search for a better form of government, however, was not devoid of realism. This becomes most visible in his analysis of what led to the degeneration of states. Based on real-life observations, Plato became convinced that the desire of riches was one of the major factors driving the degeneration process. For him wealth had a social function, and the desire that fuelled wealth accumulation was not only destructive to personal virtue, but also had social consequences by increasing tensions, and thus destroying peace and harmony. Among the aspects that Plato points to as underlying deterioration of states is the enrichment of some through lending at interest and loss of property and citizenship by others. To him, charging interest on loans had primarily negative social consequences. Although such a practice was allowed by the Athenian law, in the view of Plato the laws were "written and unwritten, were being altered for the worse, and the evil was growing with startling rapidity."[36] Interestingly, in the *Republic*, Plato expresses his contempt for the practice of lending money at interest not in the ideal state, but in a discussion of the change from oligarchy to democracy, thus suggesting that prohibiting the practice could help to prevent further degeneration.

Much stronger and more straightforward opposition to charging interest on loans can be found in Book Five of Plato's *Laws*. In it he states: "no one should give money to someone he can't trust, and no money should be lent at interest. Anyone who has received a loan will be permitted to refuse to pay it back, both interest and principal."[37] From the modern perspective, this is an extraordinary statement. To understand the reasons underlying Plato's opposition to making money through lending, it is important first to see that for him the principal function of the laws of a state was to make the citizens "as happy and as friendly to one another as possible."[38] But happiness is conditioned by goodness, and goodness, in turn, is difficult to reconcile with riches. Plato was convinced that "it is impossible for someone to be both unusually good and unusually rich" because "the gain derived from both just and unjust means is more than twice that derived from just means alone." In order to achieve relative happiness and friendliness of the citizens, the state then cannot allow making big money "through vulgar occupations, or usury" (i.e., lending money at interest), but rather promote their satisfaction through profits from farming, and only as much of it as would not lead a man to lose from his sight the main purpose to which money was intended to serve, namely "the soul and the body" of the person.[39] In the view of Plato, "civil war" was "the greatest illness" that a state could face. To avoid that, he reckoned, "neither harsh poverty nor wealth should exist among any of the citizens," and it was the role of the state to "announce a limit for both conditions."[40]

There is however one instance where Plato favors charging of interest – in the case of delayed payments for the received work. The rate of interest that Plato suggested for the payments that were not settled "within the agreed time period" was 200 percent per year.[41] Of course, one may be shocked by this figure, but once taken in its entirety, the proposal of Plato makes good sense. What he was concerned about was the just functioning of the society. And because many citizens relied on short-term income, postponement of payments could cause a dire financial situation for some, and could ultimately lead to social instability. So although in principle Plato was against charging interest on money as a way of increasing one's wealth, he had no objections to charging even extremely high interest – particularly to poorer citizens – as a penalty for delayed due payments.

Another fierce critic of usury among Greek philosophers was Aristotle. Although use of money started long before Aristotle was born, he actually was among the first who not only began a theoretical reflection on the function of money, but more importantly, linked the nature of money with the issue of justice and the very existence of a community through just exchanges. In his words:

> all items for exchange must be comparable in some way. Currency came along to do exactly this, and in a way it becomes an intermediate, since it measures everything . . . Everything, then, must be measured by some one measure . . . In reality, this measure is need, which holds everything together; for if people needed nothing, or needed things to different extents, there would be either no exchange or not the same exchange. And currency has become a sort of pledge of need, by convention; in fact it has its name (*nomisma*) because it is not by nature, but by the current law (*nomos*), and it is within our power to alter it and to make it useless.[42]

As a matter of fact, Aristotle in *Nicomachean Ethics* reflects on the nature and function of money in the context of his discussion of justice, to which the entirety of Book Five is dedicated.

In general, Aristotle divides justice into two broad categories: general (legal) justice and special justice. According to Aristotle, law imposes certain constraints on people's behavior, and even forces them to do acts of courage, such as not to throw down one's weapons and desert the post in battle.[43] So legal justice regards one's relations with others in general, or one's relation to society as a whole, and takes the form of the obligation to follow society's just laws as a basic prerequisite of the common good.

Special justice, in turn, refers to relationships involving concrete individuals. As for this type of justice, Aristotle makes the distinction between distributive and corrective justice, the former governing the relation of society or the state to the private person, and the latter covering diverse dealings between individuals, and thus involving correction of any unfairness in explicit and implicit contracts.[44] What is perhaps characteristic with regard to corrective and distributive justice is that each is exercised on the basis of a different concept of equality. Distributive justice involves geometrical equality (equality based on the proportion between "person" and "thing"), meaning that the give-and-take is proportionate to one's needs and abilities.[45] In other words, it considers the well-being of individuals in relation to the common good. Corrective justice, on the other hand, is based on arithmetic equality (equality between "thing" and "thing"), meaning that the focus is on the object that is due, without any regard to the status or wealth of the individuals involved.

For Aristotle, then, justice is about relationality and commensurability. The three types of justice distinguished above reflect three important relationships: the individual to society as a whole (legal justice), the society or state to the individual person (distributive justice), and between individuals (corrective justice). Justice in each such relationship, in turn, involves a sort of commensurability.

It is in the context of his discussion of corrective justice that Aristotle takes up the issue of money. Because corrective justice is about the mean between loss and gain, or numerical proportion between "things," such as "how many shoes are equal to a house"[46] in his view, money was invented not only to facilitate exchanges of "things" (being a medium of exchange) but also to provide a standard by which the numerical proportion, and thus justice, can be achieved. Money, then, by providing a measure by which all commodities can be compared, plays an indispensable role in a community for mediating just exchanges. Differing needs, being part of the very nature of human beings, drive people to make exchanges, and money as a means for achieving equivalence in exchange has become an important factor in satisfying human needs and intensifying human interactions. Money, then, "by making things commensurate as a measure does, equalizes them; for there would be no community without exchange, no exchange without equality, no equality without commensuration."[47] Thus, for Aristotle, the importance of money does not only lie in providing convenience in exchanges (as presented in modern mainstream economics), and thus disconnecting individuals, but rather in helping a community to achieve just exchanges.

In the thought of Aristotle money has also the function of a store of value. According to him: "If an item is not required at the moment, currency serves to guarantee us a future exchange, guaranteeing that the item will be there for us if we need it; for it must be there for us to take if we pay."[48] This means that currency serves as a guarantee that in future exchanges an equal amount of need can be satisfied. He was well aware that money, just like commodities, was exposed to the vagaries of the market, and so it did not always "count for the same." Nevertheless, in Aristotle's view money was "more stable," than commodities, meaning that its value tended to be rather constant.[49] Yet this function of money as a store of value ultimately is also meant for exchange purposes, because it helps to rate "everything" according to a relatively stable value of money.

Niall Ferguson in *The Ascent of Money* distinguishes three functions of money: "a medium of exchange, which has the advantage of eliminating inefficiencies of barter; a unit of account, which facilitates valuation and calculation, and store of value, which allows economic transactions to be conducted over long periods as well as geographical distances."[50] This distinction has by now become a standard view of money in modern economics. As presented above, it actually goes back to Aristotle. Unfortunately, while Aristotle in his debate on money put the emphasis on the need of a standard of measurement to keep justice in human economic interactions, modern economics, with its assumption of humans as being self-interested, disconnected individuals, treats money predominantly as a neutral means of exchange. For Aristotle, money existed "not by nature, but by the current law (*nomos*)," and it is within the power of the community that created it "to alter it and to make it useless."[51] Whatever could fulfill the role of being a unit of account and store of value, and thus become a medium facilitating *just* exchanges in a community, could be declared by the lawful authority of the community as currency (*nomisma*). As such, money had an indispensable justice function in a given society, and thus was closely related to the very existence of community. For modern economics, on the other hand, money has become a neutral means of exchange that provides convenience in exchanges, but otherwise has no social or moral connotations.

Aristotle takes up the question of usury in the context of his discussion of wealth. He distinguishes natural and unnatural modes of wealth acquisition, between which lies an intermediate mode. The natural mode is proper to what he calls household management. It is considered "natural" because it aims at satisfying basic human wants, mainly through agriculture, which includes raising stock, farming, horticulture, the keeping of bees, fish, fowl, and so forth. Aristotle saw these as "natural" ways of making profit because "it is nature's work to provide food to what has been born, since everything finds food in the residue of what it is born from." The intermediate type of wealth acquiring is partly natural, but it also includes exchange (the unnatural mode). In the words of Aristotle, this mode "deals with things that come from the earth or with unfruitful but useful things growing in the earth – as, for example, logging and all kinds of mining." Finally the unnatural profit-making mode covers all activities that are proper to exchange. Aristotle divides unnatural exchanges into three categories: commerce and trade, lending money at interest, and wage labor. Among these, he considers lending money at interest, or usury, as the most contrary to nature and a rightly despised form of business.[52]

From the analysis of the modes of acquiring wealth and the nature of money, Aristotle came to the conclusion that usury is a "most reasonably . . . hated" money-making activity. This is so,

> because it gets its property from money itself and not from what money was supplied for. Money came into being for the sake of exchange, but interest just makes the money itself increase. That is how interest got its name, for offspring ["interest" in Greek is "*tokos*," which literally means

offspring] are like the parents that gave them birth, and interest is money born of money.[53]

It became obvious to Aristotle that usury violated something very basic in exchange activities, namely justice. By forcing barren money to increase by itself, usury made the exchange not commensurable, and thus was unjust of its very nature.

In short, Aristotle's condemnation of usury was anchored in the nature of money. Because money's primary function was to facilitate just exchanges, lending money at interest caused incommensurability in exchanges. For him, money generating more money through payment of interest was morally unacceptable, or simply unjust. As a result, Aristotle opposed the practice of lending money at interest primarily not on the basis of the negative influence such practice had on society, as was the case of Plato, but on the basis of its distortion of just exchanges. He saw the social impact of usury through the prism of injustice it caused in exchanges.

However, Aristotle agreed with Plato's criticism of usury as causing personal degeneration. For Aristotle, the practice of usury had an adverse effect on cultivation of the human character, especially the virtue of liberality, understood by him as a habit of giving to proper recipients and taking from the right sources,[54] which in present terms would be close to generosity. As a matter of fact, in *Nicomachean Ethics*, Aristotle takes up the issue of usury while discussing the vice opposing liberality, namely meanness. By demonstrating that usury involved taking what belonged to others,[55] he managed to present usury as detrimental to the practice of the virtue of generosity, especially toward the poor, which in turn was an important component of social justice at the time.

Similarly to the Greeks, the Roman philosophers in principle viewed income from agricultural endeavors, or "natural" economy, as most appropriate for a noble man. For Cicero (106–43 BC), among the most undesirable, or "vulgar," forms of income were tax collecting and usury.[56] Also Cato in his work *On Agriculture* argues that the lending of money for increasing profits was very dishonorable. By pointing to the laws of "ancestors," Cato states that the usurer was considered as "much less desirable a citizen" than the thief. According to him, those laws "required that the thief be mulcted double and the usurer fourfold."[57]

With regard to charging interest on loans, just as in Roman law, philosophical views also oscillated between limiting and prohibiting it. The limiting mode can be found for example in Cicero. Having been personally involved in lending at interest,[58] Cicero overall held the position that it was the responsibility of government to provide legal protection of creditors, and to enforce the payment of debts.[59] Yet at the same time he was appalled by the practice of some people charging high interest rates.[60] This makes him an advocate of lending at interest, but at rates set within reasonable limits. As a result, usury meant for him *high interest rates*, or interest rates that were beyond reasonable and widely acceptable bounds.

A stark contrast to the view of Cicero – namely prohibition – can be found in Seneca. While reflecting on what was happening in the Roman society of his time, Seneca looked deeper into human nature. One of the vices that he saw as eating into human minds and souls was avarice. The conclusion he reached, and which he put into the mouth of Demetrius, a well-respected person of his time, was this:

> some forms of wealth deceive our eyes and minds alike. I see there letters of credit, promissory notes, and bonds, empty phantoms of property, ghosts of sick Avarice, with which she deceives our minds, which delight in unreal fancies; for what are these things and what are interest, and account books, and usury, except the name of unnatural developments of human covetousness? . . . what are your documents, your sale of time, your blood-sucking twelve per cent interest? These are evils which we owe to our own will, which flow merely from our perverted habit, having nothing about them which can be seen or handled, mere dreams of empty avarice.[61]

Seneca then condemned usury both on the ground that it was an unnatural selling of time, and because it had a negative social effect through "sucking the blood" of other people. In reality, however, he was not totally against paying interest on loans. Nevertheless, for him interest could only take the form of gratitude of the debtor toward his creditor.[62] Thus, for Seneca, a sort of interest on a loan should be paid, yet the only obligation to do so was a *moral obligation* on the part of the debtor derived from the fact that benefits had to be reciprocated, as in the case of gifts carrying a moral obligation to reciprocate.[63]

In addition to different views on wealth, the lending of money, interest, and usury, ancient Roman literature also sheds light on the effects these all had on individuals and entire societies. One can easily deduce from it that many people lived under a heavy burden of debts, which caused much misery and suffering. Plutarch in *The Lives of the Noble Grecians and Romans,* while praising the achievements of a certain Lucullus in "the cities of Asia," also adds how the province was "plundered and enslaved by taxfarmers and usurers," and how widespread were the phenomena that "private people were compelled to sell their sons in the flower of their youth, and their daughters in their virginity, and the states publicly to sell their consecrated gifts, pictures, and statues."[64] Moreover, some of the debtors, before being enslaved, were given up to torture, "inflicted with ropes and by horses, standing abroad to be scorched when the sun was hot, and being driven into ice and clay in the cold." In the face of such suffering, "slavery was no less than a redemption and joy to them." And it is for getting rid of such "evils and oppressions" that Lucullus was praised by Plutarch.[65]

Condemnation of usury in religious thought

Perhaps the strongest denunciation of usurious lending in the ancient world came from religious circles. At a relatively early stage, the Jewish religion took a very critical stance on charging of interest on loans. Later, Christian and Islamic traditions also became vehement critics of usury.

The Hebrew Bible recognizes that a loan at times could become a real necessity of life.[66] Yet the condition attached to lending was that interest on loans was not to be exacted: "If you lend money to my people, to the poor among you, you shall not deal with them as a creditor; you shall not exact interest from them."[67] The underlying reason for such prohibition was that once the Jews had been brought out of slavery in Egypt, they were supposed to be free, and should not allow one form of slavery to be replaced by another. For their leaders it was not too difficult to see the enslaving potential of debts. "Independence, self-reliance, self-support was the condition aimed at and encouraged in the Hebrew state" while borrowing was meant to be a form of support only in times of dire need.[68] As a result, economic equity and protection of the weak and poor became an essential part of the Law of Moses. Perhaps the most obvious expression of this is the concept of the year of jubilee (every forty-nine years), which stressed redemption of ancestral property (mainly land) and freeing the Israelites enslaved due to inability to pay debts. Additionally, every sabbatical year (every seventh year) all debts were supposed to be cancelled and every Hebrew enslaved by debt set free.[69]

The ideal of an equitable society as expressed in the Law of Moses was nevertheless often challenged by practice. In the First Book of Samuel, David, while being chased by the king Saul, is said to have attracted to his ranks "everyone who was in distress, and everyone who was in debt, and everyone who was discontented."[70] The story of Elisha meeting a certain widow points to even a grimmer picture of the suffering of entire families because creditors did not hesitate to enslave debtors, or their children, to recover their debts.[71] Such a condition would be hard to imagine had the prescriptions of the Law of Moses been followed. Neither the utterances of the prophets, such as Ezekiel, condemning abusive lending,[72] nor inspiring prescriptions, as expressed in Psalms,[73] seem to have altered much the plight of debtors. Even after the painful Babylonian exiles (sixth century BC), usurious practices and suffering caused by them were widespread.[74] In short, "the notion of an unprofitable loan proved liable to abuse during Israel's long history."[75]

The practical failures in enforcing the prohibition of charging interest on loans, however, did not result in abandoning the principle. The texts of the Bible that do raise the issue of lending at profit, and problems associated with it, point to a clear stance condemning usurious lending (in the sense of charging interest). Furthermore, despite the fact that the Bible never developed a systematic teaching presenting reasons why charging interest was wrong of itself (as for example in the case of Aristotle), based on the life experiences of the biblical authors, it nevertheless categorized profitable lending as evil per se. The experiences gained over centuries appear to have led to the conviction that the interest on loans was distorting something essential to the fabric of Jewish society, namely equity. Unprofitable lending was not merely "an obligation of fraternal charity, a duty of mercy and generosity which the rich owed to the poor."[76] It had a deeper meaning of preserving a certain level of equity in society, the most thorough expressions of which were the prescriptions concerning the sabbatical year and the year of jubilee.[77]

While the stance of the Old Testament condemning usury (lending at interest) is relatively clear, this is not so in the New Testament. As a matter of fact, we find no direct ordinances on the ethics of interest there. Nevertheless, some authors point to certain texts to prove that Jesus was at least tolerant of the practice of lending at interest. For example, Divine uses the parable of the talents found in the Gospels of Matthew (25:14–30) and Luke (19:11–27) to claim that it "bears witness to the existence of commercial lending at interest without adverse or favorable comment."[78] However, it should suffice to state here that the existence of lending at interest at the time of Jesus does not mean that he condoned it. Had Jesus accepted it, it would mean he turned against one of the core tenets of the Law of Moses – prohibition of usury. Yet in the same Gospel of Matthew Jesus himself said: "Do not think that I have come to abolish the law or the prophets; I have come not to abolish but to fulfill. For truly I tell you, until heaven and earth pass away, not one letter, not one stroke of a letter, will pass from the law until all is accomplished."[79]

Undoubtedly, as in the case of Jewish communities, the Christian communities also were not free of usurious practices, or lending at interest. It appears that in the patristic period, at times even the clergy were not free of the sin of usury, as reflected in the reprimands of Cyprian of Carthage (c. AD 200–258).[80] The very fact that the Fathers of the church repeatedly condemned usury is proof of the existence of the practice. Yet despite the difficulties in implementing certain ideals in the early church, the Fathers put much effort into upholding its core values.

Looking at patristic literature, one can clearly see how united the Fathers of the church were in condemning usury. Through their preaching and writing they denounced the practice not only on theological grounds – as being contrary to biblical teaching – but also on the grounds of the very nature of money as barren, on ethical grounds as unjust, and on spiritual grounds as harmful to the growth of usurious lenders. For example, among Eastern (Greek) Fathers, Saint Basil (330–379), playing on the Greek word *tokos*, which can mean childbirth, interest, or usury, attacks moneylenders very strongly. For him, the usurious lending process makes money to reproduce itself. As a way of explaining, Basil further argues:

> And the interests are produced by eating up the houses of the debtors. Seeds spring up in time; and animals in time bring their offspring to perfection; but the interest is produced today, and today again begins its breeding. . . . Everything that increases, when it reaches its proper size, stops increasing; but the money of avaricious men always increases progressively with time. The animals, after transmitting to the offspring the power of bearing, desist from conception; both the money of the money-lenders and the accruing interest produce, and the capital is redoubled. Do not, then, make trial of this unnatural beast.

He concludes that lending at interest is actually harmful to both the lender and the borrower because to both it brings some form of loss – to the latter in money and to the former in soul.[81] A similar line of argument can also be found in the writings of Gregory of Nyssa (330–395).[82]

Also the Latin Fathers strongly condemned usury. Where, however, they differ slightly with the Greek Fathers is that the Latin Fathers tend to stress more the unjust outcome of usury as it makes one collect more than one has given. For Lactantius (c. 240–320), a worshiper of God should be cautious while lending money not to practice usury, because "to receive back more than he might have given is unjust."[83] In the treatise *De Tobia*, Saint Ambrose (c. 340–397) denounces the charging of interest on a loan, stating that "whatever is added to the principal is usury."[84] Likewise, Saint Augustine (354–430) defines a usurer as anybody who looks to gain more than he has given, be it money, corn, wine, oil, or anything.[85] Of course, the harmful aspect of usury was to the Latin Fathers not only in the injustice done to the borrower, but also in the damaging effect on the character and soul of the lender.[86]

What is perhaps worth adding here is the church Fathers' awareness of the tension between the spiritual-moral depravity of usury and the civil laws permitting a charge of interest on loans. Saint Augustine was particularly dissatisfied with the permissiveness of law. In his letter to Macedonius, Augustine criticizes both the civil law permitting the charge of interest and judges "who order interest be paid." For him, a usurer is like a thief stealing from what belongs to others. To resolve the problem, Augustine suggests that usury should be "given back in restitution," but at the same time he is aware that "there were no judges to whom a debtor could have such recourse."[87]

Overall, by grounding their pronouncements in biblical teaching and theological interpretation, the Fathers expanded the debate on usury beyond the sphere found in Aristotle, namely the virtue of justice, adding to it a warning about the harm that usury caused not only to the character but also to the soul of usurious lenders. Interestingly, while occasionally stressing justice in the act of lending, the Fathers did not consider the justice issue from the perspective of the lender. Apparently it was the overall social condition of the time and the special attention of Christianity given to the poor and marginalized, as well as the prevailing perception that lenders were always among the rich, that prompted the Fathers to see the function of justice more as protecting those most vulnerable to borrowing. It was only the scholastics during the golden period of the Middle Ages, thus in very different social circumstances, that gradually took up the issue of justice viewed also from the perspective of the lender.

The Old Testament, by hinting at the possibility of charging interest on money lent to non-Israelites,[88] although open to interpretation (see Chapter 5), left a crack in the otherwise solid edifice of denunciation of usury. In contrast, the Koran is very firm in condemning usurious lending. It leaves no space for any rationalization: "Those that live on usury shall rise up before Allah like men whom Satan has demented by his touch; for they claim that usury is like trading. But Allah has permitted trading and forbidden usury."[89]

What apparently influenced the Islamic stance on usury was the fact that the prophet Muhammad himself had experience as a merchant, and therefore was very familiar with financial dealings. This could have been an important reason why, while in both Ancient Greece and Rome trade was not a noble engagement, Islam actually very much favored the making of profit from trade. It encouraged people to expand their capital, but *not through lending at interest.*

The prohibition of usury in Islam comes primarily from its concern about justice in exchanges. Moreover, such justice should be kept without distinguishing between a Muslim and a non-Muslim, meaning that the Islamic prohibition of usury is universal. This concern for justice is clearly expressed in the condemnation of *riba*, which sometimes is translated as usury, but in fact appears to have a broader meaning. Ibrahim Warde claims that *riba*

> is not necessarily about interest rates as such, and it certainly is not exclusively about interest rates. It really refers to any unlawful gain derived from the quantitative inequality of countervalues *(inequality of exchange values in real terms)*. Interest or usury . . . would then be only one form of *riba*.[90]

As such, the Islamic prohibition of *riba* is also meant to put constraints on capital increases and ultimately on the growth of the gap between the haves and the have-nots of society. Gain, nevertheless, is allowed from pooling resources and sharing the risks of the enterprise, similar to the partnerships (*societas*) of the Middle Ages (see Chapter 4).

In order to assure the equality of exchange, the Koran suggests that the one contracting a debt, be it small or big, should put the agreement in writing, and include in it the date of payment. The agreement should also have witnesses. Such process of borrowing, in the words of the Koran, "is more just in the sight of Allah; it ensures accuracy in testifying and is the best way to remove all doubt." Yet this prescription also leaves some flexibility for quick transactions "concluded on the spot" where fulfilling the agreement may meet practical difficulties. In such cases there would be "no offense" if one did not put the agreement in writing.[91] Moreover, in Islam debtors are under a moral obligation to pay debts. It is seen as a prerequisite of justice to pay due debts. This requirement of justice in paying debts is so important that all the sins of a martyr can be forgiven "except for his unpaid debts."[92] But the Koran also states that if the debtor is in a difficulty, the lender should "grant him a delay until he can discharge his debt." And it adds that by way of charity, the lender could even remit such debt.[93]

Undoubtedly, in the Muslim world, as in other traditions, there have been people charging interest on loans. Diverse interpretative traditions have also grown. But, nevertheless, the principle has remained clear: "Allah has laid His curse on usury."[94]

To conclude, it can be stated that in the ancient world, charging interest on lending was relatively widespread. But so was condemnation of usury. Various forms of opposition to usurious lending can be found across legal, philosophical, and religious literature in Greek, Roman, and other cultural contexts. The medieval scholastics, equipped with the accumulated knowledge of the ancient world, looked anew at the ethical aspects of borrowing–lending transactions and the problem of usury, and ultimately developed a refined theory of usury. Now we turn to their contribution to the debate.

Notes

1 J.T. Noonan, *The Scholastic Analysis of Usury*, Cambridge, MA: Harvard University Press, 1957, p. 1.
2 E.H. Brown, *The Web of Debt: The Shocking Truth about Our Money System and How We Can Break Free*, 3rd ed., Baton Rouge, LA: Third Millennium Press, 2008, p. 56.
3 L.S. Yang, *Money and Credit in China: A Short History*, Cambridge, MA: Harvard University Press, 1971, p. 6.
4 S. Zarlenga, *The Lost Science of Money: The Mythology of Money – the Story of Power*, Valatie, NY: American Monetary Institute, 2002, p. 14.
5 Brown, *The Web of Debt*, pp. 56–57.
6 Zarlenga, *The Lost Science of Money*, pp. 12–13; Brown, *The Web of Debt*, pp. 56–57.
7 Zarlenga, *The Lost Science of Money*, p. 13.
8 P. Steinkeller, 'The Ur III Period', in R. Westbrook and R. Jasnow (eds.), *Security for Debt in Ancient Near Eastern Law*, Boston: Brill, 2001, p. 48. Graeber also points to the fact that loans to peasants often were advanced with the aim of appropriating their land (D. Graeber, *Debt: The First 5,000 Years*, Brooklyn, NY: Melville House, 2011, pp. 64–65).
9 R. Westbrook, 'Introduction', in Westbrook and Jasnow (eds.), *Security for Debt*, p. 2.
10 Graeber, *Debt*, pp. 65 and 219.
11 R. Westbrook, 'The Old Babylonian Period', in Westbrook and Jasnow (eds.), *Security for Debt*, p. 74.
12 R. Jasnow, 'Pre-Demotic Pharaonic Sources', in Westbrook and Jasnow (eds.), *Security for Debt*, p. 38.
13 Proverbs 22:7. See also Deuteronomy 15:6 and 28:43–44. Throughout this book the quotations from the Bible are from the *New Revised Standard Version* translation.
14 In Jasnow, 'Pre-Demotic Pharaonic Sources', p. 42.
15 Matthew 18:23–35.
16 B.W. Frier, 'Interest and Usury in the Greco-Roman Period', in *The Anchor Bible Dictionary*, New York: Doubleday, 1992, vol. 3, p. 424.
17 N. Ferguson, *The Ascent of Money: A Financial History of the World*, New York: Penguin Press, 2008, p. 31.
18 G. Davies, *A History of Money: From Ancient Times to the Present Day*, Cardiff, Wales: University of Wales Press, 2002, pp. 71–74 and 92–93.
19 'The Code of Hammurabi'. Available at: http://www.sacred-texts.com/ane/ham/index.htm (accessed 25 June 2012).
20 Zarlenga, *The Lost Science of Money*, pp. 31–33.
21 Ibid., p. 30.
22 T.F. Divine, *Interest: An Historical & Analytical Study in Economics and Modern Ethics*, Milwaukee, WI: Marquette University Press, 1959, p. 11.
23 Ibid., pp. 19–20.
24 Ibid.

25 Frier, 'Interest and Usury', p. 424.
26 Divine, *Interest*, pp. 19–20.
27 A. Bloom (trans.), *The Republic of Plato*, New York: Basic Books, 1991, VIII, 556a-b.
28 Divine, *Interest*, p. 22; see also Elliott, C., *Usury: A Scriptural, Ethical and Economic View*, Millersburg, OH: Anti-Usury League, 1902, p. 261.
29 Divine, *Interest*, p. 22.
30 M.T. Cicero (W. Miller, trans.), *De Officiis*, London: Heinemann, 1928, II, XXI.
31 McCall, B.M., 'Unprofitable Lending: Modern Credit Regulation and the Lost Theory of Usury', *Cardozo Law Review*, 2008, vol. 30:2, 560.
32 Ibid., 560–561.
33 Bloom, *The Republic of Plato*, IV, 433a.
34 Ibid., IV, 443d-e.
35 Ibid., VIII, 543.
36 M. Hutchins (ed.), *Great Books of the Western World, vol. 7, Plato: The Seventh Letter*, Chicago: Encyclopedia Britannica, 1952, 325d.
37 T.L. Pangle (trans.), *The Laws of Plato*, New York: Basic Books, 1980, V, 742c.
38 Ibid., V, 743e.
39 Ibid., V, 743d.
40 Ibid., V, 745a.
41 Ibid., XI, 921b-d; Divine, *Interest*, p. 15.
42 Aristotle (T. Irwin, trans.), *Nicomachean Ethics*, Indianapolis: Hackett, 1999, V, 1133a.
43 Ibid., V, 1129b.
44 Ibid., V, 1130–1133b.
45 Ibid., V, 1131b.
46 Ibid., V, 1133a.
47 Ibid., V, 1133b.
48 Ibid., V, 1133b.
49 Ibid.
50 E.g., Ferguson, *The Ascent of Money*, p. 23.
51 Aristotle, *Nicomachean Ethics*, V, 1133a.
52 Aristotle (P.L. Phillips Simpson, trans.), *The Politics of Aristotle*, Chapel Hill, NC: University of North Carolina Press, 1997, 1258b and a respectively.
53 Ibid., 1258a.
54 Aristotle, *Nicomachean Ethics*, IV, 1120a.
55 Ibid., IV, 1121b–1122a.
56 Cicero, *De Officiis*, I, XLII.
57 M.P. Cato and M.T. Varro (W.D. Hooper, trans.), *On Agriculture*, Cambridge, MA: Harvard University Press; W. Heinemann, Ltd., 1934, p. 3.
58 M.T. Cicero (A.P. McKinlay, trans.), *Letters of a Roman Gentleman*, Boston: Houghton Mifflin, 1926, XLVII.
59 Cicero, *De Officiis*, II, XXIV.
60 Cicero, *Letters of a Roman Gentleman*, XLVII.
61 L.A. Seneca (A. Stewart, trans.), *On Benefits*, Kessinger, n.d., VII, 10.
62 In Divine, *Interest*, p. 21.
63 Marcel Mauss, in the essay *The Gift*, points to a rule he had discovered in the gift phenomenon throughout cultures, namely that gifts carry three interlocking moral obligations: to give, to receive, and to reciprocate (M. Mauss (W.D. Halls, trans.), *The Gift: The Form and Reason for Exchange in Archaic Societies*, New York: W.W. Norton, 2000[1925]).
64 Plutarch (J. Dryden, trans.), *The Lives of the Noble Grecians and Romans*, New York: Modern Library, 1932, p. 606.

65 Ibid., p. 607. See also e.g., Petronius (W. Burnaby, trans.), *The Satyricon of Petronius Arbiter*, New York: Modern Library, 1929.
66 E.g., Deuteronomy 15:7–8; Leviticus 25:35.
67 Exodus 22:25; see also Leviticus 25:35–38.
68 Elliott, *Usury*, p. 17.
69 Leviticus 25 and Deuteronomy 15, respectively.
70 1 Samuel 22:2.
71 2 Kings 4:1–7.
72 Ezekiel 18:13.
73 E.g., Psalms 15:5, 112:5.
74 Nehemiah 5:1–13.
75 B. Chilton, 'Debts', in *The Anchor Bible Dictionary*, New York: Doubleday, 1992, vol. 2, p. 114.
76 Divine, *Interest*, p. 8.
77 Leviticus 25; Deuteronomy 15.
78 Divine, *Interest*, p. 25.
79 Matthew 5:17–18.
80 Saint Cyprian (M. Bevenot, trans.), *The Lapsed. The Unity of the Catholic Church*, Westminster, MD: Newman Press, 1957, p. 6.
81 Saint Basil (A.C. Way, trans.), *Exegetic Homilies*, Washington, DC: Catholic University of America Press, 1963, Homily 12.
82 E.g., C. McCambley, 'Against Those Who Practice Usury by Gregory of Nyssa', *Greek Orthodox Theological Review*, 1991, vol. 36:3–4, 287–302.
83 Lactantius (M.F. McDonald, trans.), *The Divine Institutes, Books I – VII*, Washington, DC: Catholic University of America Press, 1964, VI, 18.
84 In L.M. Zucker, 'S. Ambrosii: *De Tobia*. A Commentary, with an Introduction and Translation', *The Catholic University of America Patristic Studies*, vol. 35. Washington, DC: Catholic University of America, 1933, p. 65.
85 Saint Augustine (P. Schaff, ed.), 'Expositions on the Book of Psalms', in *A Select Library of Nicene and Post-Nicene Fathers of the Christian Church*, vol. 8, Edinburgh: T & T Clark, 1996, Psalm 36:6.
86 Saint Leo the Great (J.P. Freeland and A.J. Conway, trans.), 'Sermons', in *The Fathers of the Church*, vol. 93, Washington, DC: Catholic University of America Press, 1996, Sermon 17:3.
87 Saint Augustine, 'Letter 154', in R.P. Maloney, 'The Teaching of the Fathers on Usury: An Historical Study on the Development of Christian Thinking', *Vigiliae Christianae*, 1973, vol. 27:4, 260.
88 Deuteronomy 23:19–20.
89 N.J. Dawood (trans.), *The Koran*, London: Penguin Books, 1974, 2:275.
90 In A. Ali, 'Globalization and Greed: A Muslim Perspective', in P.F. Knitter and C. Muzaffar (eds.), *Subverting Greed: Religious Perspectives on the Global Economy*, Maryknoll, NY: Orbis Books, 2002, p. 147.
91 Dawood, *The Koran*, 2:282.
92 R.I. Beekun, *Islamic Business Ethics*, Herndon, VA: International Institute of Islamic Thought, 1997, p. 47.
93 Dawood, *The Koran*, 2:280.
94 Ibid., 2:276.

4   The scholastic theory of usury and its ultimate marginalization

The commercial revolution of the twelfth century enormously increased the frequency and size of financial dealings compared to the economically depressed previous centuries. This also brought back the debate on usury. The medieval scholastics were at the heart of the renewed elaboration of the theory of usury. The Protestant Reformation, however, challenged their work by bringing into play different approaches toward usury, which ultimately caused division in the Christian interpretation of the usury prohibition. The developments that took place in post-Reformation thought further exacerbated that division. The result was that the monetary views of Aristotle and the scholastic theory of usury became marginalized. The aim of this chapter is to present how these shifts took place.

The scholastic condemnation of usury

The scholastic method, formed around the year 1200, was a rational investigation of a vast array of problems approached from opposing points of view meant to reach "an intelligent, scientific solution that would be consistent with accepted authorities, known facts, human reason, and Christian faith."[1] An important aspect of scholastic thought was a revival of the thought of Aristotle. Because the scholastics were Christian philosophers and theologians, their thought also included the teachings of the Bible, of the church Fathers (important carriers of Christian thought between the second and the eighth centuries) and of the ecumenical councils (broadly represented and gathered to settle church matters, particularly doctrinal in nature). In addition, the scholastics occasionally incorporated into their debates Roman law and philosophy. Their aim was an honest search for truth based on diverse spheres of thought available at the time.

Economic boom and renewed debate on usury in the middle ages

Equipped with the thousand-year-old Christian doctrine, Aristotelian thought, and other sources of knowledge (philosophical and legal), the scholastics also began to discuss some of the crucial economic issues of their times. Their concern, however, was primarily moral, as for them economic activity was a human activity and as such could not have taken place in some kind of moral vacuum, which is precisely what modern economics has done by assuming economic processes to be "amoral." Thus in scholastic thought economic issues always had moral connotations. Zarlenga even calls the scholastics "the moral economists."[2] Perhaps the hottest economic issue taken up by them was that of usury.

At least partly, the reemergence of the concern with usury in the late twelfth and thirteenth centuries was due to the commercial boom of that period. Apparently, usury, or even moneylending, did not pose a major problem in earlier medieval Europe when economic activities remained depressed. The commercial revival brought along "a speculative credit boom," as moneylenders had no qualms about charging high rates of interest, which civil law permitted.[3] Thus the renewed debate on usury was not initiated for moralizing purposes, but was rather a response to the public outcry over interest-bearing moneylending activities. It was "the consequence of growing awareness of the need in society to regulate financial transactions."[4] The scholastics saw it as their duty to take up the issue, because, as put by William of Auxere (1160–1220), "if men were silent against usurers, the stones would cry out if they could."[5]

Undoubtedly, the monastic revival had also its say in the debate on usury. As a matter of fact, the very establishment of the Franciscan Order was itself a reaction to the commercialization of life in various urban centers of the thirteenth century. The preaching of Francis of Assisi, who himself was the son of a merchant, and who ultimately denounced the wealth of his family, was a powerful symbolic backlash against "unregulated pursuit of profit" of that time.[6] For the friars, the root of all evil was avarice, and the monastic ideals to which they committed themselves were meant to help them to cultivate habits overcoming this human vice. It was this focus on avarice that formed the moral basis for their condemnation of usury. Although among the Franciscans there were some attempts, for example that of Duns Scotus (1265–1308), to intellectually evaluate the prohibition of usury,[7] their overall impact was predominantly in the sphere of spiritual-moral reaction to the issue of usury.

The Dominicans, another order established in the thirteenth century, began to develop a different approach condemning usury, based on the thought of Aristotle, Roman law with its natural law tradition, biblical teaching, and the Christian tradition. The most influential among them was Thomas Aquinas (1225–1274).

Similarly to Aristotle, Aquinas takes up the issue of usury in the context of his deliberations with regard to the virtue of justice. For him the principle is clear: "to take usury for money lent is unjust in itself, because this is to sell what does not exist, and this evidently leads to inequality which is contrary to justice." In elaborating this principle, Aquinas points out that for certain things, such as wine or wheat, the use of them means consumption. In the case of such commodities, granting the use of the commodity automatically means granting the thing itself. Consequently, if someone tried to sell separately for example wine and the use of wine, that would mean benefiting twice from selling the same thing, an unjust act. He then distinguishes that category of things from the objects, such as houses, of which use can be separated from the ownership, meaning that granting the use of them is not equal to the transfer of owner-ship (in the case of a house it would for example mean to rent it out). Aquinas places money in the former category. Based on that, he comes to the conclusion that "the proper and principal use of money is its consumption or alienation whereby it is sunk in exchange." Thus it is in the nature of money that makes it "unlawful to take payment for the use of money lent."[8]

In the view of Aquinas, commensurability of values in exchange is crucial to the proper understanding of the function of money. For him, just as for Aristotle, natural wealth, such as food, clothing, and shelter, is a different cat-egory from the wealth artificially created by men. Aquinas places money in the category of artificial wealth.[9] As such, money functions as a standard that of itself cannot be bought or sold. It mediates exchanges in which things (other than the standard itself) are bought and sold and serves as basis of valuation to keep exchanges within the confines of justice. In such perception of money as an unsalable standard measure in economic exchanges Aquinas anchors his objection to usury.

Following the tradition of the church Fathers, Aquinas also points to the possible tension between the spiritual-moral depravity of usury and the civil laws allowing the charging of interest on loans. He admits that in human affairs justice is normally governed by civil laws. But he objects to the claim that because civil law permits usury, there was no problem with it. To argue his stance, Aquinas points out that human laws often leave certain actions unpunished because they take into consideration "the condition of those who are imperfect." He also admits the difficulty with the attempt to legally punish "all sins." But then, by referring to the view of Aristotle, Aquinas states that permitting usury by civil laws does not change the fact that "to make money by usury is exceedingly unnatural."[10] This is why, at least on moral and spiritual grounds, usury should still be condemned.

For Aquinas, the attainment of ultimate happiness is inseparable from eternal law, or God's rational plan for the created world. Yet in his system of thought it is natural law that mediates eternal law, or in other words, "natural law is the participation of eternal law in the rational creature." It is so because human reason, itself God-given, "reflecting on the creation made by God can deter-mine how God wants us to act or what constitutes our own flourishing and happiness."[11] Natural law, then, also means rational ordering of the world. By emphasizing that usury is primarily about inequality within exchange relation-ships, Aquinas points out that usury disturbs not only *natural justice*, but also *divine (eternal) law*. As a result, the fact that Aquinas anchored a condemnation of usury in natural law helped him to preserve the prohibition of usury as found in the Bible, the teachings of the Fathers, Greek philosophy, Roman thought and law, or Islam, and thus to present it as a view that should be universally held.

Some, nevertheless, take a very critical stance toward Aquinas's condemnation of usury. Thomas Woods, for example, attempts to undermine the argumenta-tion of Aquinas from two angles. One of them concerns Aquinas's claim that lending money at interest would be like "selling the same thing twice." And to this Woods answers: "So what? What exactly is wrong with that, particularly since both parties agree to the terms?"[12] But one can immediately ask: when does the mere fact that two parties agree to something make the agreement just of itself? From ethical (and often legal) perspectives, there are at least two instances that cause a contract to be considered as tainted: coercion and lack of sufficient relevant information as to the terms of the contract one enters.

The second criticism put forward by Woods concerns Aquinas's endorsement of investment partnerships (*societas*), which in the view of Woods lacks logical coherence with what Aquinas said about usury. According to Aquinas, when someone entrusts money to a merchant or a craftsman in a sort of partnership, that person does not transfer the ownership of the money. As a result, he still bears the risk of the venture, even if the work is done by the merchant or the craftsman. Based on that, the one who has entrusted money to the partnership is entitled to the profit from the undertaking.[13] At the same time his condemnation of usury is based on the fact that as in the case of other fungible goods (such as wine or wheat), it is unjust to charge for the thing itself and for its use. This is so, because granting the use of such a thing automatically means transferring the ownership of it.[14] According to Woods, this poses "serious intellectual difficulties" in the argumentation of Aquinas, because the fact that in partnerships the use of money is given to somebody else without transfer of the ownership "contradicts" Aquinas's claim in the debate on usury that with regard to money its "use and ownership are inseparable."[15]

What Woods apparently fails to see, however, is that there is a difference in the concept of "use" in the case of the lending of money and in partnership itself. In the lending of money there is a transfer of ownership and the borrower totally controls the use of the borrowed money. The only responsibility he has toward the lender is to return the amount borrowed. In partnerships, on the other hand, despite the apparent transfer of funds, the use of money was not separated from ownership, because the one investing in the partnership bore the risk of loss in the venture, and thus could set limits on the use of the invested funds. In partnership, then, a designated partner (or partners) used the invested money *on behalf* of the owners of the funds and only "in accordance with the common venture."[16]

To sum up, by the time of Aquinas there was a widespread agreement that usury should be prohibited. In principle, three reasons were given as undergirding the condemnation of usury: first, money belonged to the fungible category of goods, and therefore was not a productive asset; second, money was a fixed medium of exchange carrying a fixed price; and third, the ownership of money meant only the right to use the money to purchase goods or assets and so the lender was not allowed to "charge separately for the use and ownership of money."[17] Doubtless to say, for Aquinas, usury was sinful from the spiritual perspective (the very first question Aquinas asks with regard to usury is whether it is a sin to earn money by loaning money).[18] However, following the Aristotelian view of money, Aquinas became convinced that usury primarily had to do with the very nature of money. The result was that he categorized usury, as the use of money against the dictates of the nature of money, to be also unjust from the moral perspective.

Finally, although a significant proportion of the medieval discussion on the issue of usury was conducted in the context of commutative (or corrective) justice, at times it was additionally presented as a problem of distributive justice. At least for some, usury was also unjust by the fact that charging interest on money lent caused a redistribution of wealth from the poor to the rich. An argument condemning usury from the perspective of distributive justice can for example be found in *Commentaria Apparatus in Quinque Libros Decretalium* by Pope Innocent IV (c. 1195–1254). Saint Bernardino of Siena (1380–1444) also argued that usury only made the needy worse off.[19]

Interest – a legitimate compensation to the lender

The development of the scholastics' views on usury, as outlined above, did not however end there. The scholastics gradually noticed the need for further elaboration. By anchoring the condemnation of usury in natural justice, Aquinas realized that the lending of money without interest also creates a certain inequality in exchange from the perspective of the lender. This is so because to the borrower such a loan becomes also a benefit, and as such it carries with it the obligation to compensate for the benefit received.[20] Actually, for Aquinas what is due to another may be due in a legal or a moral sense. While what he calls "legal debt" is about rendering to another what originally belonged to that person, and now is due by virtue of having been stolen, or having been received as a loan or deposit, "moral debt" arises from giving to another what is one's own.[21] As a result, in the case of a loan, the borrower has the obligation to repay the legal debt, meaning to return the amount borrowed, and the obligation to repay the moral debt, meaning to reciprocate the benefit. However, the moral due does not have the meaning of debt in the strict sense (is not a matter of justice proper) but in the sense of the demands one is expected to meet in order to live a virtuous life.[22] Moreover, the teaching of Aquinas, especially on restitution, also seems to open up prospects of a limited compensation for a loss incurred (*damnum emergens*). Such compensation, nevertheless, could not be required at the beginning of a loan.[23]

Aquinas, by including in the debate on usury the perspective of the lender, opened the possibility to consider what could be rightful claims for compensation on the part of the lender. In addition to recouping for loss to capital, Cardinal Hostiensis (c. 1200–1271) put forward prospects of charging beyond the principal as compensation for "*lucrum cessans*," or forgone profit that the lender could make by investing the lent funds in another venture. Pierre de Jean Olivi (1248–1298) also took a similar stance on *lucrum cessans*. Such provision, however, was meant only for those who lent out of charity, and thus were not professional lenders.[24] It nevertheless was very significant because it opened options for rightful claims for compensation of forgone profit on the money lent.

Through scholarly debates, the scholastics gradually gained a broad consensus that usury should be condemned on the basis of the principle that in a loan of *mutuum*, the good borrowed must be returned "to an equation of values"[25] to meet the demands of commutative justice. Because money was considered as having relatively stable fixed value, the mere passing of time did not provide sufficient grounds for charging over the principal in a loan of *mutuum*. Time-value of money just by itself was not a reason by which one could claim interest on money lent. The lender, however, was rightfully entitled to compensation on two grounds: emergent loss (*damnum emergens*) – a direct or indirect cost incurred in the process of making the loan as well as risk of one's capital, and cessant gain (*lucrum cessans*) – a forgone opportunity of gain by the means of money lent. The scholastics had a common understanding that there was nothing in a loan of *mutuum* itself that could justify charging interest. Rather, it was other circumstances accompanying the loan that provided basis for legitimate compensation. Such compensation was itself part of commutative justice.

Regrettably, in some modern works the two grounds for legitimate compensation – emergent loss (*damnum emergens*) and cessant gain (*lucrum cessans*) – are not seen as an honest search for justice in moneylending practices. For example Chown presents them among "a number of loopholes" invented "to permit interests to be charged."[26] Obviously Chown is unable to approach usury as the scholastics did: as a justice issue. Instead he judges it from a much later utilitarian perspective as an obstacle to "the growing needs of commerce."[27] In similar vein, Reinhart and Rogoff claim that, because "the church enforced usury laws that were intended to prevent Christians from lending to each other at interest," so "in order to gain access to larger wealth pools, borrowers (sometimes with the help of theologians) had to think of ways to try to circumvent church law."[28] Amazingly, while talking about "Eight Centuries of Financial Folly" – as the subtitle of the work suggests – Reinhart and Rogoff mention usury only once in the entire book. What these and similar views miss totally is that the usury prohibition was *not* an obstacle to prosperity. The examples of Islamic societies, in Venice and others, which thrived without violating the prohibition of usury (of course, this does not mean that *all* members of those societies respected the principle of usury), fly in the face of what modern economists and commentators on finance tend to say about usury.

It is worth then restating that for the scholastics, the concept of interest meant nothing else but a just compensation to the lender. As a matter of fact, the very notion of interest takes its meaning from the legitimate compensation to maintain an equity of values within a financial relationship.[29] Already in Roman law, interest carried the meaning of "the compensation for damage or loss suffered by the creditor resulting from the debtor's failure to return the loan (itself gratuitous in principle) at the date specified by the contract."[30] The Latin verb *intereo* actually means "to be lost." Thus, in its origin, interest carried the meaning of loss, not gain.[31] And it was this understanding of "interest" that made the scholastics distinguish between usury and interest – the former seen as money demanded in excess of the amount lent, which disrupted the equity within a financial relationship, and the latter meaning just compensation to the lender.[32] For them the principle was clear that it was always unjust to engage in usury.

The late scholastics of the sixteenth and seventeenth centuries, responding to changing economic circumstances, continued the tradition of condemning usury. For example, for Juan de Lugo (1583–1660), a Spanish Jesuit, usury meant "gain immediately arising as an obligation from a loan of *mutuum*." The crucial characteristics of such a loan were constancy in number, weight, and measure of the article lent, and that it immediately became the property of the one borrowing it with the obligation to return an article of the same kind and quality.[33] Such were also the features of so called fungible goods, or the goods where one could take the place of another. Money was considered to be "the perfect example of a fungible good."[34] In this way the late scholastics upheld the principle condemning usury on the basis of the equivalence of values of the goods in transaction. Because by then the entire debate of usury was anchored in the demands of justice, they also recognized legitimacy of compensation for emergent loss (*damnum emergens*) and cessant gain (*lucrum cessans*) in the lending of money.

Since the Middle Ages, then, the teaching of the Catholic church has understood usury as unjustified gain from a loan, or in other words, as taking unfair advantage in moneylending. The church authorities time and time again reaffirmed the denunciation of the practice of usury. None of these decisions has ever been repealed. The scholastic theory of usury was formally reconfirmed by Pope Benedict XIV in his encyclical *Vix Pervenit* (1745). In it, the pope condemns usury, but endorses legitimate compensation due to the circumstances accompanying a loan, which are extrinsic to it. He equally approves "honest gain" made through partnerships.[35] In the nineteenth century there were some fourteen decisions issued by the Congregations of the Holy Office, the Penitentiary, and the Propaganda declaring that the faithful who lend money at moderate rates of interest were "not to be disturbed."[36] Up to now, such a view of usury has represented the official stance of the church. Unfortunately, as will be presented in the following chapters, the church authorities did not notice the change taking place in the banking industry over centuries, which gradually transformed money, lending, and so-called interest into something very different from what the church authorities thought them to be.

The scholastic theory of usury, however, was not left without challenge. Just as in the ancient world, usury prohibition continued to face problems on the level of practice. Yet beginning in the sixteenth century, the practice of usurious lending was gradually aided with theoretical challenges.

The Protestants on usury

The impact of the Protestant Reformation lies not so much in its opposition to the Catholic church, but rather in the shift of perception of how one should realize Christian ideals. By emphasizing the individual and the subjective in the form of *sola gratia* (only grace), *sola fide* (only faith), and *sola scriptura* (only scripture) – meaning that a person could be saved only by the grace of God, only by personal faith, rooted in the teaching of the scripture as the only source of Christian doctrine interpreted individually – the Protestant movement succeeded in distinguishing itself from the Catholic approach stressing the "both . . . and" (grace and good works, faith and reason, the Bible and apostolic tradition as the sources of Christian doctrine). Such a shift within Christianity had a profound impact on the perception of usury, and laid the foundation for a gradual removal of a neatly organized scholastic theory of lending at interest from the moral radar of financial dealings.

Luther's condemnation of usury

Only for the brief period between 1523 and 1525 did Martin Luther (1483–1546) appear to be somewhat less critical of the practice of usury. The main reasons were peasant revolts, the leaders of which advocated the abolition of private property.[37] Otherwise Luther can be considered as a vociferous critic of usury. In his view,

> When money is lent and a charge made or more taken back than was originally made over, that is usury, and as such is condemned by every law. Hence those are usurers who charge 5 or 6 more on the hundred on the money they lend . . . nor can they be saved unless they do penance.[38]

For Luther, anyone who charged interest on loans was "a thief, robber and murderer," and therefore was to be denied Christian burial if death occurred before repentance. He appears to be particularly critical of the "great ogres of the world who can never charge enough per cent."[39] The prime targets of Luther's denunciations were Jews who had become influential moneylenders.[40]

It is unlikely, and thus contrary to the claim of Zarlenga, that Luther "was not aware of the advanced usury concepts developed by the Scholastics."[41] Luther, himself an Augustinian monk and an ordained priest, was trained in scholastic philosophy and theology. Moreover, he also seems to have been very familiar with the thought of Aristotle: "I know my Aristotle . . . I have lectured on him, and I understand him better than do St. Thomas or Scotus."[42] Nevertheless, he absolutely rejected the natural philosophy of Aristotle, because for him Christian theology far exceeded it. In his words, "the whole of Aristotle is to theology as darkness is to light."[43] Nevertheless, having been trained in scholastic thought he was not able totally escape its influence. This can for example be deduced from his perception of money as being sterile and the condemnation of monopolistic banking anchored in the scholastic view that monopoly induces economic coercion.[44]

Luther ultimately not only distanced himself from the scholastic theory of usury, but became very critical of what the scholastics accepted as a legitimate compensation accompanying a loan, meaning a moderate rate that falls under the categories of emergent loss (*damnum emergens*) and/or forgone profit (*lucrum cessans*). According to him, "the greatest misfortune of the German nation is easily the traffic in interest . . . The devil invented it and the Pope, by giving his sanction to it, has done untold evil throughout the world." As for extrinsic titles for compensation, he saw them to be a "pretty sham and pretence by which a man can oppress others without sin."[45]

Apparently, in order to be true to the Reformation dictum of *sola gratia* (only grace), *sola fide* (only faith), and *sola scriptura* (only scripture), Luther had no other option but to turn against the scholastic universalist theory of usury. This is why, while the scholastics in their debates on usury drew from the Bible, the writings of the Fathers, Aristotle, Roman law, and other available sources, Luther built his argument solely on a biblical basis.

It was, then, the biblical prohibition of usury that for Luther was permanently binding. His favorite biblical passage used in the arguments against the practice of usury is the statement of Jesus from the Gospel of St. Luke that one should lend expecting nothing in return.[46] This is why, in a loan contract, any claim above the principal was against the teaching of the Bible, and eventually usury. In order to connect his theory of usury with the realities in which people lived, Luther tended to point to the destructive social effects of lending at interest. This, in turn, suggests that his view of usury was actually stricter compared to that of the scholastics. According to George O'Brien:

> Luther tore the whole of this [scholastic] beautiful fabric to the ground, and carried back the teaching on usury to the primitive bare prohibition of all gain on loans, with the inevitable result that it could not be lived up to in the facts of modern life, and that it consequently fell into disrepute.[47]

Calvin's justification of usury

Far more revolutionary and having much greater impact on later developments were the usury views of Calvin. They were expressed in a letter to his friend, Claude de Sachin. In it, Calvin, like Luther, puts the biblical teaching on usury at the heart of his argument, but then adds his own interpretation. He departs from the position that "if all usury is condemned tighter fetters are imposed on the conscience than the Lord [Jesus] himself would wish." It is here that he already distances himself from both the scholastics and from Luther.

As for Luther's favorite biblical passage from the Gospel of St. Luke, in which Jesus states that one should lend expecting nothing in return, Calvin agrees that Jesus "wished to restrain men's abuse of lending." Yet then he explains that Jesus' statement should be rather interpreted as a command "to lend to those from whom there is no hope of receiving or regaining anything." And from this he deduces that while such should be the practice toward the poor, Jesus did not forbid charging interest on lending to the rich. In terms of the prohibitions of usury in the Old Testament, Calvin claims that they could be applied only to the Jews and their particular circumstances, and therefore were irrelevant where the conditions were different. As a result, he finds the biblical teaching on usury either irrelevant to the circumstances of his time (Old Testament) or as open to interpretation (New Testament).[48] But this does not mean that Calvin abandoned the Reformation principle to place the Bible at the heart of his teaching. With regard to the usury prohibition, Calvin reduced its role predominantly to matters of charity.

With regard to charging interest on loans, Calvin claims that it should follow the principle of equity. According to him, "usury must be judged, not by a particular passage of Scripture, but simply by the rules of equity."[49] Calvin was convinced that just as in the case of the renting of an asset where interest is charged, an interest can also be charged on money lent. Otherwise, why renting a house as a physical entity could beget money and money itself could not. But there is a catch in this logic. Calvin simply mingles two types of transactions that already in Roman law were treated as different forms of contracts – *commodatum* and *mutuum*. The former meant lending of a nonconsumable good to which an obligation to return the identical good was attached and that permitted additional charges for use of the good lent. The latter, on the other hand, referred to the lending of consumable goods combined with an obligation to later return goods of identical type and quantity, which in principle had to be gratuitous, but that gradually allowed borrowers to promise additional fees (*stipulatio*), although such promise was perceived as a separate agreement. While renting a house represented *commodatum* type of transaction, lending of money belonged to the contract of *mutuum*.

By mixing the two types of transactions, Calvin was able to argue that money, just as other assets, was barren only when it was not used, but could beget more money when employed for productive purposes. On the basis of such logic, justice also required that interest should be charged on money lent. To be true to Calvin, he did not propose that such a requirement should be universal because this at times could be against charity. Based on the biblical teaching of Jesus, the view of Calvin was that one should lend to people in dire need without expecting any interest to be paid (the charity principle), but at the same time a modest interest rate (usually 5 percent at that time) could be charged from other borrowers (the "equity" principle). In fact, Calvin perceived usury as morally abhorrent, but took the stance that the sinful human condition forced its acceptance. In his own words: "It could be wished that all usury and the name itself were first banished from the earth. But as this cannot be accomplished it should be seen what can be done for the public good."[50]

Overall, then, Calvin considered the issue of usury rather as a form of lesser evil in the midst of the fallen human condition. Moreover, it appears that the letter expressing his opinions on usury was never intended for publication. His views favorable to usury, nevertheless, were soon "cited without the restriction he imposed, and his authority was invoked justifying usury of every sort."[51] Apparently, for some, Calvin's views became very useful.

Although the justification of usury by Calvin had its nuances, it eventually marked a clear break with the scholastic tradition. In terms of practical outcomes, one may conclude that Calvin reached a similar point to that of the later scholastics, namely that in lending of money, a modest interest rate should be permitted. However, such a conclusion can be very misleading. For the scholastics, usury was primarily about violation of the principle of justice (understood as equivalence of values). And it was again the principle of justice that allowed charging compensation on the basis of loss accompanying the loan (*damnum emergens*) or forgone profit (*lucrum cessans*). The change in the economic conditions simply demanded a new *application* of the principle to those conditions. For Calvin, on the other hand, money was not different from other assets, so interest could be justifiably charged on money lent. Thus while Calvin claimed that the charging of interest on money lent was intrinsic to a contract, the scholastics argued that it was only extrinsic circumstances accompanying the loan that could provide the grounds for just compensation.

In the end, the scholastic view actually preserved the meaning of interest found already in Roman law as a legitimate claim due to *loss* suffered. In Calvin's theory, on the other hand, interest was more like a justified share in the productive outcome of the loan, thus carrying a positive meaning of *gain*. For Calvin, "equity" in charging interest on loans meant that the lender was still supposed to *gain* (get interest payment) even if the loan failed to produce profit. This was a very crucial paradigm shift in the perception of loan transactions.

What lies at the heart of the shift in understanding "interest" is differing views between Calvin and the scholastics with regard to the nature of money. Continuing the Aristotelian tradition, the scholastics considered money to be barren, not to be able to produce anything of itself. For Calvin, on the other hand, money was just like other assets, such as a house or land, which could be used for productive purposes. Money, in the same way as many other assets, was barren only when it remained unemployed, but could be fruitful when put into use. Thus Calvin, by attributing to money the characteristics of capital, replaced a very coherent, neatly nuanced scholastic theory of money with a simplified view of the fruitfulness of money. Money itself became an asset that once invested could produce more money, and the lending of money became a way of increasing money. The foundation for growing wealth disparity was laid (Hilaire Belloc even described the Reformation as "a rising of the rich against the poor").[52] What put limits on the productive (begetting) potential of money was a "price" for money, or in other words the market rate of interest. This eventually became the dominant money paradigm in modern economics.

Yet Calvin's views of money brought along something perhaps even more important – a growing preoccupation with money. Once money was forced to be fruitful, a market for multiplying money quickly developed. This, in turn, brought along cycles of the money craze. One of the most famous examples of this is the so-called tulipmania that took place in Holland from the 1620s to 1637.[53] During that period, the bulbs of tulips (the flowers introduced from Turkey at the end of the sixteenth century) became a source of wild speculation, by which their prices were pushed to unprecedented highs – the average price of a single bulb surpassed the annual income of a skilled worker. In the

1630s many people, including some poor families, were borrowing money to buy tulips. Needless to say, when the bubble burst in February of 1637, as the prices dropped drastically in a single week, many could not pay their massive debts and went bankrupt. However, perhaps due to the enormous size of the debts, the debtors were not forced to repay all their debts. Since then recurring bubbles (the rise of certain asset prices beyond what incomes from the real economy are capable of sustaining) have become part of economic realities. Interestingly, for Investopedia, the tulipmania simply "reflects the general cycle of a bubble," which people apparently have no other choice but to accept as a *normal* aspect of modern economy.[54]

The fact that the first money mania took place in Holland, however, was not an accident, for it was there that by the beginning of the seventeenth century the ideas of Calvin became particularly strong and widely accepted.[55]

As Calvinism began to dominate some societies, including the Anglo-Saxon ones, usury, for centuries functioning as moral radar on financial dealings, began to lose its effectiveness. This also caused a break in the moral tradition shaped by the Middle Ages, which stressed a search for objective criteria in condemning usury anchored in commensurability of exchanges, namely justice. The impact of such a break on later developments was immense, as now it was at most the legal system that was charged with the responsibility to set interest rates. The problem with rate regulation, however, is that it is arbitrary. Without a clear principle, it becomes rather difficult to judge *what forms the basis of justice in moneylending* and *what rate of interest could be considered just*. Throughout the remaining chapters we will continue to show that in the context of the workings of the modern moneylending industry this has become a very valid concern.

Marginalization of Aristotelian and scholastic views

By defining itself in opposition to the Roman Catholic Church, the Protestant Reformation ultimately turned also against the Aristotelian/scholastic theory of usury. This subsequently caused gradual marginalization of the view of money as a legitimate creation of government (*nomisma*), and ultimately led to further confusion of *what* money really was, *who* had the power to issue it, and for what purpose (*why*).

Break with the Aristotelian/scholastic theory of usury

From the historical perspective, the Protestant Reformation not only brought along a new split within Christianity (the previous one, with Eastern Christianity, took place in the eleventh century). Perhaps more importantly it accentuated growing differences in perceiving the world at large. The medieval world, while not free of diversities, disputes and even disagreements, was overall relatively united, mainly due to a sharing of the same religious faith and common metaphysical principles. It was a more static, contemplative world, a world that philosophically was focused on abstract universals dealt with deductively and on balancing the good of an individual with the attainment of common good. The Reformation brought to the fore ideas that made the impression that a brand new world was being created. The focus of this "new" world was predominantly on the autonomous individual, the study of nature (including the human person) conducted through the inductive method, and the perception of knowledge as a useful tool for practical solutions.

At least to some thinkers, in this "new" post-Reformation world there was no place for the views of Aristotle. Among those who clearly wanted to end Aristotle's dominance in diverse spheres of thought was Francis Bacon (1561–1626). "Of all the enemies of the New Philosophy, Aristotle and the Aristotelian spirit appear to have been regarded by him as the most dangerous."[56] In his fervor, Bacon would even go as far as launching very personal attacks on Aristotle, describing him as "impatient, intolerant, ingenious in raising objections, perpetually concerned to contradict, hostile to and contemptuous of earlier thinkers, and purposely obscure."[57] Put simply, in order to let Bacon's natural philosophy (inductive, scientific and applicable) grow, Aristotle had to go.

It is not difficult to see that in such an anti-Aristotelian climate the scholastic prohibition of usury, itself rooted in Aristotle, was also prone to attacks. In the essay *Of Usury*, Bacon begins with a statement that "usury is a *concessum propter duritiem cordis*,"[58] or "a concession because of the hardness of heart." Just as Calvin, Bacon builds his argument in defense of usury on the biblical concept of human hard-heartedness. For him, "since there must be borrowing and lending, and men are so hard of heart as they will not lend freely, usury must be permitted."[59]

Interestingly, Bacon seems to be very aware of problems caused by usury. He lists several "discommodities of usury," as he calls these problems. First, usury "makes fewer merchants," as charging interest rates on money lent causes more people to hold their money for lending rather than investing purposes. Second, it makes merchants poorer because a bigger share of their earnings goes into paying debts and interest on money lent. Third, usury causes less income from the custom duties for governments due to the previous two problems. Fourth, it causes concentration of wealth in a few hands, while the flourishing of a state happens when wealth is spread more equally. Fifth, usury forces down the price of land, as keeping money for earning more money through lending reduces the amount of money that can be employed for its chief purposes such as merchandizing or purchasing. Sixth, it siphons resources meant to stir up diverse investments, improvements and inventions. Lastly, usury brings to ruin the estates of many, thus breeding "a public poverty."[60]

Yet Bacon also sees the usefulness of usury, or what he calls "the commodities of usury." He first points out that in trade, while in some respects usury hinders the development of trade, it can also have a positive influence because a great portion of merchandizing is done by young merchants who rely more on borrowing, the lack of which would bring trade to a standstill. Second, usury is an important means for the supply of money, otherwise many people in need of money would be forced to sell some of their assets (such as land), and gradually "bad markets would swallow them quite up." Third, Bacon argues, it is hard to imagine that people would be willing to lend money without profit, and lack of lending would cause great inconvenience. This is why, despite the fact that he was aware of various negative consequences of usury, he still was against abolishing it.[61]

In the end, Bacon proposed as a solution to set two rates of usury, one at 5 percent for common borrowers, and the other, higher one, for special purposes, such as merchandizing (for Bacon merchandizing was "the most lucrative" trade, and therefore could "bear usury at a good rate"), which would require a license. This way he thought he could reconcile "commodities and discommodities of usury" so that, on the one hand, "the tooth of usury be grinded, that it bite not too much," and, on the other hand, "that there be left open a means to invite monied men" to provide lending to those with special needs (e.g., merchants).[62]

The conclusions reached by Bacon show his inability to understand money as an abstract construct defined by law, as proposed by Aristotle. Moreover, his statement that all states had allowed charging interest on money lent flies in the face of historical evidence. As presented earlier, the moral stance condemning usury was widespread, and even in the legal system the approach toward usury was rather mixed, with periods when charging interest on lending was prohibited. However, perhaps the greatest problem with Bacon's views of usury was his moral minimalist point of departure based on the argument of the hardness of the human heart, thus further opening a door for human vices to play their role in financial dealings and wealth concentration.

In similar vein, the revered "father of modern economics," Adam Smith (1723–1790), embraced charging of interest on lending. For Smith, "interest" is the *revenue* (note the difference with the scholastics seeing interest as "loss") derived from lending money. This is how he explains it:

> It is the compensation which the borrower pays to the lender, for the profit which he has an *opportunity* of making by the use of money. Part of that profit naturally belongs to the borrower, who runs the risk and takes the trouble of employing it; and part to the lender, who affords him the *opportunity* of making this profit.[63]

The problem in Smith's argument is that he expects the borrower to pay back the debt and the interest even if the opportunity for making profit does not materialize. According to him, if the interest "is not paid from the profit which is made by the use of the money," it "must be paid from some other source of revenue, unless perhaps the borrower is a spendthrift, who contracts a second debt in order to pay the interest of the first."[64] Regardless of what may occur, the lender should get his money back, including his earning in the form of interest, no matter whether the borrower manages to make profit from the borrowed money or not. This is where Smith clearly differs from the scholastic and Islamic understanding that the right to share profits from an enterprise comes not from an "opportunity" to make profit, but from the actual profit made.

In the end, Smith takes the stance that the law should not prohibit charging interest on lending, because even if it does, it will not prevent the charging of interest anyway. The reason is that many people are in need of borrowing, and "nobody will lend without such a consideration for the use of their money as is suitable, not only what can be made by the use of it. but of the difficulty and danger of evading the law." This is why, according to Smith, it is the responsibility of the legal system to set the interest rates and to enforce their payments.[65]

Almost two centuries after Francis Bacon, Jeremy Bentham (1748–1832) still carried on the anti-Aristotelian campaign. For him Aristotle was "that celebrated heathen, who, in all matters wherein heathenism did not destroy his competence, had established a despotic empire over the Christian world." After this statement, similarly to Bacon, Bentham's attack on Aristotle discretely shifts to a more personal level. He accuses Aristotle of bestowing "uncommon pains" on many people, and of gaining a "great number of pieces of money that had passed through his hands (more perhaps than ever passed through the hands of a philosopher before or since)."[66]

In the *Defence of Usury*, Bentham launches his stance on usury, which is: "there can be no such thing as usury." The crucial reason for it is the difficulty to establish what rate of interest could be more adequate than another. Put simply, just as in the case of other commodities where prices are not fixed, so in the case of money, the price for lending should not be fixed.[67] As a result, Bentham argues, government should not attempt to establish any legal interest rates. The only guide for the amount of interest on lending that is acceptable is a customary convention. And the custom is supposed to result from "free choice." Bentham also claims that historical evidence of legal rates of interest proves that as far as past times are concerned, it was the legal rate that provided the most reliable basis for how high interest rates should be charged.[68]

Interestingly, Bentham's "historical evidence" does not include places and times that law forbade charging interest on money lent. For example, Bentham mentions the 10 percent interest rate at the time of Henry VIII,[69] but does not say that it was forbidden before him. In the section on "the Prejudices against Usury," he also does not blame the Bible for condemning usury, but ascribes it to Aristotle's control of the Christian world.[70] All this shows how selective Bentham was in picking his examples.

Overall, then, within the ranks of the new philosophy, there appeared a split in the views regarding usury. One, which could be termed the legal faction, proposed price controls over interest charged, or usury laws (e.g., Bacon and Smith). The other one, the laissez-faire noninterference faction, argued for the removal of legal controls of the interest charged in moneylending (e.g., Bentham).

The legal faction continued the old tradition and attempted to keep interest on lending within the sphere acceptable by most citizens. It is this tradition that in the post-Reformation developments gained strong support and, as a result, usury gradually came to be identified with the charging of interest on loans above the legal limits (predatory lending). In England, for example, at the end of the sixteenth century the legal ceiling of interest on lending was set at 10 percent, but then it was reduced to 8 percent in 1624 and to 6 percent in 1651. Nevertheless, interest rates actually charged were often much higher than the legal limits, forcing poor people "into a situation of debt, and effectively into prison, if they could not pay debts."[71] Despite criticism, directed primarily at failures of the legal system to control usury, apparently there was no improvement.[72]

In nineteenth-century England, however, the utilitarian arguments of Bentham against usury began gaining popularity, particularly among bankers, who began pushing for deregulation. This eventually led to the abolition of the Usury Laws in 1854, and the shift to the noninterference stance on usury. It is not difficult to imagine that this caused a rapid rise of exploitative loan schemes, and only gradually some countermeasures were introduced, such as the Money-Lenders Act (1900) and the Consumer Credit Act (1974).[73]

Various countries, nevertheless, have opted for legal limits on the interest charged in moneylending. Despite the theoretical break with the scholastic tradition, usury laws have expressed an awareness of the need to keep at least a certain approximation of commensurability in monetary exchanges (the main concern of both Aristotle and the scholastics). Up to now they are still present in the jurisdictions of many countries.

Marginalization of Aristotle's view of money

Throughout the Middle Ages, money was increasingly viewed as correlated with the intrinsic values of the metals it was made of. The gap between the Aristotelian and the metallist understandings of money was growing. It reached its peak in the work of Nicholas Oresme (1320–1382). In *De Moneta*, Oresme took the stance that in order to fulfill the mediating role in acquiring natural riches, money itself must represent some form of "riches," and thus must be made of some precious materials, such as gold or silver. Although Oresme's ultimate concern was equivalence of values (commensurability) in exchanges, or simply justice, by making money and wealth inseparable, he caused *the standard* of exchange itself to become sellable.[74] This was an obvious departure from Aquinas's view that money was a standard meant to mediate exchanges, which of itself could not be bought or sold. Moreover, while Aquinas placed money in the category of artificial wealth, in the thought of Oresme, money became part of natural wealth. The monetary stance of Oresme, then, not only further intensified the growing metallist perception of money, but also mingled money with other categories of natural wealth. This was a shift of unparalleled proportions.

The monetary views of Bentham, several centuries after Oresme, reflect a growing departure from the Aristotelian understanding of money. According to Bentham, although money does not beget more money of itself, with money that one borrows, "he might get a ram and a couple of ewes" and then after some time "he would find himself master of his three sheep, together with two, if not three, lambs." As a result, argues Bentham, that person could later sell the ram and the ewes to pay back the principal and a lamb to pay the interest, and in the end "he would be two lambs, or at least one lamb, richer than if he had made no such bargain." Amazingly, Bentham accuses Aristotle (and apparently also the scholastics) of "theological and philosophical conceits" because they claimed that money was barren, and yet, as presented in his example, by adding some "complexion" to one's thinking, the barren money could actually produce more money.[75]

Unfortunately for Bentham, Aristotle and the scholastics had showed much more sophistication in their thinking than he did. First of all, in the example of Bentham there could be no actual increase of money in circulation. It is a mere shift of money from one hand to another that made Bentham think that money increased. In reality, there was no increase of money in the system as such. Second, the perceived "complexion" in his thinking was nothing more than a confusion of two distinct forms of goods (sheep and money) that since antiquity had been considered as belonging to separate categories. The fundamental problem with Bentham's thinking (and all those similar to his) is that in case nature, due to some calamity or disease, does not provide the expected produce (no new lambs are born, or worse, the ram or ewe dies), an actual decrease in the outcome may occur. And yet if one is still forced to pay back not only the original loan, but also the interest, the result could be more impoverishment and debt enslavement. This is why the scholastics (and also Islamic finance), having anchored the entire issue in equivalence of values in exchanges, put the stress on sharing in the *actual profit* made, and were so critical of charging actual interest on the basis of a mere *opportunity to make profit*.

Among those greatly contributing to the marginalization of Aristotle's monetary views was also Adam Smith. In his *Wealth of Nations*, after a brief overview of how different commodities had money function as an instrument of commerce, Smith portrays metals as the most ideal commodities to take the role of money. According to him, "different metals have been made use of by different nations for this purpose. Iron was the common instrument of commerce among the ancient Spartans; copper among the ancient Romans; and gold and silver among all rich and commercial nations."[76] For Smith, only money that itself had an intrinsic value could fulfill its role as the medium for exchanging valuables, while "a public stamp" on money had basically a convenience function to guarantee "the quantity and uniform goodness" of the metals contained in coined money and to avoid tedious examining of the metallic content of money during each transaction.[77]

As a matter of fact, Smith was aware of paper money produced by banks. Nevertheless, he had his own explanation of how it worked: "A paper money consisting in bank notes, issued by people of undoubted credit, payable upon demand without any condition, and in fact always readily paid as soon as presented, is, in every respect, equal in value to gold and silver money; since gold and silver money can at any time be had for it."[78]

There is no doubt that Smith was particularly fond of the Bank of England – a privately created central bank. For him, it was "the greatest bank of circulation in Europe," with stability that was "equal to that of the British government."[79]

Unfortunately for Smith, in his laissez-faire zeal to keep money power in private hands, he was either unaware of how the bank really worked, or was intentionally concealing it. Already in 1707, a concerted attack by goldsmiths (in fact, a run on the Bank of England) took place. They demanded only £30,000 of the bank's notes to be redeemed in gold. The directors of the bank simply refused to bend to the demand, but they were still willing to redeem the notes of other customers. As it turns out, the notes were not necessarily "payable upon demand without any condition," and "always readily paid as soon as presented," as claimed by Smith. In fact, the Bank of England itself was prone to repeated crises. Zarlenga points out that "between 1694 and 1870, 25 years never passed without a crisis at the Bank."[80]

Moreover, according to Smith, to restrain a banker from issuing promissory notes, "when all his neighbours are willing to accept of them, is a manifest violation of that natural liberty which it is the proper business of law not to infringe, but to support."[81] In reality, the Bank of England used its growing political power to gradually push for more and more privileges. By the early 1740s, it already gained partial control over the issue of banknotes.[82] When one takes into consideration the fact that this was all happening over thirty years before Smith published the *Wealth of Nations* (1776), it becomes obvious that the above statements of Smith had more in common with ideological slogans than economic realities.[83]

Yet perhaps the strongest marginalization of the monetary views of Aristotle can be noticed among economists of the Austrian School. Most of its representatives have clung to the noninterventionist approach to market mechanisms (laissez-faire) and the perception of money as "a naturally-based commodity standard created by the marketplace."[84] Having opted for such a point of departure, they have become profoundly anti-Aristotelian, without even mentioning his name.[85]

Perhaps the most renowned view of Austrian leanings denying the legal authority of the power to create money comes from Ludwig von Mises. According to him, "the concept of money as a creature of law and the state is clearly untenable. It is not justified by a single phenomenon of the market."[86] The representatives of the Austrian School sometimes call history as the witness supporting such a view.[87] They also tend to claim that historical data supports their stance of money as intrinsically bound to some particular commodities, especially gold and silver.[88]

In reality, however, historical data taken in their entirety, and not just selectively, do not support such claims. Histories of both West and East provide compelling evidence that diverse societies used monies for which value did not depend on the "weight and fineness" of the metal used, or the state stamp as guaranteeing "weight and fineness" of the metallic content, and gold or silver, despite their availability, not necessarily became "dominant" money. For example, already Sparta for about three and a half centuries used the system in which the value of money (iron discs) appears to have been partly decreed, but mainly determined by the number of units in circulation, not by the value of the metal of which it was made.[89] Similarly, the Roman Republic gradually adopted copper coins (*aes grave*), for which the exchange value far exceeded the value of the commodity they were made of. It was this system that helped republican Rome to grow powerful. Interestingly, Rome chose bronze as the material for its fiat money, although it also had stockpiles of gold and silver cast into bars.[90]

A long monetary history in China even more strongly contradicts the stance that money has to be intrinsically equated with the value of various commodities. For centuries the Chinese perceived money creation as a core prerogative of the state, and in the course of time it was bronze coins that gained the reputation of "proper" money. The classical Chinese monetary view is that in contrast to commodity monies like gold and silver, the value of bronze coins was in their quantity and convenience in small exchanges. Already during the Han dynasty (206 BC – AD 220), there were some voices calling for the abolition of bronze coins and the adoption of more valuable commodities as media of exchange, but in the end they did not gain sufficient support.[91] During the Song dynasty (960–1279), bronze coins became so widely accepted that by the twelfth century, "Song coin assumed the role of the international currency of the trading world of East Asia, and to some extent of the Indian Ocean as well." This brought trouble in the end, because supplying coins for such a vast and expanding market turned out to be unsustainable. As a result, unable to issue a sufficient amount of coins, the Southern Song turned to pure paper money.[92]

The Mongol Yuan dynasty (1280–1368) rejected coin in favor of paper money, originally backed by bullion but later practically inconvertible into gold or silver. This marked a critical shift in Chinese economy away from the reliance on coin. Nevertheless, mistaken monetary policies of the Yuan, and later of Ming (1368–1644) in the form of issuance of excessive quantities of pure paper money caused another shift to precious metals, particularly silver, as "real" money. As a result, silver gradually gained the function as a store of value, a measure of value, and a medium of exchange. This is why the period between mid-fifteenth and mid-sixteenth centuries is sometimes referred to as a "silver century."[93] However, demand for coin in China grew again in the late seventeenth and eighteenth centuries. So in the end it turned out that "the greater utility of coin as an instrument of petty exchange" made coins "a premium over silver bullion."[94]

Yet perhaps the statement of Graeber with regard to how the Chinese really perceived money sums it up best: "For Chinese theorists . . . Aristotle's argument that money was simply a social convention was hardly radical; it was simply assumed."[95]

In short, for the scholastics, usury meant inequality (lack of commensurability) within money lending–borrowing relationships. The crucial element in the scholastic theory of usury was that there was nothing intrinsic in the loan of *mutuum* that justified charging interest (anything above the principal). Rather, it was the extrinsic titles such as actual loss or forgone opportunities of profit that provided basis for charging some interest. Therefore, in contrast to our modern understanding of interest as *gain*, the scholastics' effort was to preserve its meaning as found in Roman law where interest was nothing else but a title to compensation for *loss* incurred by the lender. The developments initiated by the Protestant Reformation led to a direct opposition not only to the Catholic Church, but to Aristotle and, ultimately, to the scholastic theory of usury. As the influence of the Reformation movement spread, particularly in its Calvinist form, gradually the usury principle became blurred and the monetary views of Aristotle became marginalized. These changes exacerbated a growing problem of abuse of the money power.

Notes

1 J.A. Weisheipl, 'Scholastic Method', in *New Catholic Encyclopedia*, vol. 12, New York: McGraw-Hill, 1967, p. 1145.
2 S. Zarlenga, *The Lost Science of Money: The Mythology of Money – the Story of Power*, Valatie, NY: American Monetary Institute, 2002, p. 177.
3 C.J. Mews and I. Abraham, 'Usury and Just Compensation: Religious and Financial Ethics in Historical Perspective', *Journal of Business Ethics*, 2007, vol. 72, 3.
4 Ibid., p. 3.
5 In Zarlenga, *The Lost Science of Money*, p. 177.
6 Mews and Abraham, 'Usury and Just Compensation', p. 4.
7 E.g., R.I. Mochrie, 'Justice in Exchange: The Economic Philosophy of John Duns Scotus', *Journal of Markets & Morality*, 2006, vol. 9:1, 35–56.
8 T. Aquinas, *Summa Theologiae*. Available at: http://www.newadvent.org/summa (accessed 11 March 2010), 2a2ae 78, 1.
9 Ibid., 1a2ae, 2, 1.
10 Ibid., 2a2ae 78, 1.
11 C.E. Curran, *Catholic Social Teaching 1891–Present: A Historical, Theological, and Ethical Analysis*, Washington, DC: Georgetown University Press, 2002, p. 25.
12 T.E. Woods, *The Church and the Market: A Catholic Defense of the Free Economy*, Oxford: Lexington Books, 2005, p. 111.
13 Aquinas, *Summa Theologiae*, 2a2ae 78, 2.
14 Ibid., 2a2ae 78, 1.
15 Woods, *The Church and the Market*, pp. 111–112.
16 B.M. McCall, 'Unprofitable Lending: Modern Credit Regulation and the Lost Theory of Usury', *Cardozo Law Review*, 2008, vol. 30:2, p. 571.
17 Ibid., p. 566.
18 Aquinas, *Summa Theologiae*, 2a2ae 78, 1.
19 McCall, 'Unprofitable Lending', p. 567.
20 Aquinas, *Summa Theologiae*, 2a2ae 78, 2.
21 Ibid., 2a2ae 31, 3 and 80, 1.
22 Ibid., 2a2ae 78, 2; 80, 1; and 106, 5.
23 Ibid., 2a2ae 62, 4; J.T. Noonan, *The Scholastic Analysis of Usury*, Cambridge, MA: Harvard University Press, 1957, pp. 115–117.
24 Woods, *The Church and the Market*, p. 113.
25 B.W. Dempsey, *Interest and Usury*, London: Dennis Dobson, 1948, p. 171.
26 J.F. Chown, *A History of Money: From AD 800*, London: Routledge, 1994, p. 121.
27 Ibid., pp. 119–120.
28 C.M. Reinhart and K.S. Rogoff, *This Time Is Different: Eight Centuries of Financial Folly*, Princeton, NJ: Princeton University Press, 2009, p. 69.

29 Mews and Abraham, 'Usury and Just Compensation', p. 4.
30 T.F. Divine, *Interest: An Historical & Analytical Study in Economics and Modern Ethics*, Milwaukee, WI: Marquette University Press, 1959, p. 3; see also p. 53.
31 In McCall, 'Unprofitable Lending', p. 567.
32 Mews and Abraham, 'Usury and Just Compensation', p. 1.
33 Dempsey, *Interest and Usury*, p. 164.
34 B.W. Dempsey, *The Functional Economy: The Bases of Economic Organization*, Englewood Cliffs, NJ: Prentice-Hall, 1958, p. 436.
35 Benedict XIV, '*Vix Pervenit* (On Usury and Other Dishonest Profits)', 1745. Available at: http://www.papalencyclicals.net/Ben14/b14vixpe.htm (accessed 12 November 2011).
36 T.F. Divine, 'Usury', in *New Catholic Encyclopedia*, vol. 14, New York: McGraw-Hill, 1967, p. 499.
37 Zarlenga, *The Lost Science of Money*, p. 191.
38 In Divine, *Interest*, p. 68.
39 Ibid., pp. 68–69.
40 J.D. Singleton, ' "Money Is a Sterile Thing": Martin Luther on the Immorality of Usury Reconsidered', 2009. Available at: http://www.econ.ucdenver.edu/home/workingpapers/zinke.pdf (accessed 7 January 2012), p. 5.
41 Zarlenga, *The Lost Science of Money*, p. 191.
42 M. Luther, *Three Treatises*, Philadelphia: Fortress Press, 1960, p. 94.
43 In Singleton, 'Money Is a Sterile Thing', pp. 8–9.
44 Ibid., p. 5.
45 In Divine, *Interest*, p. 69.
46 Luke 6:35.
47 In Zarlenga, *The Lost Science of Money*, p. 191.
48 In Elliott, *Usury*, pp. 73–78. The quotations are from p. 74.
49 Ibid., p. 77.
50 Ibid., p. 75.
51 In Divine, *Interest*, p. 88, footnote 51.
52 In Zarlenga, *The Lost Science of Money*, p. 194.
53 Although the financial literature tends to point to the Mississippi and South Sea Bubbles of 1720 as marking the beginning of financial bubbles, the Dutch tulipmania represents an important historical shift toward money mania.
54 'Tulipmania'. Available at: http://www.investopedia.com/terms/t/tulipmania.asp (accessed 5 January 2012).
55 E.g., M. Weber, *The Protestant Ethic and the 'Spirit' of Capitalism*, New York: Penguin Books, 2002.
56 E. Abbott, *Francis Bacon: An Account of His Life and Works*, London: Macmillan, 1885, p. 339.
57 S. Gaukroger, *Francis Bacon and the Transformation of Early-Modern Philosophy*, Cambridge: Cambridge University Press, 2001, p. 112.
58 F. Bacon (B. Vickers, ed.), *The Essays or Counsels, Civil and Moral*, Oxford: Oxford University Press, 1999, p. 94.
59 Ibid.
60 Ibid.
61 Ibid., pp. 94–95.
62 Ibid., pp. 95–96.
63 A. Smith, 'An Inquiry into the Nature and Causes of the Wealth of Nations', in R.M. Hutchins (ed.), *Great Books of the Western World*, vol. 39. Chicago: Encyclopedia Britannica, 1952, p. 22; italics added.
64 Ibid.
65 Ibid., pp. 40–41.

66 J. Bentham, *Defence of Usury*, La Vergne, TN: Dodo Press, 2009, p. 38.
67 Ibid., p. 4.
68 Ibid.
69 Ibid.
70 Ibid., p. 38.
71 Mews and Abraham, 'Usury and Just Compensation', p. 6.
72 Ibid.
73 Ibid., p. 8.
74 N. Oresme, 'A Treatise on the Origin, Nature, Law, and Alterations of Money', in C. Johnson (ed.), *The De Moneta of Nicholas Oresme and English Mint Documents*, London: Thomas Nelson and Sons, 1956.
75 Bentham, *Defence of Usury*, p. 39.
76 Smith, *Wealth of Nations*, p. 11.
77 Ibid.
78 Ibid., p. 140.
79 Ibid., pp. 137 and 138, respectively.
80 Zarlenga, *The Lost Science of Money*, p. 286.
81 Smith, *Wealth of Nations*, p. 140.
82 N. Ferguson, *The Ascent of Money: A Financial History of the World*, New York: Penguin Press, 2008, p. 49.
83 See also D. Graeber, *Debt: The First 5,000 Years*, Brooklyn, NY: Melville House, 2011, pp. 354–355; D.K. Foley, *Adam's Fallacy: A Guide to Economic Theology*, Cambridge, MA: Belknap Press of Harvard University Press, 2008.
84 M. Skousen, *Vienna and Chicago: Friends or Foes?* Washington, DC: Capital Press, 2005, p. 7.
85 In fairness, while many economic scholars of the Austrian leanings tend to avoid Aristotle in their monetary reflections, Joseph Schumpeter did take up his monetary views, but in the end struggled vigorously with them (J. Schumpeter, *History of Economic Analysis*, London: Routledge, 1997[1954], p. 63; note particularly the content of footnote 6). Jörg Guido Hülsman, on the other hand, in *The Ethics of Money Production* on several occasions refers to Aristotle. However, he mostly makes reference to Aristotle's *Politics*, and thus avoids the discussion of Aristotle's view of money as *nomisma* found in *Nicomachean Ethics*, where he actually puts money into an ethical context (J.G. Hülsman, *The Ethics of Money Production*, Auburn, AL: Ludwig von Mises Institute, 2008).
86 L. von Mises, *The Theory of Money and Credit*, Lexington, KY: Pacific Publishing Studio, 2010, p. 24.
87 E.g., Mises, *The Theory of Money and Credit*, p. 27.
88 E.g., M.N. Rothbard, *The Mystery of Banking*, 2nd ed., Auburn, AL: Ludwig von Mises Institute, 2008, p. 8; Mises, *The Theory of Money and Credit*, pp. 20–21.
89 Zarlenga, *The Lost Science of Money*, p. 32.
90 Ibid., pp. 51–54 and 41.
91 R. von Glahn, *Fountain of Fortune: Money and Monetary Policy in China, 1000–1700*, Taipei: SMC, 1997, pp. 251 and 39, respectively.
92 Ibid., pp. 247–248.
93 Ibid., pp. 248 and 250, respectively.
94 Ibid., p. 253.
95 Graeber, *Debt*, p. 301.

5 Abuse of money power

Beginning in the late Middle Ages, despite the prevalent understanding of money as commodity money issued by kings or princes, there was in reality a gradual shift taking place in both the nature of money and who held the power over its issuance. The aim of this chapter is to demythologize the view of the state as the abuser of monetary power and to show that already in the Middle Ages, a hidden abuser of the money system began to appear on the stage.

Kingly "abuse" of monetary power

For centuries, tapping into monetary power for private gain was very tempting. This is why the issuance of money was a strictly protected prerogative of rulers. In the thirteenth century, however, a major monetary shift took place, which later not only immensely influenced the dynamics of money creation, but also caused moral concerns as to what monetary power really meant.

Medieval shift in monetary power

Since antiquity, while money systems in the Western world were increasingly driven toward commoditization (China was a notable exception), coining gold was still kept strictly as a sacred prerogative of the supreme sovereign, and local rulers were allowed at most to mint silver coins.[1] In Rome, for well over three hundred years, coining gold was "a jealously guarded privilege of the Caesars as Pontifex Maximus." Later, it was continued by the emperors as Basileus of Byzantium (an eastern successor of the Roman Empire) for almost another nine hundred more years.[2] The silver/gold ratio in the Roman Empire (including its Byzantine extension) was kept at 12 to 1, and because the emperors held the prerogative of minting gold, they also controlled the difference in the gold/ silver ratio between west and east, thus amassing huge wealth, particularly in Constantinople.[3] This fixed ratio functioned as a fiat system in the world of commodity money. The gold coins issued by the emperor in Rome or Byzantium were "the only full legal-tender money having a forced circulation in all parts of the Empire," and, as a result, the imperial taxes and tributes were collected in gold coins or their exact equivalent in silver (twelve times the weight of gold).[4]

Only after the first fall of Constantinople in 1204 did local rulers in Europe free themselves from the monetary dominion of the Roman empire. It was "one of the most significant monetary events in history."[5] In 1225, Europe began minting its own gold coins, with rulers of Naples and Lyon among the first.[6] This marked the dawn of a new era in monetary history, called by Del Mar (1836–1926) "the Kingly period."[7] This is also when the commodity theory of money really began to take shape and to gradually dominate monetary debates and policies for several centuries.

Perhaps the biggest beneficiary of the venture that toppled Constantinople was Venice. As early as the sixth century, Venice already gained extraordinary trading privileges within Byzantium's control and could gradually engage in trade with the East and with Muslims. Such privileges were further strengthened particularly when the Byzantine emperors needed the assistance of Venice's naval force.[8] This helped Venice to tap into the difference in the gold/silver ratio between West and East and to rise to prominence. By the beginning of the twelfth century, Venice already had Europe's greatest shipyard and a rapidly growing navy, which, in turn, further intensified its connections with the Orient and eventually allowed Venice to control trade with the East for several centuries.[9]

Muslims were also able to take advantage of the gold/silver exchange ratio. Already in 695, the Muslim leader Abd El Melik first coined gold, thus sending a powerful message to the Byzantine emperor about sovereignty. After 695, the Muslims struck their gold and silver coins at the Eastern rate of about 7 to 1. This of course was a great challenge to the sacred prerogative of the Byzantine supreme sovereign, but the weakening empire could not do much to remedy the situation. Beginning in the eighth century, trade with Muslims was tantamount to tapping into the disparity in the gold/silver exchange ratios between East and West.[10] This is why Venice was so keen to gain Byzantium's permission for trade with Muslims.

Interestingly, the Muslims and Venice were to rise to prominence and for centuries dominate huge areas essentially without violating the prohibition of usury. This is not to say that among the Muslims and the Venetian Christians no one attempted to get rich through usurious means or other chicaneries. The point here is that the dominant trend was different than seeking profit from a mere *opportunity* for profit by means of loans with interest (usury).[11] The secret to that was that profits were considered as an outcome of shared risks in ventures. The share in *actual profits* was the sum and substance of the prevailing business structure. Such an anti-usurious approach "encouraged the flow of capital into trade rather than pawn shop lending," contributing to the development of real economy, and not merely speculative lending where money is supposed to "breed" more money.[12]

It is not difficult to imagine that once European kings and princes seized the coinage prerogative, they often tried to make full use of it. Unfortunately, at times, they turned monetary power into a "right" for personal enrichment. As a result, some kings and princes considered their coinage power as one of their vital sources of revenue.[13] Yet the rulers' minting power nevertheless also had limits, normally due to the natural availability of metals used for coins. This was particularly true during the so-called silver famine of the fourteenth century. Facing growing military expenses and, at the same time, limited possibility to tax the clergy and nobles (who actually held most of the wealth), kings and princes often turned to debasement, meaning to issuing more monetary units made of the same amount of metal used for coining money, which decreased its intrinsic metallic value. Having realized the benefits of debasement, kings and princes often did not hesitate to resort to it as a solution to their financial problems. Edward II of England (1284–1327) and Philip IV of France (1268–1314) are often presented as the most famous medieval abusers of coining power. In fact, frequent debasement between the mid-1300s and 1400s has led some to refer to the period as a time of "kingly abuse" of monetary power.[14]

Another way of altering the value of money was in fact even simpler – by proclaiming a change in the legal value of coins. This became particularly popular in the sixteenth and seventeenth centuries. The Holy Roman Emperor Charles V (1519–1556) is said to have twice raised in Holland the amount in silver coins to match his gold coins – in 1524 from 9 or 10 for 1 to over 11 to 1, then in 1542 he reduced the figure to 10 for 1, and in 1546 again raised it to over 13 to 1. Del Mar considers these alterations of the value of money as one reason behind the Dutch revolution of 1572 and establishment of the republic.[15] In a similar vein, Edward VI of England (1537–1553) raised the value of his silver coins for three consecutive years, thus making a profit of over 113 percent the first time he did so, 128 percent the second time, and 356 percent the third.[16] Such practices were not uncommon.

Oresme's critique of debasement

The abuse of monetary power by kings and princes however did not occur without criticism. Among the fiercest medieval critics of debasement was Nicholas Oresme. In his work *De Moneta*, Oresme took the stance that debasement was immoral, unjust (ch. XV), unnatural (ch. XVI), and even worse than usury (ch. XVII). The basis of his argument was that the intrinsic quality of the monetary medium guaranteed also its stability. For him, money was "an instrument for the exchange of natural riches," and in order to fulfill the mediating role of acquiring riches, money itself had to be made of a precious and rare material, such as gold.[17] When there was a limited availability of gold, silver could also serve the coining need, and if neither gold or silver were enough, metals such as copper could also be used. Thus for Oresme the soundness of money depended on a fixed weight of precious metal, and the stamp of the issuing authority (a prince) was supposed to guarantee the quantity and fineness of the metal in the coin. Yet despite the fact that the prince as "the most public person and of the highest authority" stamped issued coins, money was "essentially established and devised for the good of the community," and therefore it belonged "to the community and to individuals."[18]

Because money did not belong to the prince, he had no right to alter the standard, or the weight, or the metallic ratio when more metals were employed for coining money. If he did so, he caused injustice to the community. Although

Oresme admitted the possibility for the prince to rightfully alter the monetary standard, he allowed it only in extreme and rare situations, such as finding a new source of supply of metal(s) used for coinage. Moreover, whatever alterations were necessary, they had to be conducted only with the consent of the community to which the money belonged, because only such a community had the power to change the money it used.

Long after Oresme, the kingly abuse of the monetary power was still criticized by many, including Adam Smith.[19] Up to now, the stigma of kingly debasement is often used as an argument against government's right to issue money. Yet a closer look at the views of Oresme helps us quickly realize that his arguments are very one-sided. First of all, once money becomes equated with precious metals, and ultimately with wealth, gradually those who control the supply of such metals, control money and wealth. Oresme did not consider the moral question of money supply. An expanding economy needed an increase in money as medium of exchange. The question, of course, was how to obtain the increase in money stock. Calling in the coins, melting them down, and reminting with a reduced content of precious metals was one way of increasing the amount of money in circulation. It is worth noting that some of the well-known kingly abuses of monetary power happened around the time of the silver famine.

Second, debasement of coinage was done not only by kings and princes. Ordinary people also practiced debasement. They debased by clipping, sweating, or other methods of reducing the quantity of fine metal in the coins.[20] Apparently familiarity with such methods was growing, and so was debasement by common people. The result was that "when under a subsequent edict of debasement and re-coinage they [coins] came to the mints, the princes really gained little or nothing by the transaction, and merely gave the force of law to what was already an accomplished fact." Even very serious penalties, such as torture, hanging, and drawing and quartering seemed to have little deterring effect. "These penalties were boldly risked every day by people who had never committed any other offense."[21] Nowhere in *De Moneta* does Oresme take up the issue of debasement by ordinary people.

Third, perhaps the biggest problem with Oresme's critique of debasement is that he claims an Aristotelian base for it. For Oresme, money is "a balancing instrument for the exchange of natural wealth" and, as a result, "the property of those who possess such wealth."[22] Although any sort of money could function as an "instrument for the exchange of natural wealth," for Oresme money itself has to have a "balancing" power. Only money that has a high intrinsic value could fulfill this function. Nowhere does Aristotle claim that money has to have an intrinsic value to balance "the exchange of natural wealth."

In fairness, in Chapter Nine of *Politics*, Aristotle indeed mentions the use of "iron, silver, and anything else of the sort" as potential material for minting coins, and specifies the need of stamping them for the sake of convenience, lest the coins have to be measured every time.[23] Yet, as argued to this point, on the subject of money, Aristotle was primarily concerned with justice or, more precisely, how money could provide commensurability in economic exchanges.

In immediate communities, money as *nomisma* (taken by its face value) could easily fulfill such a role. Much more problematic was how to keep commensurability in exchanges with "foreign sources," about which Aristotle speaks in *Politics*. Aristotle admits that in the remote past it was the "size and weight" (thus intrinsic value) of some commodities that served as such a measure. Yet it appears he could also easily accept the solution of using the *nomisma* money in exchange with "foreign sources," as long as the mark indicating "how much there was"[24] would be accepted by both parties as the measure of what was exchanged.

As a matter of fact, at the time of Oresme more than only metallic money existed. The English tally sticks are an example.[25] Although tallies were basically a system of account, because of their diverse and widespread use (e.g., as tax payments, as payments for soldiers' services and laborers' work, for purchase of goods such as wheat, and as records of debit and credit cleared only some time later) they actually functioned as money. A crucial aspect of the function of tally sticks was that the issuing side was also bound to accept them as payments. Apparently, tally sticks were in use for more than five hundred years, and "may have made up the bulk of the English money supply" during most of the Middle Ages.[26] Moreover, unlike metal money, tally sticks were in the total control of the crown. It was this type of "medium of exchange" that carried far more Aristotle's view of money than Oresme's.

Fourth, in *De Moneta*, Oresme does not discuss at all bills of exchange, which at his time were used extensively by bankers. Although Davies claims that "Oresme was perfectly aware of the use of credit and in particular of bills of exchange,"[27] nowhere does he take up this issue. It is in itself remarkable, because bills of exchange played an important mediating role in economic exchanges. Yet apparently due to the fact that they did not represent intrinsic "natural riches," bills of exchange were not worthy of consideration as having the function of money.

In the course of history, a conviction grew that the view of sound metallic money contributed enormously to plunder and the sufferings of many peoples, particularly in South America and Africa. Even as late as 1849, the infamous California gold rush "led to the worst slaughter of Indians" in American history.[28] At the turn of the twentieth century, Del Mar pointed out that about half of the stock of precious metals that existed at that time had been "obtained through conquest and slavery."[29] Adam Smith and the followers of his monetary views had no qualms about equating the value of gold and silver money with the cost of labor, because labor was "the real measure of the exchangeable value of all commodities" (thus the so-called labor theory of value).[30] According to Smith, "the discovery of the abundant mines in America reduced, in the sixteenth century, the value of gold and silver in Europe to about a third of what it had been before." This was so simply because "the fertility" of the newly discovered mines added to a substantial reduction of the cost of labor "to bring those metals from the mine to the market."[31] Smith does not ask how the labor was obtained and what the real cost of mining was. So the correlation between changes in the value of gold and silver in Europe and the cost of bringing these commodities "from the mine to the market" is simply based on Smith's belief that it was due to the "the fertility" of mines.

Overall, then, Oresme is representative of the failure to bring to light what Aristotle really meant by money. As a result, the preoccupation with the issue of usury and the un-Aristotelian view of strong metallic money caused an important shift toward privately created money to slip from the moral radar of the scholastics. They particularly "missed the fact and the importance of bank created deposits as money."[32]

Rising power of private banking

In 1204, the joint force of a diverted Fourth Crusade and Venice toppled Constantinople. This event not only caused the destruction of one of the greatest cities of the world at that time, a great loss of life, and the disappearance of ancient literary works and masterpieces of art, but also significantly altered the monetary dynamics of the medieval world. After the plunder of Constantinople, plenty of gold and silver was shipped to Europe, providing it with a vital monetary boost.[33] It was in the context of such monetary shifts taking place at the beginning of the thirteenth century that European banking began to take shape.

Formation of the medieval banking powers

One peculiar group that was able to tap into the finance of the twelfth and thirteenth centuries were the Knights Templar (the Poor Knights of the Temple of Solomon), formed between 1114–18, after the First Crusade captured Jerusalem (1099), to protect pilgrims in the Holy Land. Established in France, the order very quickly expanded its presence in the Middle East, Cyprus, Germany, parts of Iberia, and even the British Isles. Within a short period of time, the Templars became rich and influential and were able to gain strong credibility.

Although the spread of the order was mainly due to endowments from the wills of various nobles,[34] the Templars' wealth also had other sources. One of them was the handling of pilgrims' funds. At the time of growing popularity of long pilgrimages, pilgrims could deposit money in one location and make withdrawals at different locations to cover expenses. The Templars could also lend money in one place and settle the debt at a very remote location. "In effect," as stated by Baigent and Leigh, "the modern origins of banking can be attributed to the Order of the Temple." Their financial acumen quickly helped them to earn sufficient trust, so at the peak of their popularity the Templars "handled much if not most of the available capital in western Europe." They also developed credit facilities for commercial purposes. In the course of time, the order even became an important lending institution for rulers, collected taxes, and even owned and ran the depository of the French treasury.[35]

The Templars' quick rise to prominence, however, began to change in the second half of the thirteenth century, when Christians lost to Muslims vital sites in the Holy Land, including Jerusalem. A combination of factors such as changing views of the role of the Templars in the Holy Land, the rising power of rulers in Europe (such as the power to coin gold), and perhaps simple envy led to growing resentment and even accusations of immoral conduct and heresy, particularly in France. In 1307, King Philip IV had ordered the arrest of members of the Order. What followed were years of suppression of the Templars, during which many were interrogated, tortured, and even executed. Among the obvious reasons for the suppression of the Order were the "short-term financial advantages which the spoliation of such a wealthy Order could bring to a monarch whose ambitions consistently outran his resources."[36] Exerting huge influence over the pope, in 1312 King Philip IV succeeded in dissolving the Order. Some sources suggest that many of its members found refuge in Scotland, where they rendered not only military support to their leaders, but also greatly contributed to Scottish banking.[37]

Another group that had vast networks in Europe, the Middle East, and the Muslim world were the Jews. Apparently, they already functioned as middlemen in commerce between Muslim Spain and the old Hansa (early tradesmen operating predominantly in the Baltic Sea, which were later superseded by the Christian Hanseatic League in the twelfth and thirteenth centuries).[38]

Yet even after the suppression of the Templars, the Jews could not take full advantage of their vast networks. One reason is that at the end of the thirteenth century, the Jews themselves began to face suppression in various places in Europe. They were expelled from England in 1290. In France, they suffered expulsion several times, including a serious persecution in 1394. Italian republics also tended to exclude Jews from money business. For example, in Venice Jews could settle permanently only in the sixteenth century.[39] Muller has compared the role of the Jews in medieval Europe to "a sponge," because through lending at high interest they were "sucking up money from untaxable estates [mainly those of the noblemen and clergy], only to be squeezed by the monarch."[40] Apparently, charging high interest rates on lending was itself, at least partly, a defense against the uncertainties of being "squeezed."

Unfortunately, the fact that Jewish moneylenders often charged high interest rates is attributed to a single source – the Book of Deuteronomy. In it, the claim goes, Jews were forbidden to charge interest on loans to their fellow Israelites, but were allowed to collect interest on loans to foreigners.[41] Even Thomas Aquinas struggled with this statement, and concluded that the Jews were permitted to "take usury from foreigners, not as though it were lawful, but in order to avoid a greater evil," meaning engaging in usury with their own people.[42]

Yet looking at the biblical texts in their entirety, one can conclude that the supposed leniency in charging interest on the money lent to foreigners is more controversial than it first appears. The basic problem is that the text of Deuteronomy 23:19–20, seemingly allowing to lend at interest to foreigners, can easily be challenged by other biblical texts, such as Leviticus 24:22: "You shall have one law for the alien and for the citizen," or Numbers 15:16: "You and the alien who resides with you shall have the same law and the same ordinance."

The problem then goes deeper than what simplified explanations tend to present. At the heart of it lies proper understanding of the Jewish perception of a "foreigner." Calvin Elliott distinguished three groups of those who were considered by the Jews as not having Hebrew blood: the proselytes (or converts to Judaism); those from the surrounding countries who happened to live among the Jews; and the natives belonging to the tribes considered archenemies of the Jews, such as the Canaanites, the Hittites, the Hivites, and the Philistines whose land the Hebrews were supposed to take over as their "promised land." According to Elliott, it was only the context of enmity toward the third group of "foreigners" that could be viewed as allowing the Israelites not to give the same rights to those people.[43]

Elliott's explanation not only makes the biblical teaching on relating to foreigners much more consistent, but also upholds the clear principle that under ordinary circumstances lending at interest was morally unacceptable. The fact that it became quite common that the Jews charged interest on lending to foreigners was perhaps only partly due to the interpretation of some biblical texts that leaned toward their own convenience. It is much more likely that usurious lending to foreigners resulted from the same human weakness that made the Jews charge interest from their own people, that made some rulers abuse Jews living in their territories without being challenged by church authorities, or that made some religious leaders think that it was better that the "outsiders" (the Jews) got involved in usurious lending rather than their own flock (the Christians).[44]

All in all, the Jews did influence European moneylending business, but their role appears to have been overstated, as others played their role too. Throughout the Middle Ages, some Italian banking houses became particularly prominent. Already in the thirteenth century Venice had private local banks. By the early fourteenth century, finance in Italy, according to Ferguson, "had been dominated by three Florentine houses of Bardi, Peruzzi and Acciaiuoli." Unfortunately, in the 1340s all three went bankrupt, mainly due to the default of their principal debtors, King Edward III of England and King Robert of Naples.[45] Nevertheless, Italian banking houses continued to dominate the money market. Increased commercial activity, especially after the Black Death of 1348, placed the Italian republics such as Venice, Florence, and Genoa right at the heart of the trade and money business. Among the banking houses that rose to prominence in the second half of the fourteenth century were the Medici of Florence. It was their way of conducting money deals, mostly currency exchanges, while sitting at benches behind tables that earned them the name *banchieri*, from which the word "bankers" derived.[46] By the time of the Renaissance, the Medici already exerted huge influence. In the middle of the fifteenth century, their bank had branches reaching as far as London.

Growing diversification of banking

Throughout the Middle Ages, banking gradually began to include an increased number of diverse activities. In its earlier stages, it primarily concentrated on money changing, pawnbroking, and deposit banking. Some, like the bank of St. George, which started in Genoa in the early thirteenth century, were simply deposit banks, meant for safekeeping and the transfer of funds and not lending. The Lombards, in turn, were essentially pawnbrokers, charging high interest rates on loans, additionally conditioned by borrowers' pledges backed by their property. As the medieval world had many different currencies circulating, some banks acted also as moneychangers. The Flemish moneychangers, who gradually also moved into deposit banking, alongside the Italian merchant bankers and the Lombards, formed the backbone of the economic rise of Bruges, which, beginning in the fourteenth century, acquired the name of "the trading capital of Northern Europe."[47]

Among the tools that increasingly gained popularity in the financing of trade was the bill of exchange. Ferguson, and others who take an evolutionary approach toward money, claim that the bill of exchange has medieval origin.[48] Del Mar, on the other hand, argues that such a view is "entirely erroneous," as bills of exchange were already known in the ancient world.[49] Nonetheless it was in the course of the Middle Ages that banks gradually began to play an important mediating role in circulation of bills of exchange. As settling trade payments with bulky coins or bullion was impractical and often vulnerable to theft, bills of exchange increasingly functioned as money substitutes.

Doubtless to say, an important aspect of bank operations was lending. The growth of commercial activity made many merchants look for opportunities to borrow, while bankers were also eager to lend. Yet the prohibition of usury stood in their way to fully exploit mutual wants. Under such circumstances, bills of exchange provided a way of getting around the prohibition. Although they were primarily a tool of financing trade, the bills could also be utilized in lending through a form of "dry exchange."[50]

Some moneylenders, however, did not heed the usury prohibition. This was particularly true about the Jewish moneylenders. Despised, forced to live in ghettos (e.g., in Venice), or at times abused, they nevertheless realized that the mediation of borrowing/lending amid the commercial expansion of medieval Europe provided them with good business opportunities. The networks they developed in many places of the then known world played to their advantage. Expelled from one place, they simply moved to another. For example, many of the Jews expelled from Spain in 1492 first went to Portugal, and later to Antwerp, and then to Holland, contributing to the growth of Amsterdam.[51] The political atmosphere of Holland particularly suited them, as beginning in the second half of the sixteenth century Holland outlawed religious persecution. Additionally, Holland's acceptance of Calvinism, with its leniency toward usury prohibition, and her thriving commerce opened before the Jews living there vast business opportunities. As a result, their numbers grew quickly. In Amsterdam, in the beginning of the seventeenth century there were only about two hundred Jews, but a century and a half later, their number increased a hundredfold.[52]

Among those exemplifying changing moods toward the usury prohibition and growing preoccupation with money at the time of the Renaissance was also the German family named Fuggers.[53] They began to rise to prominence in the financial sector at the end of the fifteenth century, and soon became one of the richest families in Europe. The core businesses of the Fuggers included the control of silver mines in Tyrol and copper mines in central Europe, the rights to mint coins, handle some church finances (as Catholics, they gained the "natural" trust of church authorities), and moneylending. It was diversification of their operations, but also closeness to the church and political authorities, that brought the family wealth and influence. The Fuggers charged interest of up to 30 percent on small loans, but as little as 2 percent on large ones.[54] It is worth recalling that by the sixteenth century, the debate on usury was already well advanced, and charging interest on loans on the grounds of compensation for emergent loss (*damnum emergens*) or a forgone opportunity of gain (*lucrum cessans*) was becoming an acceptable practice. For example, Leonardus Lessius (1554–1623), a Jesuit late scholastic, marks 6.25 percent as the highest rate on loans.[55] So when the Fuggers lent at 2 percent, such interest on moneylending was definitely within the acceptable scope as far as usury is concerned. Of course, it was a totally different matter when they charged the interest of 30 percent. Still, at the end of the sixteenth century the Fuggers' power was brought down by the Spanish financial crisis.[56]

In short, in late medieval Europe and during the Renaissance, the growing influence of private banking and preoccupation with money caused a gradual weakening of the moral function of the usury prohibition. If not openly violating the prohibition, many at least found ways of getting around it. Corruption and weakened moral power of church authorities, combined with the split caused by the Protestant Reformation and the increasingly more lenient perception of usury, further exacerbated the problem. Yet despite it all, the usury prohibition still at least to some degree functioned as a form of moral radar with regard to financial dealings. An expression of its influence is the usury laws that were gradually adopted by many countries.

Deepening abuse of monetary power

By the end of the sixteenth century, the roots of private banking were entangling diverse forms of the business structures known at the time. What went completely unnoticed, however, was how banks through issuance of loans (double-entry bookkeeping) began to expand the amount of money in circulation, and gradually usurped for themselves an increasing monetary power.

Banks gaining monetary power and the growth of economic instability

The first country in which particular interests snatched money power was Holland. After the revolution of 1572, which had led to the independence of the Dutch republic, "the burghers [took] the monetary system into their own hands by establishing private or individual coinage."[57] With the free coinage law in operation, soon no fewer than fourteen mints competed for seignorage (gain from minting coins) in the United Provinces.[58] Although the republic sought uniformity of minting, it did not succeed. As a result, merchants had to deal with multiple currencies in circulation. It was in this context that in 1609 the Amsterdam Exchange Bank (the Bank of Amsterdam) was established to resolve the problem of the exchange of the multiplicity of currencies. The Bank of Amsterdam allowed merchants to open accounts denominated in a standard-ized currency and through the system of checks and direct debits helped them to carry on commercial transactions without the need of coins for each of the actual transactions. In other words, payments could be settled by debiting one party's account and crediting the account of the counterparty.[59]

In the course of the seventeenth century, the English were particularly keen on copying several Dutch inventions, such as the establishment of the East India Company, the development of the colonies or policies with regard to admin-istering those colonies, banking and monetary system, and land registries.[60] In 1653, the English even deposed their king and also formed a republic. Moreover, while the Dutch dropped free mintage in 1648, eighteen years later England adopted the Free Coinage Act, on the basis of which people were allowed to request the mint to refine and coin their bullion of silver or gold for free. As such, the Free Coinage Act granted an enormous monetary power to the mer-chant and finance class.[61] Despite widespread perception that governments were in charge of money supply, in reality a huge shift toward private control over money was taking place. Banks were right at the heart of that shift.

Establishment of the Bank of Amsterdam in 1609 is sometimes cited as an event that marks an important turning point in financial history. In theory, the Bank of Amsterdam was a deposit bank belonging to the city of Amsterdam and, as such, was not supposed to make loans. It was expected to function as a precious metals system. Profits of the bank were supposed to come from diverse fees. The bank was founded to serve as a 100 percent reserve bank, meaning that its deposits were totally backed by precious metal and coin. Among the admirers of such a bank was Adam Smith. In his words, at Amsterdam "no point of faith is better established than that for every guilder, circulated as bank money, there is a corresponding guilder in gold or silver to be found in the treasure of the bank."[62]

Yet apparently the bank at times did not live up to the standard it had set, nor to the image it had gained. Although in 1614 the Municipality of Amster-dam established separately the Bank of Lending, the Bank of Amsterdam also gradually got involved in issuing credit, albeit to a very limited number of exclusive customers. One of them was the city itself. Another was the Dutch East India Company. According to Zarlenga, "the large secret overdrafts" to this company "changed the nature of the bank into a covert bank of issue," or a bank creating money through the process of issuing loans. In principle, the bank tried to keep overdrafts in balance. Its deposits are said to have stood in 1760 at close to nineteen million florins, and its metallic reserve at over sixteen million.[63] In the 1780s, the bank again got involved in heavy lending, and in

1790, when the French invaded Holland, they found the bank not only empty, but in fact, insolvent.[64] In 1814, toward the end of the Napoleonic wars, the Netherlands Bank was established on the ruins of the Bank of Amsterdam, but it was already a very different type of bank, modeled on the Bank of England.

Despite aberrations in keeping the standard, the Bank of Amsterdam was nevertheless rather an exceptional type of a banking institution when compared with the banks of issue, or lending banks. As a matter of fact, it was through issuance of credit (lending) that private banks got involved more and more in creating money. It worked like this:

> Deposits were received in coinage, or if a bill was deposited, drawn upon another bank, ultimately coinage could be collected from that bank. However, the loans would not have to be made in coinage, but could be in credits to the borrowers account at the bank – in bookkeeping entries. The borrower would have the ability to write checks on that account. Such checks might not actually be cashed, but be credited to another account on the books of the same bank. Once their clients got into the habit of conducting business with bills of exchange (checks) rather than actual coins, it became possible for the bankers to greatly multiply the apparent amount of money in circulation, in the form of these credits.[65]

This marked perhaps the greatest shift with regard to money, and formed the basis of the system, which carries today the positive sounding name of "fractional reserve banking."

According to Ferguson, "by lending amounts in excess of its metallic reserve," the Riksbank of Sweden, established in 1656 (and taken over by the state in 1668), "may be said to have pioneered the practice of what would later be known as fractional reserve banking."[66] In reality, multiplying the amount of money in circulation (creating money) in the form of bookkeeping credits had been known since the Middle Ages. Apparently it was the method that already the Templars brought back from the Crusades. The double-entry method was also known to Italian bankers, particularly in Genoa,[67] and to the fourteenth century deposit banks situated in the Venetian region Rialto.[68] Nevertheless, in the Middle Ages it was still a secretive banking practice, which played a more supplementary monetary role. In the seventeenth century, however, the practice of fractional reserve began to accelerate, and private interests began to exert an enormous power over the creation of money. Gradual shifts occurring in the ways banks conducted their operations allowed them to gain substantial control over the very process of money creation. Issuance of debt and bookkeeping entries began to play an increasingly important role in this process.

Doubtless to say, expanding economies and the growing preoccupation with getting rich by the lending of money caused rapid growth of banks. At the same time, however, bank failures also increased, which in turn caused growing instability of entire economies. Del Mar, in his work published in 1896, provides a long list (75 entries) of bank suspensions over the period between 1696 and 1891. Many of the entries speak not only of individual banks, but of widespread systemic bank failures.[69] In order to stabilize the system, bankers managed to outmaneuver rulers as well as governments of the rising nation-states and establish bankers' banks, namely central banks. As it turned out, these banks, often privately owned (although some of them eventually nationalized), gradually also gained control over the issuance of national currencies.

The Bank of England is often considered to be a model of a central bank. In reality, however, it is an example of yet another step in private interests getting a grip on the ancient prerogative of money issuance. Established in 1694, the bank's prime interest was in lending to the government. At a time of frequent wars, the bank made it possible to finance the growing expenses of the English government by transforming the government debt into a form of IOU (I-owe-you) obligations, or simply by monetizing government debt. Beginning in 1742, the bank also managed to establish "a partial monopoly on the issue of banknotes," which was a form of "promissory note that did not bear interest," the purpose of which was to "facilitate payments without the necessity of the transacting parties to have current accounts."[70] The amount of bank notes that the bank was allowed to create was set to equal the money it lent to the government – in other words, the bank used government debt as the collateral. This in turn meant that government debt became even more valuable than gold or silver, as the payment of the debt could fail only together with the nation.[71] Indeed, it was a brilliant move and an extraordinary privilege given to a private institution.

Despite repeated difficulties, the Bank of England managed to keep renewing its charter and soon became the central money institution in the country. Although only very gradually, the result was that through the Bank of England, certain private individuals began to exert an enormous power over England's money supply. Nathan Rothschild, who took control of the bank in 1820, is said to have declared: "I care not what puppet is placed upon the throne of England to rule the Empire on which the sun never sets. The man who controls Britain's money supply controls the British Empire, and I control the British money supply."[72] In 1946, with the strong backing of the Church of England, the Bank of England was nationalized. But by then it could function only as "independent" of political (government) influence. In the view of Zarlenga, over all those years the government "could have created its own paper notes based on the same security and not paid any interest on it to anyone," and thus could have easily fulfilled the functions of the bank.[73]

For several centuries, the money created in the fractional reserve banking system was still supposed to be backed by *real* (read: metallic) money. By the nineteenth century this requirement became homogenized and internationalized, forming the so-called gold standard. It survived until World War II, at the end of which the Bretton Woods conference (1944) decided that major currencies would be pegged to the US dollar, while the US dollar would have a fixed exchange rate with gold. This new system, however, did not last long. In 1971 the US dollar was freed from the requirement of being backed by gold, thus giving rise to a new monetary system based on fiat currencies. Once the dollar reached the status of international currency, it provided its issuer, the Federal Reserve, another privately owned central bank,[74] with tremendous influence over world affairs. In the post-1971 world order, fiat currencies have become tradable, comparable to many goods or services.

The removal of the gold standard has opened for banks an enormous potential for creating money, practically limited by customers' ability to borrow, or their "credit." The supposed-to-be stabilizer – the central bank – cannot do much to actually keep the financial system stable. As Michel Chossudovsky noted during the Asian currency crisis of 1998, "Privately held money reserves in the hands of 'institutional speculators' far exceed the limited capabilities of the World's central banks. The latter acting individually or collectively are no longer able to fight the tide of speculative activity."[75] As a result, the present banking system is inherently prone to deep crises.

It is this innate instability in the financial system and the realization of the inability of central banks to really cope with bigger crises that gave rise to a sort of bank of bankers' bank – the International Monetary Fund (IMF). After the experiences of the Great Depression, its main purpose was to prevent another depression of such magnitude. Among the crucial factors underpinning the founding of the IMF was the belief of "a need for *collective action at the global level* for economic stability."[76] The 2007–2009 financial crisis showed clearly the inability of the present "stabilizing" system to provide real stability. Peter Doyle, an IMF economist who had worked for the fund for twenty years, quit the fund in 2012, stating in his resignation letter that one of the main reasons for his departure was the fund's failures to issue timely warnings before the crisis by suppressing the findings, which he described as "a failing in the first order."[77]

While the IMF is assumed to have a "stabilizing" function for the worldwide banking system, the Bank for International Settlements (BIS) is often reckoned to be "a bank for central banks." Established in 1930, the BIS in its origin had the role of an international gold clearinghouse. By balancing credits and debits between member states, the BIS undeniably contributed in minimizing actual gold shipments. After 1971, when the US dollar was unitarily freed from the requirement of being backed by gold, the BIS ultimately shifted its activities into other areas. At present, it is an international organization of over fifty central banks, in which private banking interests are strongly represented. One of the tools through which the BIS pulls strings is the requirement for the "independence" of central banks from their respective governments. As such, the BIS deals almost exclusively with central banks, and keeps a significant portion of the world's foreign reserves.[78] The BIS is now also known for setting basic standards (policies are still made by individual banks) for banks, such as capital adequacy requirements and transparency of reserve requirements – the Basel Accord (since 2010, the Basel III has already been agreed upon, but its implementation will take some years). These requirements, however, despite their façade of providing financial stability, are nothing more than attempts to preserve the present privately controlled banking system.

John Kenneth Galbraith once described the ease with which banks create money as "a method so simple the mind is repelled."[79] Over the past four centuries, this ease to create money through debt (economists prefer to call it "credit supply") has contributed immensely to fuelling new "financial products," speculative activities in the economy, bubbles, investment manias, and growing cycles of booms and busts. Governments, including governments of the rising democracies, found it increasingly difficult to control the money power.

Struggle over government control of the money supply

In the eighteenth century, recurring voices began to show discomfort over what constituted money and the growing influence of private interests over control of the supply of money. Already John Locke (1632–1704) in his *Essay on Money and Bullion* wrote: "It is a very common mistake to say that money is a commodity . . . Bullion is valued by its weight . . . money is valued by its stamp."[80] Apparently, Locke viewed the stamp as the essence of money and not the intrinsic value of the material money was made of. For him money was nothing more than pledge for wealth, meaning that money and wealth were two distinct categories. Some years later, George Berkeley (1685–1753), an Anglican bishop in Ireland, in *The Querist* argued that paper money and a publicly owned and controlled bank were the most suitable for economic development of countries such as eighteenth-century Ireland.[81]

The French philosopher Charles de Montesquieu (1689–1755), in *The Spirit of Laws*, also questioned the money system that was taking shape at his time. He seems to have been particularly concerned about "the paper which represents the debt of a nation."[82] In the view of Montesquieu:

> Some have imagined that it was for the advantage of a state to be indebted to itself: they thought that this multiplied riches by increasing the circulation. Those who are of this opinion have, I believe, confounded a circulating paper which represents money, or a circulating paper which is the sign of the profits that a company has or will make by commerce, with a paper which represents debt. The first two are extremely advantageous to the state; the last can never be so.[83]

The financing of government expenses through the means of "the paper which represents the debt of a nation" was increasingly used as a form of money created by banks. Obviously, Montesquieu was very critical about the practice of financing public needs through expanding public debt and charging interest on the paper debt (money) created by private institutions. For him money and credit were two different realities, and while he saw no problem with money circulating as paper, he argued there were "no advantages" in the system where the public had to pay interest on the paper representing a nation's debt.[84]

In effect, Montesquieu belonged to the few who still dared to ask very basic questions: why could not government issue (paper) money needed to carry out its public function without the bother of going into debt and paying interest on it? Why could private banks do so but government could not? Yet at his time the system of private control over the money supply and monetization of government debt had only begun to take shape. Ferguson's exaltation of the system as a great financial innovation[85] shows how in the course of time sufficiently strong stress on the virtues of the private over the public sector affects our perception of surrounding reality.

While some European minds were raising concerns over the private influence of money, it was the United States of America that became a battleground for public versus private control of the money supply and the test ground for the Aristotelian concept of money as *nomisma*. Beginning in the seventeenth century, the Americans made several attempts to introduce government money. Four of them appear to be of particular importance.

The first occurred at the time of frequent monetary distress experienced by many states due to the scarcity in the supply of British silver coins for the North American colonies. Even the use of foreign coins, such as the Spanish dollar, apparently did not resolve the problem of monetary privation. To ease the shortage of money, local governments in the colonies began to use diverse commodities as legal tender. Perhaps the most obvious example of such distress occurred during the so-called country pay period (1632–92), in which even agricultural products were made legal tender.[86] During that period, the Massachusetts Bay Colony went as far as establishing in 1652 an illegal mint for the production of coins that were declared as legal tender in the colony. Although the mint was soon ordered to end operations, it nevertheless continued producing coins for over thirty years, all dated 1652, giving the impression that no new coins were put into circulation. Yet even this act of defiance did not resolve the problem of monetary privation in the state. The mint was permanently closed in 1685.

Several years later, in 1690, the government of the same colony attempted another step to ease its monetary distress. Taking advantage of the authorization to pay the troops helping English soldiers to fight the French in Quebec, it gained permission to issue bills of credit distributed in denominations of five, ten, and twenty shillings. These bills were likely the first fiat paper money created in the West, as they were not backed by any commodity. This new form of money was indeed revolutionary in the sense that "rather than a promise to pay, it was a promise to receive – to accept the paper bills for all moneys due to Massachusetts, valued at 5% above the note's face amount."[87] The declaration that the bills of credit were as good as silver coins was indeed extraordinary. As a matter of fact, while paying taxes the bills were actually worth more than "hard" money. Despite the fact that originally the bills were not officially declared as legal tender, they were quickly accepted as such. Soon other colonies began to copy the Massachusetts model and issued their own in-fact paper money. The money system of Pennsylvania, which was introduced in the 1720s, was among the most successful stories of the pre-Revolution fiat monies, sometimes referred to as Colonial Scrip.[88] However, two Currency Acts, one of 1751 (restricting the issuance of paper money by the colonies of New England), and the other one of 1764 (extending the restriction on the emission of paper money to all the colonies of Britain in North America), put an end to the experiment.

The third important attempt in government issuance of paper money took place in 1775, at the start of the Revolution. With the primary intent to finance the war, the Continental Congress emitted bills of credit called continental currency or, in short, "continentals." Perhaps the most crucial feature of the continentals system was that it was not originally intended to be permanent. In fact, the variety of currencies circulating in the colonies was upheld, including British coinage and the currencies issued by respective colonies. The difficulty the new money faced was that the Congress had no power of taxation, so in reality the Continental Congress could only count on the willingness of individual states to accept the continentals as their legal tender. As one can imagine, the process was not an easy one, and the new currency quickly lost its value. Yet, historically speaking, despite the ultimate collapse of the continentals, the system did contribute greatly to winning independence and the formation of a new democratic country.

The fourth, arguably most serious undertaking in introducing government paper money in recent history took place during the American Civil War of the 1860s. The greenback, as the new money authorized by Congress was called, was declared legal tender "receivable for all duties and taxes to the U.S.," with the exception of import duties and interest on bonds, which were still to be paid in coin.[89] Over twenty-two centuries after Aristotle, a government of a democratic country introduced paper money that closely resembled the Aristotelian *nomisma* – the money legally sanctioned by a lawful authority. It appears that Abraham Lincoln initially was not very enthusiastic about the project, which led Zarlenga to the conclusion that "Lincoln supported the banker's privilege to create money."[90] Nevertheless, at the end of the war, in his monetary policy (1865), Lincoln seems to have taken a very different stance on money.

The spirit of the policy outlined by Lincoln was indeed very Aristotelian. According to him, "money is the creature of law, and the creation of the original issue of money should be maintained as the exclusive monopoly of national government." Lincoln further claims:

> Government, possessing the power to create and issue currency and credit as money and enjoying the right to withdraw both currency and credit from circulation by taxation and otherwise, need not and should not borrow capital at interest as a means of financing governmental work and public enterprise . . . The privilege of creating and issuing money is not only the supreme prerogative of government, but it is the government's greatest creative opportunity.[91]

This was, as contended by Rowbotham, "one of the world's great political declarations; a masterpiece of succinct advocacy and irrefutable justice."[92] However, several weeks after presenting his monetary policy, Lincoln was assassinated. At the end of the 1870s, the decision to convert greenbacks into gold led to yet another collapse of government-issued money. Interestingly, the greenbacks continued circulating until 1994.

Unfortunately, up to now the issuance of greenbacks still faces a strong criticism. For example, according to Rothbard, "greenbacks began to depreciate in terms of specie almost as soon as they were issued." In order to present a more detailed picture of the greenback's depreciation, Rothbard states that in June of 1864, the greenback dollar "plummeted" from 52 cents to 40 cents against gold.[93] In fact, the greenback reached as low as 36 cents on July 16, 1864.[94] But all that plummeting happened for a brief period of several months. Zarlenga's graphic presentation of the greenback versus gold over the entire period of its use (1862–1879) shows that already in the second half of 1864 the greenback quickly began regaining its worth against gold. By the end of 1865 it was worth 68 cents. The greenback's appreciation further strengthened once the war was over. In 1870 the greenback rose to 85 cents, and by December of 1878 it was on par with gold. In January 1879, it became "freely convertible into gold, dollar for dollar."[95] The broader perspective of the greenback's performance shows that Rothbard's presentation, focusing only on a war period of just a few months, distorts the real picture. In the end, what brought down the greenback was not the loss of its market value against gold, but the *ideology* of "sound" money instigated by various religious and academic circles.[96]

The chartering and structuring of the banking system immensely added to the failure of the government control over money supply in the United States. On its face, the National Banking Act of 1863/64 appeared to be wise because it put in place some important regulations covering the diverse aspects of bank operations, such as minimum capitalization, reserve requirements, or limiting interest rates the states set in their usury laws. Yet, in reality, the Act was a bargain between powerful representatives of the banks and the government involved in a war and badly in need of money. As it turned out, "the government got what it needed at the time – a loan of substantial sums for the war effort and a sound circulating currency for an expanding economy – but the banks were the real winners."[97] With the passage of the National Banking Act, the US government was allowed to issue $450 million in greenbacks, while the private bankers gained the right to create $1.49 in their own money for each greenback.[98] As one can immediately see, this added immensely to the money supply so strongly criticized by Rothbard. Salmon P. Chase, the treasury secretary at the time, apparently later called his support for the Act "the greatest financial mistake" of his life.[99]

After the National Banking Act, the number of banks began to increase rapidly, as did the volume of issued bank notes. The expansion of the fractional reserve system was possible because of the claim that paper notes issued by banks could at any time be redeemed in species, which after the Civil War practically meant in gold. This claim, however, was a mere fiction, as there was never enough gold to make such redemption viable. Bank bankruptcies became part of the system.

Nevertheless, it was that "empty" claim of the possibility to redeem in species the paper notes issued by banks at any time that in the end gave the bankers' legal and practical monopoly over the country's money supply. In the 1890s, a populist movement broke out to challenge that monopoly and to give the government a say in the issuance of money. It was one of the last serious attempts to break the power of the banks over the control of the nation's money. The culmination of the private influence over money creation in the United States (and beyond) was the establishment of the Federal Reserve in 1913. Bankers emerged as absolute winners of the struggle over the control over the country's money while both the *nomisma* and the "sound" (fully backed by gold) money factions became the losers.

The attempts to get government control over the process of money creation still find widespread criticism, particularly from the libertarian wing, perhaps best represented by the Austrian School. Murray Rothbard, for example, goes into great detail to show that all the efforts of introducing government money in the United States were a total failure.[100] Taking the typical antigovernment monetary stance of the Austrian School, Rothbard argues that the consequences of those attempts were disastrous, due to politics and the practice of undermining "hard" (gold) money. The tool he uses to prove that is Gresham's law, which according to him says that "when *government* compulsorily overvalues one money and undervalues another, the undervalued money will leave the country or disappear into hoards, while the overvalued money will flood into circulation."[101]

This is an ideologically charged definition (note that Wikipedia under the entry "Gresham's law" uses Rothbard's definition), because the crucial part of Gresham's law speaks about *what* happens when new, intrinsically less valued money ("bad money") is put on par with the money already in circulation ("good money"), and not so much about *who* does it. For Rothbard that "who" is only government, whereas in fact it could be anybody with the ability and will to debase the money in circulation. The notes issued by banks in a fractional reserve system actually could lead to a similar outcome, but in a more covert way. Nevertheless, Rothbard's definition of Gresham's law suggests that there was only one culprit – government.

To sum up, beginning in the Middle Ages, issuance of money into circulation faced increased abuse. While the dominant narrative tends to present rulers, and by extension governments, as the abusers of the monetary power, it was the private banks that gradually gained an enormous influence over money supply. The paper bills issued by several North American colonies and later by the US government were outstanding attempts by lawful governments to regain the ancient prerogative of controlling the issuance of money. Unfortunately, those governments did not have sufficient experience and perhaps even the means to defend against diverse challenges, including the variety of money in circulation, counterfeiting, and various ideological campaigns discrediting fiat money. In the end, the banking lobby turned out to be powerful enough to extend its grip over the private control of money supply.

Notes

1 S. Zarlenga, *The Lost Science of Money: The Mythology of Money – the Story of Power*, Valatie, NY: American Monetary Institute, 2002, p. 85.
2 A. Del Mar, *History of Monetary System*, Honolulu, HI: University Press of the Pacific, 2000[1896], p. 83.
3 Zarlenga, *The Lost Science of Money*, p. 144.
4 Del Mar, *History of Monetary System*, p. 319.
5 Zarlenga, *The Lost Science of Money*, pp. 85 and 144, respectively.
6 Del Mar, *History of Monetary System*, pp. 76–77.
7 Ibid., pp. 386–387.
8 The so-called Golden Bull of 1082, which granted Venice's merchants the privilege to trade throughout the entire Byzantine empire exempt from taxes, is an example of how Venice was keen to keep a relatively good relationship with Constantinople and maintain access to trade with the Orient (J.P. Farrell, *Financial Vipers of Venice: Alchemical Money, Magical Physics, and Banking in the Middle Ages and Renaissance*, Port Townsend, WA: Feral House, 2010, pp. 73–74).
9 Zarlenga, *The Lost Science of Money*, p. 118.
10 See, e.g., Del Mar, *History of Monetary System*, pp. 125–148; Zarlenga, *The Lost Science of Money*, pp. 83–85 and 100–101.
11 Farrell, for example, notes that Venice's oligarchy was actually eager to present itself as operating within the set legal constraints of the time in the form of usury prohibition, and used other methods to strengthen its trading power (Farrell, *Financial Vipers of Venice*, p. 159).
12 Zarlenga, *The Lost Science of Money*, p. 122.
13 Ibid., p. 155.
14 Ibid., p. 154.
15 Del Mar, *History of Monetary System*, pp. 317–321.
16 Ibid., p. 328.
17 N. Oresme, 'A Treatise on the Origin, Nature, Law, and Alterations of Money', in C. Johnson (ed.), *The De Moneta of Nicholas Oresme and English Mint Documents*, London: Thomas Nelson and Sons, 1956, II, 5.
18 Ibid., V, 10 and VI, 11, respectively.
19 A. Smith, 'An Inquiry into the Nature and Causes of the Wealth of Nations', in R.M. Hutchins (ed.), *Great Books of the Western World*, vol. 39, Chicago: Encyclopedia Britannica, 1952, p. 12.
20 Del Mar, *History of Monetary System*, p. 345.
21 Ibid.
22 Oresme, *A Treatise*, VI, 10.
23 Aristotle (P.L. Phillips Simpson, trans.), *The Politics of Aristotle*, Chapel Hill, NC: University of North Carolina Press, 1997, 1257a30.
24 Aristotle, *Politics*, 1257a30.
25 A tally stick was a piece of wood that had been notched and then split in half. One half was kept by the recipient, while the other was stored with the government to prevent counterfeit. In other words, the two pieces had to tally. Tally sticks were far more difficult to forge than other forms of money.
26 E.H. Brown, *The Web of Debt: The Shocking Truth about Our Money System and How We Can Break Free*, 3rd ed., Baton Rouge, LA: Third Millennium Press, 2008, p. 59.
27 G. Davies, *A History of Money: From Ancient Times to the Present Day*, Cardiff, Wales: University of Wales Press, 2002, p. 230.
28 Zarlenga, *The Lost Science of Money*, p. 219.
29 In ibid.

30 Smith, *Wealth of Nations*, p. 13.
31 Ibid., p. 14.
32 Zarlenga, *The Lost Science of Money*, p. 180; see also J.T. Noonan, *The Scholastic Analysis of Usury*, Cambridge, MA: Harvard University Press, 1957, pp. 171–178.
33 In Zarlenga, *The Lost Science of Money*, p. 145.
34 M. Barber and K. Bate, *The Templars*, Manchester: Manchester University Press, 2002, pp. 161–211.
35 In Zarlenga, *The Lost Science of Money*, p. 146.
36 Barber and Bate, *The Templars*, p. 17.
37 Zarlenga, *The Lost Science of Money*, p. 148.
38 Del Mar, *History of Monetary System*, p. 271.
39 Zarlenga, *The Lost Science of Money*, p. 122.
40 J.Z. Muller, *Capitalism and the Jews*, Princeton, NJ: Princeton University Press, 2010, p. 25.
41 Deuteronomy 23:19–20.
42 Aquinas, *Summa Theologiae*. Available at: http://www.newadvent.org/summa (accessed 11 March 2010), STh 2a2ae, 78: 1.
43 C. Elliott, *Usury: A Scriptural, Ethical and Economic View*, Millersburg, OH: Anti-Usury League, 1902, pp. 18–25.
44 Apparently some Jewish spiritual leaders, such as Moses Maimonides (1138–1204), were convinced that in order to avoid befriending non-Jews, it was necessary to charge even high interest rates on lending to Gentiles (e.g., M.A. Ali, *Prohibition of Usury: Islamic and Jewish Practices*, Denver, CO: Outskirts Press, 2009, p. 10; 'Usury', *Jewish Encyclopedia*. Available at: http://www. jewishencyclopedia.com (accessed 10 September 2010)).
45 N. Ferguson, *The Ascent of Money: A Financial History of the World*, New York: Penguin Press, 2008, p. 41. In the view of Farrell, Venice was the real culprit that caused the collapse of the Bardi and Peruzzi companies by manipulating the silver/gold ratio (Farrell, *Financial Vipers of Venice*, pp. 167ff).
46 Ferguson, *The Ascent of Money*, p. 42.
47 Ibid., p. 167.
48 Ibid., p. 43.
49 Del Mar, *History of Monetary System*, pp. 195–196.
50 Zarlenga, *The Lost Science of Money*, p. 159.
51 Farrell points to several mercantilist similarities between Amsterdam and Venice and argues that the declining power of Venice caused some of its influential families to transfer northward. Those families formed the backbone of the rise of Amsterdam (Farrell, *Financial Vipers of Venice*, pp. 215–216).
52 Zarlenga, *The Lost Science of Money*, p. 235.
53 According to Farrell, the Fuggers got their training "in the techniques of banking and accounting" in Venice (Farrell, *Financial Vipers of Venice*, p. 185).
54 Ibid., p. 164.
55 B.W. Dempsey, *Interest and Usury*, London: Dennis Dobson, 1948, p. 180.
56 C.P. Kindleberger, *A Financial History of Western Europe*, London: Routledge, 2006, p. 45.
57 Del Mar, *History of Monetary System*, p. 288.
58 Kindleberger, *A Financial History*, p. 48; Ferguson, *The Ascent of Money*, p. 48.
59 Ferguson, *The Ascent of Money*, p. 48.
60 Del Mar, *History of Monetary System*, p. 326.
61 Zarlenga, *The Lost Science of Money*, p. 269.
62 Smith, *Wealth of Nations*, p. 208.
63 Zarlenga, *The Lost Science of Money*, p. 231; Ferguson, *The Ascent of Money*, p. 48.
64 Del Mar, *History of Monetary System*, p. 332.

65 Zarlenga, *The Lost Science of Money*, p. 162.
66 Ferguson, *The Ascent of Money*, p. 49.
67 Zarlenga, *The Lost Science of Money*, pp. 157 and 162, respectively.
68 Farrell, *Financial Vipers of Venice*, p. 168.
69 Del Mar, *History of Monetary System*, pp. 402–411.
70 Ferguson, *The Ascent of Money*, p. 49.
71 Zarlenga, *The Lost Science of Money*, p. 282.
72 In Brown, *The Web of Debt*, p. 63.
73 Zarlenga, *The Lost Science of Money*, p. 282.
74 Brown, *The Web of Debt*, p. 24. The Federal Reserve was declared to be a private corporation by a federal circuit court in the 1982 case *Lewis v. United States*, 680 F.2d 1239 (ibid., footnote 4).
75 Ibid., p. 5.
76 Stiglitz, *Globalization and Its Discontents*, London: Penguin Books, 2002, p. 12; italics his.
77 P. Doyle (2012) 'Resignation Letter'. Available at: http://cnnibusiness.files.wordpress.com/2012/07/doyle.pdf (accessed 24 July 2012).
78 Zarlenga, *The Lost Science of Money*, p. 608.
79 In M. Rowbotham, *The Grip of Death: A Study of Modern Money, Debt Slavery and Destructive Economics*, 4th ed., Charlbury, UK: Jon Carpenter, 2009, pp. 10–11.
80 In Zarlenga, *The Lost Science of Money*, p. 396.
81 G. Berkeley, *The Querist*, Rockville, MD: Serenity, 2008.
82 C. Montesquieu, 'The Spirit of Laws', in R.M. Hutchins (ed.), *Great Books of the Western World*, vol. 38, Chicago: Encyclopedia Britannica, 1952, p. 183.
83 Ibid.
84 Ibid.
85 Ferguson, *The Ascent of Money*, p. 49.
86 Zarlenga, *The Lost Science of Money*, p. 364.
87 Ibid., p. 367.
88 Zarlenga, *The Lost Science of Money*, pp. 370–371; Brown, *The Web of Debt*, p. 39.
89 Zarlenga, *The Lost Science of Money*, pp. 456–457.
90 Ibid., p. 458.
91 In Rowbotham, *The Grip of Death*, pp. 220–221.
92 Ibid., p. 220.
93 M.N. Rothbard, *A History of Money and Banking in the United States: The Colonial Era to World War II*, Auburn, AL: Ludwig von Mises Institute, 2005, pp. 124 and 125, respectively.
94 Zarlenga, *The Lost Science of Money*, p. 460.
95 Ibid., pp. 461 and 460, respectively.
96 Ibid., pp. 471–473.
97 Brown, *The Web of Debt*, p. 92.
98 Zarlenga, *The Lost Science of Money*, p. 469.
99 In Brown, *The Web of Debt*, p. 92.
100 Rothbard, *A History of Money and Banking*, esp. pp. 47–179.
101 Ibid., p. 47; italics added.

6 Debt money and institutionalization of usury

Among the many little-known stories of the 2007–2009 financial crisis is that of a small private bank: the Constantia Bank of Austria. At the time the crisis broke out, the bank was in comparatively good health, with a capital ratio of 16 percent, far higher than many others, including some large global banks. Yet a mere rumor that the bank was insolvent was enough to start a bank run. The result was that

> within a single day, the bank had to declare insolvency, and within hours was taken over by a consortium of big Austrian banks that bought the bank for one euro. The rescue package of the Austrian state, which in principle was available for this bank, could not be activated in time to prevent this fate: it was still in the legislative process.[1]

As a matter of fact, many small banks went bankrupt as the crisis unfolded. Often they were simply not big enough to matter.[2] But there are at least two remarkably telling things about the fate of the Constantia Bank of Austria: first, that just a *rumor* was able to wipe out a bank; and second, that the government could not save it, despite its "good health." These two facts, as it turns out, reflect how the modern banking system actually works – that it operates on the basis of fractional reserves and that "good health" means that the fraction of reserves of a particular bank simply matches the "good practice" of the sector, but is not sufficient to withstand rumors, and thus is in constant need of rescue.

Another important aspect of the present banking system, as demonstrated up to this point, is that over the past several centuries, banks succeeded in inserting themselves into the money creation process by turning debt into "money." The current money system is driven by debt. The primary aim of this chapter is to illustrate how private interests have now dominated the money supply, and to explore how debt money is created and ultimately changed the nature of usury. We will begin by challenging the prevalent view of how money developed.

Banks and the money creation process

While money should be perceived as a public good, it is now controlled by a banking system that reflects more a cartel interested in its own profits gained from an enormously privileged position. At the heart of the problem is the protection the banking cartel enjoys to create money. An ideological position on the meaning of money and on the question of who has the power to issue it undergirds the entire situation. The very account of how money developed has even become part of this ideology.

How did money develop?

The introduction of money goes back to the dawn of the formation of human societies. How money became an indispensable part of human exchange was undoubtedly a long and complex process. Graeber argues that early human societies relied on credit (money), which was predominantly about mutual trust and strengthening community bonding, and not about accumulation of wealth. The developments of that stage he sums up in the concept of "human economies," in which each human being was considered "a unique nexus of relations with others." As a result, in such economies money acted "primarily as a social currency, to create, maintain, or sever relations between people rather than to purchase things."[3] It was only during the period between 800 BC and AD 600 – which Graeber, in a nod to German philosopher Karl Jaspers, calls "the Axial Age" – that coinage and metal bullion came to be perceived as money. Histories of money generally begin their account from what happened at the beginning of this period.[4] The Middle Ages (c. 600–1450), during which metallic money often faced shortages, returned to credit money, but its function was already quite different from that of "human economies." The fourth stage distinguished by Graeber is "the Age of Capitalist Empires," extending between 1450 and 1971. Due to new geographical discoveries, accompanied by a massive influx of gold and silver, world money switched again to bullion. In 1971, when Richard Nixon abolished the practice of pegging the value of the US dollar to the price of gold, a new phase of virtual money began.

As one may quickly note, the view of Graeber, which actually falls in line with the stance of many anthropologists, is in stark contrast with a widespread perception of the three-stage development process of economic exchanges: from barter to money to credit. Such a understanding of money as a great improvement over the impracticalities and limits of barter economy – thus allowing for smoother satisfaction of people's needs as well as expansion of exchanges, both territorially and in terms of goods and services offered – and then finally followed by the gradual introduction of more complex means of exchange in the form of credit, represents a standard view of mainstream economics. Whenever economists discuss the history of how money developed, they generally stick to the three-stage theory. Such an understanding of the origins of money is well reflected, for example, in the thought of Adam Smith.[5] This is also the theory with which students around the world are fed.[6]

Occasionally the three-stage theory of money is flavored with evolutionary thinking combined with the ideology of the free market. Niall Ferguson's book *The Ascent of Money* is a very telling example of such an approach. In his view, "financial history is essentially the result of institutional mutation and natural selection," and although randomness in mutations and adaptation processes play their part, "market selection is the main driver." Ferguson admits that "the evolutionary analogy" he uses is "imperfect" as the reproduction in the natural world differs from "most financial mutation" which is more about "deliberate, conscious innovation."[7] Nevertheless, he still takes the stance that

> our financial system has ascended since its distant origins among the moneylenders of Mesopotamia. There have been great reverses, contractions and dyings, to be sure. But not even the worst has set us permanently back. Though the line of financial history has a saw-tooth quality, its trajectory is unquestionably upwards.[8]

Such an optimistic and unfortunate presentation of financial history suggests ignorance of a far more complex picture, which in reality is not evolutionary and definitely *not* driven by market forces. Yet at times historians of economy tend to maintain that evolution has indeed been very much part of changes affecting economy, which has proceeded, as mentioned above, from barter economy to a money economy and eventually to a credit economy. According to Kindleberger, this view actually "happens to be wrong" as some modes of economic exchanges and financial instruments used over the course of history tend to be very mixed.[9]

The three-stage monetary stance is not limited to only mainstream economists. It is also widespread among economists of the Austrian School,[10] as well as among supporters of the so-called community (local) currencies.[11] Interestingly, those favoring the three-stage theory typically ask the reader to first imagine a society without money or the state of barter economy.[12] The difficulty with this point of departure is that for almost a century, anthropologists were complaining that they could find no evidence of a barter stage in economic exchange. Graeber calls it "the myth of barter," and sees it more as an Enlightenment ideology attempting to undermine the notion that money was actually a creation of government. This is why "the myth of barter" is so crucial. It shows that before the government took control over money, there existed a stage of natural exchange between people. Yet in fact, Graeber argues,

> we did not begin with barter, discover money, and then eventually develop credit systems. It happened precisely the other way around. What we now call virtual money came first. Coins came much later, and their use spread only unevenly, never completely replacing credit systems. Barter, in turn, appears to be largely a kind of accidental byproduct of the use of coinage or paper money: historically it has mainly been what people who are used to cash transactions do when for one reason or another they have no access to currency.[13]

The credit theory of money, as it sometimes is called, points out that money at its most basic meaning plays an important social function by establishing, maintaining, or disrupting relationships, and therefore cannot be treated simply as a neutral (disconnected from social and moral function) means of exchange, the way modern economics does. Yet in order to fulfill this function, what is needed is a certain measure, or a yardstick, to express the value of what one owes to somebody else. Thus, as a matter of fact, a coin or a banknote is basically a quantified expression of an IOU (I-owe-you) relationship. The search for such accounting measures goes back to early civilizations. Among the first ones known to have developed accounting tools were the administrators of Sumerian temples. Obviously the purpose of having such yardsticks was to record how resources were moved around, and in particular, to keep track of debts, such as rents or loans. In principle, calculations were in silver, but, ironically, silver hardly circulated. Most of it sat idly in treasuries of the temple and palace, "some of which remained, carefully guarded, in the same place for literally thousands of years."[14] Having the yardstick without sufficient circulating currency was enough to make the Sumerian civilization thrive.

A vehement critic of the three-stage theory of the development of money (from barter to money to credit) was Alexander Del Mar (1836–1926), an American political economist and monetary historian. His account of how money developed speaks of five distinct periods.

> First, the Pontifico-royal period, which lasted from the earliest times to the epoch of the Greek republics. In the pontifico-royal period money was coined exclusively in the temples, and stamped with the sacred emblems of religion. Second, the Republican period, when money was controlled by the senates of Sparta, Clazomenae, Byzantium, Athens and Rome. Third, the Pontifico-imperial period, when the coinage was assumed by the Caesars, and so regulated by them that for thirteen centuries its essential features remained substantially unaltered. Fourth, the Kingly period, when the princes of the West, having freed themselves from the dominion of Rome, seized the coinage prerogative and exercised it independently. Fifth, the period of Private Coinage, when the goldsmiths and merchant adventurers chartered to trade with and despoil or conquer the Orient, obtained control of the royal prerogative of coinage, and thus opened the door to that last of degradations, Private Coinage. This period has not yet ended.[15]

Needless to say, when Del Mar wrote these words over a hundred years ago, his concern was private dominance over money issuance, which was not at all evolutionary, but a move toward "degradation" of money. Although in the twentieth century governments regained some control over money power, overall, money is in a deepening stage of "degradation."

Yet by favoring monetary solutions in the spirit of Aristotle, and the state controlled money system, Del Mar profoundly differed from the dominant paradigm of his time. This was also the reason why his economic and monetary views became marginalized, if not suppressed. Joseph Aschheim and George Tavlas point to two main reasons why Del Mar was rejected by his contemporaries as well as later generations of economic writers. The first is "his intellectual position" that "placed him in opposition to the views of the leaders of the profession." The second suggests "prejudice and bigotry in high places" of economic academia in the late 19th century.[16] The silencing of Del Mar eventually caused his contributions to modern monetary economics to be grossly overlooked. A notable exception to the general trend of monetary economics was the work of Zarlenga, arguing for the relevance of Del Mar's thought to modern monetary problems.[17]

Banks as money creators

As presented in the previous chapter, over the last four hundred years, a gradual takeover of the power of money by private interests occurred. "Fractional-reserve banking," one of the crucial tools driving modern banking, was a very secretive practice in the end of the Middle Ages. By the seventeenth century, as the "desire for less risk, less trouble and higher status"[18] was gaining strength, the practice of fractional reserve began to accelerate. It was this shift that gave banks increasing power over the creation of money in the form of debt (as book entries) by keeping cash reserves as minimal as possible. The ease with which banks could create debt money (in economic jargon called "credit supply") caused the state not only to play an ever-smaller role in supplying money, but to become more and more dependent on debt money. The ideology presenting the state as the "Leviathan" (at present still advocated by, for example, the *Economist*)[19] and the self-regulation of the free market as a path to an enlightened future of humanity helped to hide the real workings of the financial system. Since the end of the nineteenth century, banks and the financial system have almost totally taken over the growth of credit, so crucial to the modern money supply.[20]

One of the reasons that prevented banks for a long time from overindulging themselves in extensive credit issuance was the fact that currencies were normally pegged to the value of metals, such as gold and silver. By the end of the nineteenth century, gold became the only form backing the debt money system, called the "gold standard." The new system agreed to at the end of World War II (the Bretton Woods conference) put the US dollar at the center. By pegging the US dollar to gold at a fixed exchange rate, and other major currencies to the dollar, the latter gained an enormous prestige. Then, with the passing of less than thirty years, in 1971, the United States unilaterally announced that it would no longer honor the pegging of its currency to gold, giving rise to a new monetary system based on fiat currencies. The connection of the US dollar to gold, however, did not end in an instant. Although the real gold-value of dollars was removed, what still continued was the dollar's credit-value gained before 1971. As a result, the US dollar retained its central role as an international currency, and its "exorbitant privilege," as Barry Eichengreen calls it, continues till the present moment.[21] At the same time, through the clearing CHIPS system (the Clearing House Interbank Payments System), the Federal Reserve functions as a sort of world central bank and the "crediting" system for the US dollar.

One must admit that under the pressure of criticism, modern economics textbooks have been much more open to the idea that banks create money. Undoubtedly, through the so-called multiplier effect, banks now have the ability and power to multiply the quantity of money many times the amount originally deposited with them. This has by now become recognized by economic theory. Moreover, economic circles are increasingly willing to acknowledge that banks normally do not make loans out of preexistent money in the form of deposits, but simply create new money by adding to the depositor's account in the bank the borrowed amount, and by deducting from the account as the debt is repaid. This "new" theory, then, basically admits that banks create money simply by crediting the depositor's account, but maintains that this does not have a damaging impact on the economy at large. The theory also claims that by creating and supplying money through loans to customers, banks provide service to particular borrowers and, indirectly, to the wider economy by increasing economic activity.

There is, however, a major problem with this theory: it does not fully express what in reality happens. The main difficulty with it is that it treats the bank–customer relationship in isolation, "as a detached mathematical model."[22] Theoretically, as Reginald McKenna, once the British Chancellor of the Exchequer, put it, "every loan, overdraft or bank purchase creates a deposit *and every repayment of a loan, overdraft or bank sale destroys a deposit*."[23] In other words, repayment of debts brings the bank-created deposit back to zero, and the interest that the bank charges is basically a form of fee for the "service" provided to the borrower. Yet what happens in reality is far from what this theory says. The basic problem with this theoretical model of multiplication of money through bank-created deposits is that it does not answer what actually happens to the money "paid back" to the bank in the process of debt repayment. In the words of Rowbotham,

> As any bank manager will confirm, when money is repaid into an overdrawn account, the bank cancels the debt, but the money is *not* cancelled or destroyed. The money is regarded as being every bit as real as a deposit; it is regarded by the bank as the repayment of money that they have lent. *And that money is held and accounted an asset of the bank . . .* The only factor which disguises their indisputable ownership of the money they create is that this returning money is usually rapidly reloaned. Borrowing in the modern economy almost always outpaces repayments, which is why the money supply escalates. This means that money returning as repayments usually does not accumulate embarrassingly in the bank's own account, but is quickly reloaned, along with more debt.[24]

It is important to stress that in the process of debt repayments money created through the very act of giving a "loan" is not destroyed, but is *removed* from circulation, which at the same time causes a decrease in the total amount of deposits held by the population.[25] Thus the claim in theory that the repayments of debt destroy the *deposit* is true, but because it treats the process as an isolated event, it does not say that the *money* created in the process is not destroyed, but only withdrawn from circulation. The final outcome is that although banks consider the act of "lending" as a service, in reality, they treat as their own all the money they create. Put more bluntly, "banks create money for themselves,"[26] but they need borrowers to achieve this. At present, basically the only factor that limits banks' power to create money is the number of borrowers.[27]

Perhaps the fact that the money flowing back to banks in the form of repayments is not destroyed, but treated by banks as their own, is most visibly observable during a recession. At such times, borrowing normally becomes depressed and some banks can be flooded with repayment money from past lending. As a result, some banks find themselves with "surplus money." This money then is quickly invested in, for example, stocks and bonds, or used to boost bank reserves. Banks do not have the slightest doubt that the money flowing in as "repayments" belongs to them.[28]

During booms, because the increase in borrowing gradually also brings increase in repayments, the fact that banks tend to quickly make this money reenter the wider economy occasionally causes the system to spike lending activity. Yet at the same time the pool of potential borrowers gradually begins to shrink. Prior to the last crisis, faced with such a dilemma, some banks, with the approval of government, simply relaxed the lending requirements and began to increase subprime loans, thus expanding further the pool of borrowers. The magic wand in the form of computer generated financial inventions, such as collateralized debt obligations (CDOs), helped to spread the risk arising from subprime lending, thus providing the impression that the system was sound. Yet what many tend to forget during flush periods is the huge vulnerability built into the present banking system. A single default can cause a rapidly spreading system-wide reaction. If this happens, even the banks of last resort, the central banks, cannot do much to prevent a crisis.

Interestingly, when the bubble bursts, often the blame-game follows. During the last crisis, Wen Jiabao, the premier of the People's Republic of China, took the opportunity of the 2009 summit in Davos to point a finger at the Western powers and blame them for a whole list of factors affecting the crisis, from inappropriate economic policies, to lack of discipline in financial markets, to high consumption and the low rate of customer savings.[29] Financial heavyweights in the United States, particularly Alan Greenspan and Ben Bernanke, on the other hand, blamed the crisis on a "savings glut" in the East, or, in other words, a massive pool of liquidity produced by high rates of savings in some countries of East Asia and the Middle East, which ultimately landed in US financial markets, encouraging financiers to make bigger and riskier bets.[30] Greenspan, Bernanke and the like, then, seem to have said that interest rates stayed low not because they kept them low, but because savings from the East prevented them from rising.

Yet looked at from the perspective of the inner workings of the entire financial system, the "savings glut" theory faces a real difficulty. Undoubtedly, a lot of savings from a booming China and the oil-rich Middle East ended up in the United States, searching for investment. Nevertheless, due to relaxed lending standards, allowing banks to use those savings to enormously expand lending, combined with the ideology that the discipline of the market would correct and rid itself of any destructive factors present in it, was more than enough to create a massive debt bubble. According to Sinn, one of the crucial causes of the last crisis was not an eastern "savings glut" but rather "a glut of American toxic assets." In his view, the causes of the crisis have to be sought in a broader context of how the present financial system (mal)functions, including its interaction with contemporary economic systems and the impact of a wide variety of policies. Sinn concludes that in the search for causes of the recent crisis, "the savings glut theory might have to be replaced with an institutional deficiency theory."[31] In effect, Sinn is saying that deeply-seated problems are engrained in the functioning of the present financial system. The "abilities" of banks to create money through the issuance of debt appear to be one of those problems.

Usury in the workings of modern banking

Virtually all contemporary money comes into existence on the basis of debt. By transforming the value of whatever can take the form of collateral into "deposits" credited out of thin air, banks can immensely increase supply of money. This extraordinary privilege of creating money through debt helps banks to keep so-called interest rates low, thus removing the issue of usury from the moral radar of modern "moneylending." In reality, however, the problem of usury has been buried in the structures of the very process of "making loans."

How do banks create debt money?

Among the chief vehicles of contemporary money supply are house mortgages. In the consumer market, houses are comparatively expensive objects of consumption. As a result, housing often faces a drastic shortage of money. This is why only the spreading of repayments over long periods of time makes it more affordable for people to buy a house. Yet taking a mortgage does not immediately mean that one owns the house. The very meaning of mortgage is that one does not own a house with a mortgage on it. In other words, a person cannot claim to own the property in which she or he lives until the mortgage has been paid off. Before that happens, the bank or building society involved "retains the title deeds."[32] Mortgages, then, create only an illusion of house ownership. Over the past decades there has indeed been an increase in the number of buildings people live in or rent out. Nevertheless, as at least some studies show, the actual ownership of houses with no mortgage on them in the so-called developed economies in fact fell.[33]

Meanwhile, because mortgages eat up a substantial portion of household earnings as "repayments," and because these repayments in the banking system form the basis for more lending, mortgages in reality have by far become the main engine of money supply. At the same time, the spiraling of repayments combined with the need for ever more lending allows consumers to gradually gain access to an increasing number of goods from cars to kitchen and exercise equipment with "mortgages" on them. From such a perspective, one can better understand why the 2007–2009 crisis of repayments in the housing market turned out to be so damaging to the economy at large. Michael Rowbotham has termed this process of money creation "the tyranny of mortgage." According to him,

> The fact that an increasing number of people do not have enough money to buy a house outright is not because someone else has an excess of money. Money only comes into existence and circulates in the economy through sufficient debt being undertaken, and *housing has become one of the main avenues through which such debt-money is created* – literally "borrowed into existence" and ultimately supplied to the economy via the institution of the mortgage.[34]

For Rowbotham, house prices do not reflect how much people can afford to pay for a house, but how much "*they can be persuaded to borrow.*"[35]

Another modern form of money supply is debts created through the use of credit cards. In general, payments in modern developed economies have become more abstract and have taken the form of transferring numbers between different accounts. Paying for purchases with plastic cards is part of this accounting system. It is "a way of 'keeping score' in the economic 'game' of give and take."[36]

But what happens when the customer's account does not have sufficient numbers to make the transfer? For modern banking, this is not a problem at all. As in the case of any loan application, once the credit card holder's creditworthiness (meaning ability to pay debts) has been established, and limits of such creditworthiness are set, as long as overdrafts on the credit card do not exceed these limits, the bank automatically creates a "deposit" equal to the needed sum and credits this to the card holder's account. If the card holder "balances" (pays) the overdrafts within the billing period, normally there is no interest charged. But once the card holder misses the deadline, she or he pays dearly on outstanding balances – the interest rates on such debts can vary, depending on contexts, from 15 percent to perhaps 30 percent. In the roaring economy of the 1990s and the early 2000s, growing amounts of repayments on previous loans, wedded with a spiraling need for an increase in lending, caused an enormous increase in credit card debts. Cardholders' creditworthiness became secondary as fees and securitization of debts were designed to offset possible losses, and the increasing pressure to provide ever more lending pushed for an immense expansion of credit card use. Debts incurred on such cards have become another important vehicle of money creation. Once the crisis hit, many were caught in vicious debt cycles. Yet even if people are able to pay their card debts within the billing period, banks (credit card issuers) still make money by charging perhaps 3 percent on each transaction in which a card was involved. Additionally, people with poor creditworthiness, low incomes, or unstable jobs may be required to pay higher interest rates. In short, whatever the business costs arising from the use of credit cards, they are essentially passed on to consumers.

From the above, one may rightly conclude that if debt is what drives our modern system of money supply, then business debt must also play an important role in the creation of money. Just as in the case of private consumer debt, industrial and commercial borrowing also adds to this process of supplying money through debt. Banks simply transform the value of illiquid assets or, in other words, whatever can be treated as collateral (sometimes merely one's signature) into the liquid form of deposits that miraculously become money that can be spent. This transformation is normally called by banks "making a loan," despite the fact that in reality nothing is loaned.[37]

Interestingly, over the past few decades, in many developed countries industrial and commercial debts decreased, and household and personal debts rose in proportion to the total of the country's debt. As a result, it is still the latter form of debts that plays the leading role in the process of money creation in modern economies.

An intriguing question arising in the lending/borrowing context is why some businesses or institutions can obtain long-term borrowing even at a rate below the rate of inflation. How is it, for example, that some institutions can borrow at an interest rate of 2 percent, while inflation stays at 3 percent or more? Or, why can a "mortgage" on a car carry zero percent interest? From the perspective of the traditional understanding of borrowing, in which interest normally means the price of borrowing, such practices make no sense. The truth, as far as regular borrowing from the bank is concerned, is that interest rates are not what they used to be, a charge for the use of money belonging to others. As pointed out earlier, the bank does not lend depositors' money or its own money. In the process of lending, it creates the needed sum out of thin air, and the interest it attaches to such lending is nothing more than regular payments for the bank's "service." All the money that flows back to the bank is treated as its own, and the interest is only a fraction of it.

Interest rates, however, are crucial to other lending institutions, such as pension funds, mutual funds, insurance companies, and financial companies, sometimes referred to as nonbank financial institutions (NBFIs). As a matter of fact, these intermediaries provide now even more lending than banks. There is, nevertheless, an important difference between them. While banks create money (in the form of debt), NBFIs can lend only the money they "have," or more precisely, the money they borrow from banks at lower interest rates than they can charge from their borrowers. This practice, often called borrowing short to lend long, makes NBFIs actually function more like traditionally understood banks, with one crucial difference: they do not accept deposits. At the heart of their business lies the ability to continuously roll over short-term debts. They are thus particularly vulnerable to contractions in bank lending. As such, NBFIs not only do not create money, but also contribute to the decrease in real money in circulation. Indebtedness ultimately increases, as somewhere in the system more debt has to be incurred to keep the system running.

The crucial reason why some debts can now function as money is that money itself has become a form of information system.[38] Of course, money still is a means of exchange, and, to a degree, stores value needed for future exchanges. Money has however become principally a unit of account. It now exists primarily as figures flowing between bank accounts. One should have no doubt that

> these bank account figures are money; equivalent to and every bit as effective as coins and notes, and can be exchanged for coins and notes if anyone wishes. But generally, the figures are simply transferred from one bank account to another according to our instructions, when we write a cheque, or pay in our salary, or use a cash card. Such numerical transfers have almost entirely taken over from cash transactions. Now, once this fact is understood, that there is no physical substance behind the majority of modern money, and that all it consists of is numbers, the ease with which such money can be created is obvious. All that is required is for more numbers to be created.[39]

Debt is the vehicle through which much money as bank account figures is created. At present, practically all money is created by banks as some form of debt. In fact, the diverse currencies circulating nationally and internationally, the paper monies that facilitate the very many transactions taking place every day, are nothing more than representations of debt.[40]

In historical shifts, then, the creation of money in the form of bank deposits empowered banks to increase the amount of money in the system beyond the limits governments set on the issuance of banknotes. As a result, while banknotes were already an abstraction compared to metal money, banks managed to further abstract the meaning of money. The primary role of banks shifted to the issuance of credit (debt) and credit clearing in depositors' accounts. Yet despite this important change, "banks still prefer to act as if money is a *thing.*"[41]

The confusion incorporated into banking language further exacerbates the perception of money as a thing, and helps to keep the public in the dark. Among the most anachronistic words in banking are "deposit," "reserve," and "redemption."

Historically speaking, "deposit" had a very concrete meaning. In the times of silver and gold money, a deposit was nothing else than the amount of silver or gold in the care of a banker. The deposit receipts (paper bank notes) that the depositor received were the proofs of what had been deposited. For bankers, however, the concreteness of deposits was itself a hindrance to their money-making business. So they gradually expanded the meaning of "deposit." The result is that now, as Greco puts it, "*money is merely numbers in an accounting system,* and the balance (number) in your account on a bank ledger, while still referred to as a deposit, simply shows your current score *or credit* in the economic game."[42] Even if one deposits banknotes in the bank, the very act of depositing transforms the banknotes into mere numbers. The banknotes, in turn, become part of the bank's "reserves."

Looking at the shifting meaning of deposit, Quigley notes that banks have taken on dual roles. They accept deposits of existing money, and thus play depository roles, but also create new money through lending by depositing in the customer's account the amount lent, and thus act as banks of issue. This is why the same term deposit actually carries two very different meanings. It may refer to (1) "lodged deposits," or money deposited by customers in a bank, on which the bank may pay interest to the depositors because such deposits are in fact debt that the bank owes to the depositors; and (2) "created deposits," or the claims that a bank creates out of nothing as loans by crediting the amounts lent to the depositors' accounts in the bank, which have to be repaid together with the attached interest, because these created "deposits" represent debt the depositors owe to the bank. Quigley further points out that one of the reasons the same word is used for these two different operations is that checks could be drawn against both forms of deposits to facilitate payments to third parties. By mixing these two very diverse functions, banks succeeded in covering (at least from the general public) the fact that they are involved in creating most modern money.[43]

The term "reserves" is also misleading because the so-called reserves are nothing more than the money needed to conduct a bank's daily business. This money is kept in the vault of the bank to meet customers' cash withdrawals, cashing checks, clearing checks, and so forth, and as a deposit of the bank at the central bank needed for clearing operations with other banks (balancing the numbers). In other words, reserves are what a bank is required to have to cover its customers' demand deposits, not their fixed deposits (on which fixed interest is paid, as they are debts the bank owes to the depositors). For example, the Federal Reserve, the US central bank, requires banks under its system to keep reserves of 10 percent or more of their demand deposits (no reserves are required on time deposits). As such, reserves are in constant flux, and at the end of the day the banks with "too much reserve" lend to those "short on reserve" at a relatively low interbank lending rate. Because of these frequent changes in reserves, the requirement is calculated as average over successive, say, 14-day periods (as in the case of the Federal Reserve).

Similarly, the concept of "redemption," or repayment of a loan, still carries the meaning as if a bank loaned its money to the borrower, while in fact it does not loan anything of its own. Nevertheless, the money the bank creates out of nothing has to be redeemed by the borrower, including the interest attached to the loan. Never mind that the money lent was created by the bank in the very process of lending.

All in all, then, some terms with regard to money and banking that developed during the times of commodity money have still been in use. Yet by now their real meanings have been broadened substantially and, as such, have become very misleading.

Modern banking as driven by "institutional usury"

Even after the Great Depression, which followed the crash of 1929, the conviction that there was nothing inherently wrong with modern banking and it needed but a little repair was relatively widespread. After World War II, this conviction was challenged by Bernard Dempsey (1903–1960), a Jesuit theologian and economist, who came to the conclusion that the modern banking system operated on "institutional usury."[44] How did he arrive at such a conclusion?

Based on the comparison of several modern interest theories found in the works of economists such as Knut Wicksell, Gunnar Myrdal, Ludwig von Mises, Friedrich von Hayek, John Maynard Keynes, Joseph Schumpeter, and Irving Fisher, and the works of seventeenth-century scholastics such as Luis Molina, Leonard Lessius, and John de Lugo, on interest and usury, Dempsey argues these two schools of economic thought may appear to have little in common, but certain divergences exist in modern economics that are applicable to scholastic teaching on usury. He specifically indicates three such divergences: between natural and money interest, between savings and investment, and in income displacement caused by issuance of new money. Dempsey's ultimate argument is that these divergences form "a sufficient common ground" with the late scholastics' views on usury.[45]

The first of the three divergences to which Dempsey refers is Wicksell's theory of disparity between the natural interest rate, or the rate "determined by supply and demand if real capital were lent in kind (*in natura*) without the intervention of money,"[46] and money interest, or the interest on lending once money has been introduced into an economy. For Wicksell, when the money rate corresponds to the natural rate, this rate is the "normal rate." Yet "the actual market rate in a modern credit economy can diverge from the normal rate because of the expansibility of bank money, and with such expansion, the sum that entrepreneurs *can* pay diverges from what under contract they *must* pay."[47] As a result, the general price level rises or falls depending whether the actual rate is lower or higher than the normal rate, which in turn causes borrowers (entrepreneurs) to make a profit or suffer a loss proportional to "the degree of divergence."[48] Departing from Wicksell's view of divergence, Dempsey argues that money creation as found in modern credit system, in which investment can be "financed with funds that have never been income," actually alters the value relationships between the commodities exchanged. The ease with which new funds can now be obtained and brought into circulation enables some people "to cut into the market and buy at current price before the effect of the injection of this pseudo-income has had opportunity to operate" or, in other words, create inflation. In short, the modern credit system can generate a gain from a loan that does not involve antecedent emergent loss or cessant gain, meaning through usurious means. However, because in the entire process the usurious outcome is not easily attributable to any personal fault, "the usury is institutional, or systemic."[49]

The second divergence Dempsey speaks about refers to the disparity between savings and investment found in the thought of Keynes. In contrast to the view of orthodox liberal economics that savings induce investment, Keynes argues that this is not necessarily true because savings may reduce the demand side of the economy if they are not immediately utilized. Thus, for Keynes, savings could actually have a negative effect on productive processes, including employment.

As a result, Keynes claims that "the rate of interest and the marginal efficiency of capital" should be distinguished from one another. In arguing this, he finds very useful both the scholastic moral contempt for hoarding money and the teaching on usury, as the former had the force to put savings into productive use while the latter prohibited rewards for money "bearing" more money or, in other words, for gains from the unproductive use of savings. Because of this, Keynes even appears to have changed his perception of various scholastic teachings:

> I now read these discussions as an honest intellectual effort to keep separate what the classical theory has inextricably confused together, namely, the rate of interest and the marginal efficiency of capital. For it now seems clear that the disquisitions of the schoolmen were directed towards the elucidation of a formula which should allow the schedule of marginal efficiency of capital to be high, whilst using rule and custom and the moral law to keep down the rate of interest.[50]

In response to Keynes's views, Dempsey argues that his understanding of the scholastics' thought contains "a truth, but one very poorly presented." According to him,

> To a Schoolman, the marginal efficiency of capital would be another name for the loss emergent or gain cessant upon the relinquishing of money, the true cost of the alternative opportunities. In communities where these alternatives were numerous and would be competed for, there would arise a common price based on the community appraisal of an average profit opportunity, an average rate of marginal profit from investment.[51]

Quite obviously, Dempsey disagrees with Keynes that the scholastics set profits in opposition to the rate of interest. Pointing to the principle of justice, Dempsey argues that while the common appraisal of marginal profit and the rate of interest are distinct concepts, they in fact should be equal or, in other words, should tend toward balance. This is why, "though this possibility of *de facto* divergence meant that the *concepts* are distinct, it may be very misleading to say that the *Scholastics* labored to keep them separate when *concretely* their whole purpose was to keep them together."[52] As a result, despite the fact that Dempsey disagrees with some of Keynes's reasoning, his views helped him understand that modern economy, by providing a possibility of gain without putting capital to productive use, has in fact become a system with an incorporated element of usury.

The third divergence Dempsey finds in Mises's view of fiduciary media or "money substitutes." For Mises, as Dempsey puts it, money substitutes are "complete and perfect deputies for money."[53] Apparently following the Aristotelian view of money, Mises considers the intrinsic qualities of "money substitutes" as merely a medium of exchange, which lacks the potential to produce anything by itself. As such, these "money substitutes" are brought into circulation through credit transactions. Yet Mises notes two distinct types of credit transactions – commodity credit, which are transactions that "impose a sacrifice on that party who performs his part of the bargain before the other does"; and circulation credit, in which "the gain of the party who receives before he pays is balanced by no sacrifice on the part of the other party," meaning that the issuer of fiduciary media can incur no loss.[54] Among the two, however, Mises considers the latter, circulation credit, as vital to the expansion of modern economy, because it can bring about an additional increase in the quantity of fiduciary media. Yet for Mises, real credit expansion takes place only when credit is "granted by the issue of an additional amount of fiduciary media," and not when banks are lending anew "fiduciary media paid back to them by the old debtors."[55] Although Mises recognizes that such an increase of money substitutes does affect the purchasing power of money, his argument is that it does not have a direct effect on the interest rate, but influences the rate of interest only indirectly through displacements in the distribution of income and wealth resulting from shifts in accumulation of capital.

Having examined the view of Mises that money substitutes affect the rate of interest only indirectly, Dempsey concludes that he must disagree. He has particular difficulty in accepting the argument of Mises that the new money is "so distributed as in no way to alter the existing proportion between expenditures on consumption goods and production goods" because, according to him, it is "an extremely unlikely case in practice and difficult to describe with certainty in theory."[56] Yet he still recognizes the contribution of Mises mainly through his "great and proper emphasis on the income displacement occasioned by issues of new money, which have a cost trifling in comparison with their value and which bear no relation to previous income and costs."[57] To Dempsey, the process of such "new money" creation is usurious, yet because it is not an outcome of the personal fault of anyone working in the banking sector, but takes place on the systemic level, the usury is institutional.

Kindleberger and Aliber once observed that "in many cases the expansion of credit resulted from the development of substitutes for what previously had been the traditional monies."[58] In the second half of the twentieth century "the development of substitutes" for money expanded to enormous proportions. The process was of course well packaged, and as long as economy "worked," hardly anybody, with the notable exception of Hyman Minsky, paid attention to how unstable the economy in reality was. Dempsey, through his analysis of the modern money creation system from the perspective of the scholastic teaching on usury, also pointed to an intrinsic problem ingrained in modern banking. Nevertheless, his concern was primarily moral – to show that the current system of money creation was intrinsically unjust, because it allowed some to receive something to which there existed "no moral title." In the end Dempsey clearly saw that in the modern economic system, banks could create loans that were not loans of *mutuum*, or loan transactions involving an actual transfer of money, and therefore could make gains without any corresponding risk or loss on their part.[59] Lacking commensurability in exchanges, for Dempsey such transactions were obviously usurious. Yet because of the change in the nature of loan transactions, the nature of usury also changed – it became not so much personal as systemic.

The genius of Dempsey's insight is that the old issue of usury continues to consume the economic system. But it does so in a new, institutionalized form. He found it difficult to accept on moral grounds the system of bank-created debt money, which allows banks to make huge gains without any proportionate danger of loss. Apparently an intrinsic shift toward money banks produce in the form of debt, thus providing banks with such an extraordinary privilege of creating money, caused Dempsey to conclude that the present system was structurally unjust. Thoroughly ingrained with an element of usury, the entire system of modern banking lacks equivalence of values in exchanges (justice). Unfortunately, the dominant mantra, even after the recent widespread crisis, has continued to be that the system overall works, and only needs a few modest repairs.

In conclusion, since the seventeenth century, banks have increasingly played a central role in bubble-creating credit expansion. By the end of the nineteenth century, the expansion of credit was almost totally taken over by banks and the financial system.[60] Although not all expansions of money and credit cause the building of bubbles, as some can be absorbed by growing economies, the ease with which credit (debt) money can now be supplied increases the likelihood of asset price bubbles. In the so-called good times, or booming economies, people tend to incur more debts because the credit-supplying institutions become more confident of debt repayments, based on the assumption of a continued increase in asset prices. As a result, borrowing is more easily obtainable. The eased access to credit strengthens investors' ability to roll old debt with new debts, yet at the same time often affects the quality of debts. Subprime mortgages are a telling example of the declining quality of credit in good times. Once reality creeps in and people realize that the investment bubble is reaching its limits, often the supply of credit declines sharply. As investors lose their ability to roll their debts, panic and crashes follow. In reality, then, it is not the burst of the bubble that destroys capital, but the gradual buildup of the bubble that already dilutes the value of the assets in question.

In the second half of the twentieth century, the inherent instability of economies was of particular interest to Hyman Minsky.[61] Even in the midst of the relative stability of the postwar economic boom, in contrast to the mainstream approach that assumed economies were constantly seeking equilibrium, Minsky claimed that modern economies were actually inherently *unstable*. Earlier, Dempsey looked at the credit expansion system within modern economies and concluded that it was built on institutional usury, thus inherently *unjust*. Interestingly, taking different perspectives, both Minsky and Dempsey looked behind the veil of the dominant theories, or more precisely prevalent ideologies, and discovered hidden systemic problems. The following chapters will look more deeply into these insights of inherent instability in modern economies and the inherent injustice of our modern money system. Keeping in mind how private banks are now so involved in the creation of money, we first look at the question of what role government plays in the process of the issuance of money.

Notes

1 H.W. Sinn, *Casino Capitalism: How the Financial Crisis Came about and What Needs to Be Done Now*, Oxford: Oxford University Press, 2010, pp. 68–69.
2 N.M. Barofsky, 'Where the Bailout Went Wrong', *International Herald Tribune*, 31 March 2011, p. 8; J. Saft, 'Big Winners in Crises: The Banks', *International Herald Tribune*, 13 April 2011, p. 18.
3 D. Graeber, *Debt: The First 5,000 Years*, Brooklyn, NY: Melville House, 2011, pp. 208 and 158, respectively.
4 E.g., N. Ferguson, *The Ascent of Money: A Financial History of the World*, New York: Penguin Press, 2008, pp. 23ff.
5 A. Smith, 'An Inquiry into the Nature and Causes of the Wealth of Nations', in R.M. Hutchins (ed.), *Great Books of the Western World*, vol. 39, Chicago: Encyclopedia Britannica, 1952, pp. 5–7, 10–11, 13–14.
6 E.g., J. Stiglitz and J. Driffill, *Economics*, New York: W.W. Norton, 2000.
7 Ferguson, *The Ascent of Money*, pp. 350 and 351, respectively.
8 Ibid., p. 358.
9 C.P. Kindleberger, *A Financial History of Western Europe*, London: Routledge, 2006, p. 21.
10 E.g., L. von Mises, *Human Action: A Treatise on Economics*, 4th ed., San Francisco, CA: Fox & Wilkes, 1996; M.N. Rothbard, *Man, Economy, and State with Power and Market*, 2nd ed., Auburn, AL: Ludwig von Mises Institute, 2009; G. Callahan, *Economics for Real People: An Introduction to the Austrian School*, 2nd ed., Auburn, AL: Ludwig von Mises Institute, 2004.
11 T.H. Greco, *The End of Money and the Future of Civilization*, White River Junction, VT: Chelsea Green, 2009.
12 E.g., Callahan, *Economics for Real People*, pp. 33ff.
13 Graeber, *Debt*, p. 40.
14 Ibid., p. 39.
15 A. Del Mar, *History of Monetary System*, Honolulu, HI: University Press of the Pacific, 2000[1896], pp. 386–387.
16 J. Aschheim and G.S. Tavlas, 'Academic Exclusion: The Case of Alexander Del Mar', *European Journal of Political Economy*, 2004, vol. 20, 31–60; quotations are from p. 31.
17 S. Zarlenga, *The Lost Science of Money: The Mythology of Money – the Story of Power*, Valatie, NY: American Monetary Institute, 2002.
18 Kindleberger, *A Financial History*, p. 36.
19 E.g., 'Taming Leviathan: A Special Report on the Future of the State', *Economist*, 19 March 2011.
20 C.P. Kindleberger and R.Z. Aliber, *Manias, Panics, and Crashes: A History of Financial Crises*, 5th ed., Hoboken, NJ: John Wiley & Sons, 2005, p. 64.
21 B. Eichengreen, *Exorbitant Privilege: The Rise and Fall of the Dollar and the Future of the International Monetary System*, New York: Oxford University Press, 2011.
22 M. Rowbotham, *The Grip of Death: A Study of Modern Money, Debt Slavery and Destructive Economics*, 4th ed., Charlbury, UK: Jon Carpenter, 2009, p. 23.
23 Ibid.; italics his.
24 Ibid., p. 29; italics his.

114   *Debt money and usury*

25 Ibid.; italics his.
26 Ibid., p. 28.
27 J. Ryan-Collins, T. Greenham, R. Werner and A. Jackson, *Where Does Money Come From: A Guide to the UK Monetary and Banking System*, London: New Economics Foundation, 2011, p. 23.
28 Rowbotham, *The Grip of Death*, p. 29.
29 M. Elliot and P. Gumbel, 'The Great Fall', *Time*, 16 February 2009, pp. 33–37.
30 B. Eichengreen, 'Is Anything Being Done to Prevent Another Crisis?', *Taipei Times*, 25 May 2009, p. 9.
31 Sinn, *Casino Capitalism*, p. 36.
32 Rowbotham, *The Grip of Death*, p. 17.
33 Ibid.
34 Ibid., pp. 16 and 21, respectively; italics his.
35 Ibid., p. 33; italics his.
36 Greco, *The End of Money*, p. 102.
37 Ibid., p. 102.
38 Greco, *The End of Money*, p. 1.
39 Rowbotham, *The Grip of Death*, p. 10.
40 Greco, *The End of Money*, p. 54.
41 Ibid., pp. 101–2. The quotation is from p. 102; italics his.
42 Ibid., p. 103; italics his.
43 C. Quigley, *Tragedy and Hope: A History of the World in Our Time*, New York: Macmillan, 1998[1966], p. 55.
44 B.W. Dempsey, *Interest and Usury*, London: Dennis Dobson, 1948.
45 Ibid., p. 228.
46 K. Wicksell, *Interest and Prices*, New York: Sentry, 1965, p. xxv.
47 Dempsey, *Interest and Usury*, p. 37; italics his.
48 Ibid., pp. 37–38.
49 Ibid., p. 207.
50 J.M. Keynes, *General Theory of Employment, Interest and Money*, San Diego, CA: Harcourt Brace, 1964, p. 352.
51 Dempsey, *Interest and Usury*, p. 220.
52 Ibid.; italics his.
53 Ibid., p. 43.
54 L. von Mises, *The Theory of Money and Credit*, Lexington, KY: Pacific Publishing Studio, 2010, pp. 139–140.
55 Mises, *Human Action*, p. 434.
56 B.W. Dempsey, *Interest and Usury: The Bases of Economic Organization*, Englewood Cliffs, NJ: Prentice-Hall, 1958, p. 44.
57 Ibid., p. 222.
58 Kindleberger and Aliber, *Manias, Panics, and Crashes*, p. 64.
59 Dempsey, *The Functional Economy*, pp. 439 and 435, respectively.
60 Kindleberger and Aliber, *Manias, Panics, and Crashes*, p. 64.
61 H.P. Minsky, *Can 'It' Happen Again? Essays on Instability and Finance*, Armonk, NY: M.E. Sharpe, 1984; H.P. Minsky, *Stabilizing an Unstable Economy*, New York: McGraw-Hill, 2008[1986].

7 The myth of money as government creation

The previous chapter demonstrated how private interests have gained an enormous influence over money supply. Nevertheless, the perception that only the government or a central bank has the power to create money has successfully captured public imagination. Even students of economics (and not only them) are still peppered with ideas of government "printing" money, how government "helicopter money" affects inflation, and so on. Apparently, for some, the suggestion that private banks can create money still sounds more like an economic heresy.

The aim of this chapter is to challenge the myth of government control over money creation by showing what role government actually plays in the entire process of money supply.

Complexity of the money construct

Virtually any person asked who controls our money supply would answer that either government (the simplistic answer) or the central bank (the sophisticated answer) controls our money. As a matter of fact, both of these answers tend to be more (the simplistic answer) or less (the sophisticated answer) a myth. Having followed all our deliberations on money, by now the reader might be perplexed seeing how money, which has become such an indispensable factor of our daily life, has become a complex construct, and how the controlling power over its issuance has been blurred.

Different layers of the meaning of money

The layers of the meaning of money reflect both the intricacy of the process of money creation and the difficulty of real control of the supply of money. This is also reason why in our recent history, diverse economic, financial, or monetary crises have become increasingly frequent phenomena. Throughout this work, what we have referred to as "money supply" is nothing else than the total amount of diverse media of exchange available in an economy at a particular time. The different layers of money in a given economy (country or region such as the eurozone) are typically codified by "M" with a number attached to it.

M0 usually means "narrow money" such as currency (notes and coins), while M3 (in some cases, for example, the UK and Japan, even M4) represents the most illiquid form of money, or "broad money." The total of M0 to M3 (or M4) forms the money supply. It is up to central banks to define the content of different Ms, but overall the differences in how various central banks define the layers of money under their control are not so great.

The US Federal Reserve (the "Fed") can serve as an example of how central banks ascribe meaning to different layers of money. The Fed divides money into currency, or more precisely, notes and coins (M0), M1 (currency, traveler's checks, and demand deposits), M2 (M1 plus saving deposits, money market funds, and small, mostly individual, time deposits), and M3 (M1 and M2 plus large, mostly institutional, time deposits and other forms of money, such as American dollars circulating abroad). US Treasury deposits in commercial banks obtained through tax payments and from the sale of its securities, although also bank money, do not fall into the M1 category because they are owned by the government.[1] Nevertheless, it is through some of the deposits form of money that commercial banks become part of the money-creation machine. The vehicle facilitating the participation of commercial banks in money creation is the issuance of loans by crediting depositors' accounts. In fact, as will be explained shortly, the entire mechanism of money supply (including M0) is based on debt. This is why, in the case of the Federal Reserve System, the money supply can be defined as "liabilities of the Fed and the banking system."[2]

It is worth noting here that up to the mid-1990s, the broadest measure of money supply in the United States (M3) was still growing rather steadily, but then began to accelerate. During the first five years of this century, it already grew on average 6 percent a year. Among the reasons triggering that growth were extremely low interest rates. The removal of bank leverage limits in 2004 even further exacerbated the expansion of money supply. In 2006, the Federal Reserve ceased reporting M3, and now only publishes relevant data up to M2. Theoretically, stopping the M3 report can be explained by the fact that M3 does not provide any particular information with regard to monetary policy. Yet it also says something far more important: that, in reality, central banks influence the money supply only up to a point (certain forms of money), but cannot control the total amount of money (debt) created in the banking system. By extension, central banks do not exert real control over the growing number of diverse financial and monetary crises.

In terms of money supply, it is also important to note that over the past years, the supply of so-called currency as the percentage of the total supply of money basically did not alter. In so-called developed economies, what people in general would consider as real money, namely currency in the form of bank notes and coins, represents now only about 3 percent of the total money stock. In the case of the most popular international currencies, such as the US dollar and euro, this figure could be approximately 6 or 7 percent, mainly because of use overseas. Thus, inside the United States or the eurozone, the figure still tends to be in the range of 3 percent. Among the biggest economies, China is an exception in this case, as in 2009, when currency represented 6 percent of its total money stock. Nevertheless, the trend there is similar to that in many developed countries. In 1999, the currency still formed 11 percent of the total money supplied.

The supply of "currency"

The still relatively widespread use of bank notes and coins in our daily exchanges has made many people think that they represent money. While searching for a better understanding of the nature of money, it is worth asking what lies underneath what so many consider as "real" money. A simple answer to this question is that in the post-1971 fiat money system, bank notes and coins are a legal tender, meaning they are endowed with a legal force to be accepted as means of payment. Among the diverse layers of money, they are often referred to as currency, although in reality the term "currency" should be seen more as a unit of account. Nevertheless, in this section we keep the meaning of currency as defined by some central banks, namely bank notes and coins (or M0).

What then do bank notes issued by central banks represent? Among the crucial functions of central banks is the putting into circulation of its bank notes, which people need for various basic economic exchanges. The way a typical central bank fulfills this role is by swapping its notes (printed paper money) for bonds of the state's treasury (promises of the government to pay, or IOUs). In other words, the state treasury has to issue bonds (debt notes) to back the notes issued by the central bank. Thus treasury bonds (government debt) are a form of collateral behind bank notes. And what stands behind the treasury bonds? Put simply, the power of the state to enforce payment of taxes. The swap of central bank notes for treasury bonds, however, is not in the form of a mere exchange between two entities. The treasury-issued bonds (debt notes) are bought by the central bank from the market, and the bonds become the debt of the treasury to the central bank. On the basis of these bonds (which are interest bearing), the central bank transfers (or simply sells) its own bank notes (which are not interest bearing) at face value into the economy through the banking system, which needs them to satisfy its customers. In short, while releasing bank notes into circulation, the central bank transforms the treasury (government) bonds, or debt, into the credit held in the treasury accounts at the central bank, and bank notes are the representations of that credit.

For some, this might look like as an unnecessarily complex process, because if only government has the authority to "print" money, why can't it print bills for ordinary daily exchanges? As a matter of fact, in 1921, Thomas Edison already raised this issue. According to him,

> If the Nation can issue a dollar bond it can issue a dollar bill. The element that makes the bond good makes the bill good also . . . It is absurd to say that our Country can issue bonds and cannot issue currency [bills]. Both are promises to pay, but one fattens the usurer and the other helps the People.[3]

The process of the issuance of bank notes shows that, despite intrinsic change in the nature of money into debt money (the public perspective) or credit money (the banking perspective), the practice is a residual of the times when bank notes were promissory notes that entitled the holder to exchange them for real money, such as gold or silver. As a result, paper money now still assumes some sort of wealth backing it. Yet in reality, it is backed only by trust in ("credit" of) government enforcement of the face values of notes as good for payments of "all debts, public and private," as stated on US Federal Reserve Notes (dollars). Thus bank notes are still "notes," meaning promises that all future deals involving them will be honored. The bank note holders, however, are not entitled to any interest. Only the holders of treasury bonds (debts) that back bank notes are entitled to interest attached to them. (As one may notice here, because the government bonds are interest bearing, the interest on such notes becomes part of the public debt.) Correspondingly, there is no need for a time limit on bank note redemption. The notes are removed from circulation only when they are no longer fit for further use. It is this lack of interest attached to bank notes that make some consider them as the only form of debt-free money.[4] Others, due to the fact that bank notes are issued on the basis of government bonds that are interest bearing, argue that virtually all our money has some form of debt attached to it,[5] or is a credit obligation,[6] depending on the public or banking perspective.

As far as the printing of bank notes by the central bank is concerned, it is enough for the central bank to order them from the selected printing agency at the mere cost of printing. For example, in the case of US dollars (or more specifically, Federal Reserve Notes), the Open Market Committee of the Federal Reserve System, which is responsible for the so-called open market operations (buying and selling of government securities by the Federal Reserve) acquires Federal Reserve Notes from the Bureau of Engraving and Printing for the average cost of about 4 cents per bill.[7] One may think that the low cost of producing a Federal Reserve Note gives the issuing entity an enormous potential for profit, perhaps over $99.9 for a $100 bill. Historically, governments tended to claim all the profits made on the minting of coins, meaning they kept the difference between the face value of the coins and the entire cost of minting, including the cost of the material of which the coins were made. This became known as seigniorage. In a modern fiat money system, however, seigniorage is more complex.

Following the example of the Federal Reserve Notes, seigniorage typically has several layers. First, the Bureau of Engraving and Printing in the Treasury prints notes, which the Fed buys at cost. The payment takes the form of crediting the Treasury's account at the Fed. Whenever banks need the Federal Reserve Notes, they can buy them at face value. Banks' payment for notes takes the form of debiting their accounts at the Fed. The notes banks acquire from the Fed then become available to depositors, who can obtain them by debiting their accounts at banks. In reverse, whenever depositors bring notes to their banks, they gain credits in their account in an amount equal to the face value of the notes. Similarly, banks gain credits in their Fed accounts when they return notes to the Fed. Not all notes the Bureau of Engraving and Printing prints are immediately put in circulation. Some are simply stored in the vaults of the Fed for future use, and remain as mere engraved pieces of paper. In the entire process, only the notes in circulation earn seigniorage. Because these notes are backed by Treasury securities, "the more notes sold to banks by the Fed, the more Treasury securities it acquires, and the greater the seigniorage benefit to the Treasury."[8] The notes once "sold" into circulation at face value are never "bought" back at face value when they are taken permanently out of circulation. As a result, the whole profit from the "sale" of bills is "credited" to Treasury accounts at the Fed.

If the notes circulate overseas, the profit from what it costs to print them and from foreigners procuring them at face value also goes to the treasury. The status of the US dollar as the most popular international currency Barry Eichengreen calls an "exorbitant privilege." According to him, "about $500 billion of U.S. currency circulates outside the United States, for which foreigners have had to provide the United States with $500 billion of actual goods and services."[9] When the notes return to the country of their origin, they become part of its monetary base and have to be matched by the treasury securities in the central bank's portfolio.

The difference between seigniorage from coins and notes is significant. Following the intrinsic change in the nature of money, seigniorage from bank notes has come to take on a new form, but the seigniorage from coins retained the function from the days when money was basically in the form of precious metals. Again using the example of the US dollar, the coins are produced by the US Mint, a bureau of the Treasury, which sells them to the Fed at face value. The moment the Fed buys minted coins, it credits the Treasury accounts at the Fed. "The difference between the face value of the coins and the cost of their production is seigniorage for Treasury."[10]

Once bought, coins are added to the Fed's balance sheet as assets. They are removed from the Fed's balance sheet when sold to commercial banks. Banks then may sell them to the public. Just as between the Fed and banks, so also between banks and the public, coins are sold at face value.[11]

"Base money" and "bank money"

Overall, money in the modern fiat system, as pointed out by Hummel, can be divided into "base money" and "bank money."[12] All base money has its origin in a country's central bank. Put simply, base money is comprised of the bank notes and coins the private sector obtains from the central bank through the banking system, and of banks deposits at the central bank. These deposits are issued in exchange for securities of the country's treasury that the public bought from the treasury with previously issued base money acquired from the central bank. When the central bank buys the treasury securities, it pays by creating (adding numbers to) sellers' (banks') deposits at the central bank. Through such a process of paying by crediting banks' accounts at the central bank, debt becomes monetized, as government IOUs (treasury securities) are transformed into credit held by the public and banks. Base money is forced into circulation by the fact that all the payments from or to government can only take the form of transfer of base money and the requirement that banks have to hold enough reserves of base money to meet the needs on their demand deposits. For example, an important factor in forcing circulation of base money is payment of taxes. So when one pays taxes by writing a check, his or her bank has to relinquish the amount in question from its reserves of the base money at the central bank to the treasury's account in order to clear that check.

Because taxes can be paid only in base money, in a sense base money can be viewed as a tax credit. This is also why government (through the central bank) has the responsibility to provide the public with at least enough base money to pay taxes (although normally more might be needed to make the economy function efficiently). At the same time, government ability to enforce payment of taxes also influences the viability of base money.

Bank money, on the other hand, takes the form of deposits created by banks while issuing loans. As presented earlier, this normally is done by crediting the borrower's account with a new deposit. In effect, a bank loan provides the borrower with the deposit, or a credit that he or she can use, which is paired with a debt that the borrower is obliged to repay. Interest paid on the loan is basically a fee for the service of creating the credit/debt pair and servicing the process of repaying the debt. For the bank, on the other hand, the loan provides an asset on which the bank additionally earns interest, matched by a liability in the form of the borrower's deposit. This is why banks, under normal circumstances, tend to expand their lending. Loans, after all, enlarge the size of their assets. (For example, the total assets of Barclays have amounted to US$2.5 trillion, which is close to the size of the annual gross domestic product [GDP] of the United Kingdom!)[13] As a result, when a bank issues a loan, the total amount of bank money increases.

The question, of course, is how base money is related to bank money. Hummel answers this question by stating that "the value of bank money is based on the promise that it can be converted on demand into base money at par."[14] In other words, bank money is merely a *claim* on base money. In order to provide some sort of safety, that bank money "can be converted on demand into base money at par," banks are required to hold enough reserves of base money to meet the demands on their transaction deposits. In the current fractional reserve system, many central banks tend to set the reserve ratio requirement on demand deposits at a minimum of 10 percent (as in the case of the Federal Reserve System) or higher. These reserves can be kept in the form of vault cash and deposits at the central bank.

The modern money system, then, can be presented as a two-layered inverted pyramid, at the bottom of which is base money, which forms a far smaller portion of the pyramid. This image is very useful because it also expresses the fact that the present system is as stable as an inverted pyramid. In other words, frequent crises are built into its very nature. Because base money has its origin in central banks, the assumed role of central banks is to keep the balance of the inverted pyramid by adjusting the price (the cost) of acquiring base money that banks need for reserves. As one may observe, even if the keeping of reserves by banks at the central bank were not required, banks would still need to have sufficient amount of reserves to cover their depositors' checks[15] as well as cash to meet daily withdrawal demands of depositors.

The present banking system, then, could work without reserve requirements, and in reality some countries, such as Canada, can do without them. Nevertheless, the requirement to hold a certain level of reserves apparently reduces fluctuations in the demand of reserves (base money) and further stimulates the interbank lending market, in which banks borrow and lend reserves among themselves. Central banks normally regulate the overnight interest rates on interbank lending by raising or lowering them. When the interest rates are lowered (meaning the cost of acquiring reserves by banks is reduced), banks are encouraged to increase their lending. On the other hand, when the interbank lending rate is set higher, it reduces bank lending. The interbank lending rate set by the central bank functions as a benchmark for all short-term interest rates. Central banks, then, set a certain target for an interbank lending rate, and in order to keep that target, they either buy treasury securities to add reserves to the system, or sell them to drain the system reserves, and thus balance their supply and demand.

Government, banks, and money creation

Government, and particularly its treasury, does play a role in originating money, while central banks control how much of the currency is issued into the economy. But this forms only a fraction of the money normally present in any modern economy, as commercial banks can also influence the amount of money through the issuance of debt. After presenting different layers of the meaning of money and how the process of money creation is initiated, the aim of this section is to further elaborate the interlocking connections between the government treasury, the central bank, and the banking industry.

The treasury, the central bank, and money creation

On the whole, the money creation machine operates as an interlocked tripartite system: the treasury (government), the central bank, and commercial banks. While much of this interlocking has just been explained, it is important to further elaborate on the role of the treasury and its relation to the central bank, as well as the nature of the relationship between government and the central bank.

Normally the treasury has its accounts in commercial banks dispersed around the country. This is where government income from taxes and the sale of bonds is deposited. The account of the treasury at the central bank is meant to do the ultimate balancing of the government spending. Thus, from the monetary perspective, the treasury operations recycle the base money already issued by the central bank and provide securities backing base money. As such, the treasury can be considered as the originator of base money, but is not in actual control of how much base money is issued to the economy, as this is the task of the central bank. The fiscal responsibility of the treasury is to keep its spending within the confines of a targeted balance, meaning that its spending should be balanced by receipts mainly from taxes and the sale of bonds. This balancing of the treasury accounts at the central bank, nevertheless, still has monetary consequences as it helps to mitigate large alterations in the overall reserves of the banking system.

It is no secret that many modern governments cannot collect enough money, and therefore run budget deficits. Normally these deficits are set at a few percentage points a year, and are balanced by the sale of treasury securities. Because the treasury securities are debts, over the years these debts tend to grow. What is often misunderstood about government debt, however, is that in reality this debt does not have to be paid off. As stated by Brown, "the government's debt is never paid off but is just rolled over from year to year, becoming the basis of the national money supply."[16] Of course, treasury securities have to be redeemed on the agreed date. But the treasury can do this by selling new securities. A shortfall from tax collection can always be made up by selling treasury securities to keep government payment obligations. It is crucial, then, that government has the ability to simply roll over debts, and thus keep open the potential to continue borrowing. And because the old treasury securities can be redeemed by selling new securities, it is enough for governments to collect enough money to pay interest rates on their debts. As a matter of fact, a large portion of the interest paid on the treasury securities is often covered by the income that the central bank transfers to the account of the treasury. The interest that the treasury pays to the central bank on its securities, on the other hand, forms an important part of the central bank's income, which in effect means that much of the interaction between the treasury and the central bank has an accounting character.

At least theoretically, then, government debt can be rolled over and over *almost* indefinitely. The crucial word here is "almost." The face value of individual maturing securities can be redeemed by issuing new securities, and thus as long as a government can continue paying the interest on all of its securities, the finances of that government are considered sound. Yet history shows that sometimes the ability of certain governments to roll their debts is put into question, which means they can sell securities only by paying much higher rates. In theory, governments can pay whatever interest the market demands, but this even further exacerbates their difficulty to roll their debts, and the suspicion may lead to suspension of lending. Because in the present system viability depends on the ability to borrow, once a government loses this ability, it faces bankruptcy. Of course, on a practical level, it means that a government must find ways to avoid such a state of affairs. This is where the International Monetary Fund (IMF) is at times requested to provide assistance. In reality, however, the very instability of the system already requires occasional actions on the part of this international support institution. Yet the question can be raised whether in the face of the huge growth of debts, this institution may also at some point become insufficiently equipped to deal with the crisis.

What is also often misunderstood is the relation between government and the central bank. In the fiat money system, central banks have managed to retain a great deal of their so-called independence. This does not mean that they can act as they please. They are still subject to legislative (parliamentary) oversight. However, in practical terms, this "oversight" means keeping the lid on borrowing, which is at the heart of the modern money system. Their "independence," then, should rather be understood more in terms of being free from direct influence of the executive branch of government. Theoretically, the fact that the head of the central bank and the members of the governing board are all appointed by government is used to claim that the central bank is still an extension of government, and that its independence is kept for the greater benefit of the economy. As often happens, the reality is much more complex than the theory.

Taking the example of the US Federal Reserve System, one can see how the central banking system operates so that the link between the central bank and government is actually far weaker than the general theoretical argument suggests. The Board of Governors of the Fed consists of seven members appointed by the president and confirmed by the Senate. The full term of each member is fourteen years, far longer than the potential two terms (eight years) of the president. Appointments are also structured so that only one appointment can take place every two years. The fourteen-year term expires on January 31 of even years, while US presidents take office in odd years. As a result, during eight years the president can change at most four board members. The chairman of the board is appointed from among the board members for a four-year term, beginning midway through each presidential term. Moreover, in practice, the president appoints the chairman and members from the list proposed by the banking community, and it would be unwise for the president to go against their will. The reality, then, is that Wall Street has a far greater say about the Fed than many would imagine, and the appointments system is more or less an illusion of public control.

The Fed also spreads the impression that the vast majority of its earnings is turned over to the Treasury. It claims that 95 percent of its net earnings are transferred to the government.[17] Yet here again it is worth looking behind the façade. The Fed is in principle owned by a consortium of private banks, the biggest of which are Citibank and JPMorgan Chase & Co. The Fed is a corporation, but "so private that its stock is not even traded on the stock exchange."[18] Owners of its stock (which cannot be exchanged or traded) are paid a dividend of 6 percent, and most of the remaining profits are paid to the Treasury. This is still not a small amount – in 2010, the Fed paid to the Treasury $79.3 billion and in 2011, $76.9 billion, which was more than double the amount in the years 2007 ($34.6 billion) and 2008 ($31.7 billion).[19] Yet one must remember that this is the amount paid to the government for the use of its credit, on the basis of which the Fed issues the most commonly used currency in the world.

Brown criticizes the Fed in that "it reports as profits *only* the interest received from the federal securities it holds as reserves" but its reports do not mention "the much greater windfall afforded to the banks that are the Fed's corporate owners, which use the securities as the 'reserves' that get multiplied many times over in the form of loans."[20]

In fact, the criticism of the way the Fed operates goes even further. According to its published statements, the Fed is audited every year by PricewaterhouseC-oopers and the Government Accountability Office (GAO), an arm of Congress. Nevertheless, as Brown points out, "some functions remain off limits to the GAO," including the Fed's "transactions with foreign central banks and its open market operations (the operations by which it creates money with accounting entities)." As a result, its "most important – and most highly suspect – func-tions remain beyond public scrutiny."[21]

Although the example of the US Federal Reserve is used here, the basic mechanism by which central banks function does not differ much in many countries. Some may claim a higher degree of public ownership and closer scrutiny. For example, since its inception in 1694, the Bank of England (on which the Fed is modeled) functioned as a private bank. Then, 250 years later, under strong pressure from the Church of England, the bank was nationalized in 1946.[22] Today it is alleged to be a publicly owned bank, or a limited liability company owned by its shareholders. Yet there is a catch in the projected public ownership of the bank. In 1977, the Bank of England formed the Bank of England Nominees Limited (BOEN), a private company, with the objective "to act as Nominee or agent or attorney either solely or jointly with others, for any person or persons, partnership, company, corpo-ration, government, state, organization, sovereign, province, authority, or public body, or any group or association of them." Using Section 27(9) of the Companies Act 1976, Edmund Dell, then the Secretary of State for Trade, granted BOEN an exemption from the disclosure requirements because "it was considered undesirable that the disclosure requirements should apply to certain categories of shareholders."[23] The exemption is still kept under sec-tion 796 of the Companies Act 2006.[24] So while normally one can request knowledge of the nominal owners, the Bank of England is exempted from such a revelation.

Apparently, the nationalization of the Bank of England, the flagship of a privately owned central bank, was too big a shock to modern-day bankers, and therefore was not welcomed. So, it seems, they had to find ways to change it. Robert Owen, one of the directors of Struggle Against Financial Exploitation (SAFE), argues that BOEN has taken real control of the Bank of England through "shares owned by the secret share holders," despite the fact that to the outside world BOEN is a subsidiary owned by the Bank of England. He concludes that through this mechanism, sometime after 1977, the Bank of England was effectively privatized, and that now it is "owned covertly, if not by the banks, then by a higher banking entity that has the interests of the banks at heart, which justifies the rampant and systemic fraud perpetrated upon their customers with arrogance and impunity." Since its establishment, BOEN "only lodges 'Short Form' un-audited accounts."[25]

The example of the Bank of England is very telling because it indicates that banking interests prefer not to allow a central bank to slip from under their influence. As stated above, the actual ownership of the Bank of England has become a very murky question. And much of what really happens inside and through central banks takes place behind a murky façade. Undeniably, some central banks are state owned and the public can now access a monstrous amount of information about them. But is the public really provided with what is essential for the common good? Seemingly behind the façade, banking interests still exert a tremendous influence over central banks. As a result, central banks are far more extensions of the power of the banking system than of the government. Or, perhaps more likely, governments, normally presented, and indeed perceived, as irresponsible stewards of money, have become complacent with the workings of the system as they themselves are paid for the use of their credit by the banking system and are allowed to spend almost as much as they wish. So the insistence that governments appoint those who make decisions in central banks does not change the fact that banking interests are well represented behind the scene, and the so-called independence of central banks even further exacerbates that influence. As long as this independence is preserved, banking interests can ultimately accept state ownership of some central banks.

The more recently created monolith, the European Central Bank (ECB), is not much different than this picture. It is a far-flung monetary organization (to which eurozone member states transfer their monetary policies), which differs from other central banks in one aspect: it still does not have a single government (treasury) that could issue bonds (debt) that can be turned into euro base money.[26] Both the ECB and the central banks of the member countries may issue the euro bank notes, but only the ECB's Governing Council has the right to authorize the issuance of such notes. This is why the ECB is characterized as "centralized decision-making and operational decentralization."[27] The bonds, on the basis of which the euro is issued, which can be bought and sold only in the open market, are treasury bonds of the eurozone member countries. But, as one may notice, there is a catch here: yields on treasury bonds of diverse member countries can vary substantially. As a result, there is a great dose of compromise built into the euro system. Greece, for example, by entering the eurozone (Lynn puts it more bluntly by claiming that Greece simply "blagued" its way into the euro)[28] managed to pull its creditworthiness closer to that of Germany. Of course, the same is true about several other eurozone countries, such as Portugal, Spain, Ireland, and Italy, all of which could borrow more cheaply than before joining the euro. This was the euro crisis in the making.

The European Central Bank is controlled by the central banks of the EU states. Some of these banks are state owned, and others are private (for example, the central bank of Italy is almost totally controlled by private banks). About two-thirds of the ECB ownership falls to the central banks of Germany, France, England, and Italy. Because the United Kingdom is not a member of the euro system, the Bank of England is one of the ECB owners, but has no voting right. Far more important than the ownership structure of the ECB, however, is its continual stress on its institutional "independence" and democratic account-ability. The first part of Article 108 of the Treaty on European Union (the EU Treaty, also commonly known as the Maastricht Treaty) states explicitly that "when exercising the powers and carrying out the tasks and duties . . . neither the ECB, nor a national central bank, nor any member of their decision-making bodies shall seek or take instructions from Community institutions or bodies, from any government of a Member State or from any other body."[29] The result is that the ECB does not lend to governments but only to banks.[30]

Looking deeper behind the façade, however, one can see that this stress on independence and accountability works like smoke and mirrors in reality. It creates the illusion of public control of the ECB, giving the impression that its actions and decisions are subject to public scrutiny, while in fact banking interests exert their influence not from outside but from within by keeping the present privately controlled money creation system intact.

One may conclude, then, that the case of the European Central Bank fits the pattern of what the central banks are about. As summed up by Henry Liu,

> The independence of central banks is a euphemism for a shift from institu-tional loyalty to national economic well-being toward institutional loyalty to the smooth functioning of a global financial architecture . . . The mandate of a modern-day central bank is to safeguard the value of a nation's [and also a zone's] currency in a globalized financial market through economic recession and negative growth if necessary . . . The best monetary policy in the context of central banking is . . . set by universal rules of price stability, unaffected by the economic needs or political considerations of individual nations.[31]

There is no doubt that the overriding objective of the ECB's monetary policy is price stability.[32] This, in turn, means that its loyalty does not differ from many other central banks.

"Central bank" versus "national bank"

The prevalent banking model of the developed economies is built around a "central bank," which is either privately owned or is supposed to exercise at least a large dose of so-called independence from the influence of government. In such a system, government can actually do little to balance a formidable power of private international finance. This is why it often tends to tap into that power, thus intermingling public interests with the interests of private banking. The result is that the central bank system has successfully created the image that money creation is under public scrutiny. In reality, however, this system not only furthers the centralization of the power and concentration of wealth, but also adds immensely to the instability of entire economies. While many aspects of human reality have moved toward greater public control, money creation has been stuck in the murky structures exacerbating the problem of real control over the creation of money. One can be sure that those who have been granted the monopolistic control over credit (debt) will protect the present privately controlled money creation system by showing that, despite some occasional disturbances, the system works and that government will be there in case real troubles set in.

Throughout this study, the main focus has been on the still dominant central bank model. However, it has to be admitted that this is not the only model presently found in modern banking. Some economies operate around the model of "national bank."

For Henry Liu, the crucial difference between a central bank and a national bank is where their loyalties lie. In his view, while a central bank is committed to "the smooth functioning of a global financial architecture," a national bank has the mandate "to finance the sustainable development of the national economy." In other words, the former is meant to serve the interests of private international finance, and the latter to serve the interests of the nation and its people.[33] As an example to demonstrate the difference, Liu points to the People's Bank of China (PBoC). Although in 1995, a new banking law granted to the PBoC the status of central bank, the change was actually more nominal than functional. In the words of Liu, "It is safe to say that the PBoC still follows the policy directives of the Chinese government . . . Unlike the Fed, which has an arms-length relationship with the US Treasury, the PBoC manages the State treasury as its fiscal agent." To this he adds,

Recent Chinese policy has shifted back in populist directions to provide affirmative financial assistance to the poor and the undeveloped rural and interior regions and to reverse blatant income disparity and economic and regional imbalances. It can be anticipated that this policy shift will raise questions in the capitalist West of the political independence of the PBoC. Western neo-liberals will be predictably critical of the PBoC for directing money to where the country needs it most, rather than to that part of the economy where bank profit would be higher.[34]

From this perspective, one can more easily understand why there has been so much criticism of China's banking system, and pressure to broaden the access of international banks to China's financial market.

At the turn of the millennium, Gordon Chang was predicting the collapse of China. Although he pointed to diverse symptoms of decay, it was in the banking system where he claimed "the end of the modern Chinese state might well begin."[35] Apparently, Chang's prophesy was based on the widespread perception that the efficiency of the Chinese banking system, dominated by the state, was no match for the Western banks. Yet several years later, it was the Western banking system that was on the verge of total collapse and needed the helping hand of government to avoid meltdown. Even the lenders of last resort – central banks – were overwhelmed by the size of the debts incurred by banks. Undeniably, the PBoC has its own problems. Nevertheless, it is more the authoritarian form of the Chinese government that has been its greatest thorn, not the fact it is owned by the state. Few national banks now function in a mode similar to the PBoC. An important way in which the PBoC differs from the dominant central banking model is that it does not let its currency float. Such a stance has helped to fend off "the currency manipulations of international speculators." A huge store of dollar reserves further shields China from the assaults of speculators. Thus, China distinguishes itself by being "free of the debt web of the IMF and the international banking cartel."[36] It remains to be seen how long China will resist the pressure of the international banking lobby.

Private versus public banking

Similarly to the distinction between central bank and national bank, in the banking industry there exist two competing models – private and public banks. Throughout this work, private banks have been the center of attention, due to the simple reason that private banking has become the dominant model in the modern world, particularly in so-called developed economies. Having cleverly institutionalized usurious practices, this model now uses the banking system to gamble economic stability for private gains, mainly for bank owners and executives. Supported by an elitist neoliberal ideology (see Chapter 2), the private banking model has helped to increasingly concentrate wealth and power in the hands of the financial elite. The main vehicle driving this process is the continual power to create money through the issuance of debt (credit) out of thin air and the forcing of money to "bear" more money. Looking at the problem of control over the process of money creation, Greco has come to the following conclusion:

> The monopolistic control over credit, exercised through a banking cartel armed with government-granted privilege, allows wealth to be extracted from producer clients and, despite the trappings of democracy, the control of governments to be maintained in the hands of a few. Credit is allocated on a biased basis to favored clients, including central governments, which distorts both the system of economic rewards and exercise of political power. Under this regime, the people's own credit is privatized and "loaned" back to them at interest.[37]

The shift toward the private banking model has put gambling for more money at the heart of the events taking place in modern economies, in which higher earnings depend ever more on the ability to tap into this gambling urge. On the contrary, the wages of those whose work contributes to real economy have stagnated, or even fallen in real terms, causing a growing gap in wealth distribution and the appearance on the stage of a modern plutocracy.

The second model is public banking. According to Brown, "publicly-owned banks operate in the public interest by law. That means they support the real, wealth-producing economy. Bank profits generated from the credit of the public are returned to the public."[38] This system of lending, in which gains belong to the public, was known to the ancient world. In some early civilizations it was built around temples, which had not merely religious but also strong social functions.[39] Only gradually over many centuries, private interests snatched the control over lending and mingled it with the creation of money. Nevertheless, throughout a long financial and monetary history, public banking made remarkable comebacks. The medieval *mons pietatis*, established by Franciscan monks in Italy to ease the need for low-interest loans for the poor, is an example of such a comeback. During the Renaissance, the tradition of public banking was also gradually incorporated into the functions of some municipalities.[40] Such, for example, was the origin of the Bank of Venice, and later of the Bank of Amsterdam.

The government "loan office" of eighteenth-century Pennsylvania is among the most admired experiences of public banking. Benjamin Franklin called the money loaned by these offices "bills of credit" or "ready money."[41] In monetary history, this in-fact paper money has become known as Colonial Scrip. According to Franklin, "experience, more prevalent than all the logic in the World, has fully convinced us all, that it [paper money] has been, and is now of the greatest advantages to the country."[42] Pennsylvania's public bank equipped with paper money helped the state to experience several decades of booming economy. Even Adam Smith was full of admiration for the achievements of the colony:

> The government of Pennsylvania, without amassing any treasure, invented a method of lending, not money indeed [note, for Smith money meant gold or silver], but what is equivalent to money, to its subjects. By advancing to private people at interest, and upon land security to double the value, paper bills of credit to be redeemed fifteen years after their date, and in the meantime made transferrable from hand to hand like bank notes, and declared by act of assembly to be a legal tender in all payments from one inhabitant of the province to another, it raised a moderate revenue, which went a considerable way towards defraying . . . the whole ordinary expense of that frugal and orderly government.

Smith adds elsewhere that Pennsylvania's "paper currency . . . is said never to have sunk below the value of the gold and silver which was current in the colony before the first emission of its paper money."[43] Unfortunately, the Pennsylvanian model had to compete with the growing monopoly of the Bank of England and the private banking model. In 1764, decisions made in London dealt a final blow to the Pennsylvanian experiment with paper money and public banking.

The tradition of public banking, nevertheless, continued, and at present about 40 percent of world banks are publicly owned.[44] Over the past several decades, public banks have become particularly strong in the so-called BRIC countries (Brazil, Russia, India, and China). They now "compose about 60 percent of the banks in Russia, 75 percent in India, 69 percent or more in China, and

45 percent in Brazil."[45] Even the *Economist* has acknowledged that with the growth in size, confidence and competence of the BRICs public banks, it will become increasingly difficult for Western banks to expand their business in these emerging markets.[46] Moreover, publicly owned banks are thought to have played an important stabilizing role allowing the BRIC economies to be only mildly affected by the 2007–2009 financial crisis.[47] An increasingly growing body of research also points to the impact of public banks on the phenomenal economic growth of the BRICs. According to one study, in the first decade of this century, the GDP of the BRICs economies grew by 92.7 percent, while the economies of industrialized countries grew only by 15.5 percent.[48] Among the reasons for such incredible growth was that, in contrast to private banks' speculative investments for quick enrichment of owners and managers, public banks tend to foster growth and expand social services. This has been particularly true of the major public banks in Brazil.[49] The 2007–2009 financial crisis has apparently shifted pendulum toward public banking. Worldwide, publicly owned banks are regaining their popularity. They are now not only among the largest banks, but also among the safest.[50]

However, it is important not to forget that public banks in principle operate on the same basis as private banks. This means they are part of the fractional reserve banking system, and also create money through the issuance of debt. Of course, there are also major differences. First, earnings of public banks belong to the public, and this is also the reason why the profit motive, and by extension the level of risk, is not as high as in the case of private banks. Second, the gambling scope of public banks, particularly the trading of so-called financial products, is often far more limited, making them safer relative to private banks. Undoubtedly, after the 2007–2009 financial mess in private banking, these differences have strengthened confidence in public banking. The danger, nevertheless, is that the blinding effect of the urge for more money can kick in at any time and change again the present dynamics. Financial history is sufficiently clear in suggesting our economic memory tends to be short.

To sum up, among the greatest successes of the increasingly international banking fraternity is the creation and promotion of the image of public ownership, transparency, and overall democratic governance of central banks. There is no direct profiteering involved. The main mechanism is to make government borrow almost without limits and feel that it is in charge. The outcome of this arrangement is that the treasury gets paid by the central bank, but paid for the use of the credit that government "sells" to the central bank. For the banking lobby, however, far more important is what happens afterwards: free and privately controlled money creation. As a result, the treasury can be considered as the originator of base money, but is not in actual control of how much base money is issued to the economy. The central bank, on the other hand, controls how much base money is issued to the economy, but has limited control over how much total "money" is issued into the economy through debt by commercial banks. The workings of the present banking system, then, not only equip commercial banks with enormous power, but also add to the instability of entire economies. As such, this system is in need of renewed moral scrutiny.

Notes

1 W. Hummel, 'Government Finance: Seigniorage', in *Money: What It Is, How It Works*, 2010. Available at: http://www.wfhummel.net (accessed 22 March 2012).
2 Ibid.
3 In E.H. Brown, *The Web of Debt: The Shocking Truth about Our Money System and How We Can Break Free*, 3rd ed., Baton Rouge, LA: Third Millennium Press, 2008, p. 87.
4 M. Rowbotham, *The Grip of Death: A Study of Modern Money, Debt Slavery and Destructive Economics*, 4th ed., Charlbury, UK: Jon Carpenter, 2009.
5 E.g., Brown, *The Web of Debt*.
6 T.H. Greco, *The End of Money and the Future of Civilization*, White River Junction, VT: Chelsea Green, 2009.
7 Brown, *The Web of Debt*, p. 160.
8 Hummel, 'Government Finance'.
9 B. Eichengreen, *Exorbitant Privilege: The Rise and Fall of the Dollar and the Future of the International Monetary System*, New York: Oxford University Press, 2011, p. 4.
10 Hummel, 'Government Finance'.
11 Ibid.
12 W. Hummel, 'Understanding Money: Money Basics', in *Money: What It Is, How It Works*, 2008; W. Hummel, 'Understanding Money: The Monetary Base', in *Money: What It Is, How It Works*, 2005.
13 S. Johnson, 'Rise of the Financial Leviathan – Megabanks Fight Off Reform', *Taipei Times*, 23 July 2012, p. 9.
14 Hummel, 'Understanding Money: Money Basics'.
15 Note that checks in reality are not money but simply orders to pay money to the account of the check recipient; centralized clearing houses, sometimes the central bank itself, help banks (for a fee) to deal with huge volume of checks by determining which banks should be debited and which credited, and the settlement takes the form of transfer in reserves across accounts that banks hold at the central bank.
16 Brown, *The Web of Debt*, p. 70.
17 Brown, *The Web of Debt*, p. 167; W. Hummel, 'The Banking System: The Federal Reserve System', in *Money: What It Is, How It Works*, 2006.
18 Brown, *The Web of Debt*, p. 24.
19 'Federal Reserve Pays $77 Billion to Treasury'. Available at: http://money.cnn.com/2012/01/10/news/economy/federal_reserve_pays_treasury/index.htm (accessed 2 April 2012).
20 Brown, *The Web of Debt*, p. 167; italics hers.
21 Ibid.
22 S. Zarlenga, *The Lost Science of Money: The Mythology of Money – the Story of Power*, Valatie, NY: American Monetary Institute, 2002, p. 571.
23 R. Owen, 'Bank of England Nominees', 2000. Available at: http://forumnews.wordpress.com/about/bank-of-england-nominees (accessed 2 April 2012).
24 'Companies Act 2006'. Available at: http://www.legislation.gov.uk/ukpga/2006/46/section/796 (accessed 2 April 2012).
25 Owen, 'Bank of England Nominees'.
26 According to Sinn, the European Investment Bank in Luxembourg could issue eurobonds "in order to be able to extend credit to individual euro countries."

(H.W. Sinn, *Casino Capitalism: How the Financial Crisis Came about and What Needs to Be Done Now*, Oxford: Oxford University Press, 2010, pp. 247–250).

27 H.K. Scheller, *The European Central Bank: History, Role and Functions*, Frankfurt am Main, Germany: European Central Bank, 2004, p. 49.

28 M. Lynn, *Bust: Greece, the Euro, and the Sovereign Debt Crisis*, Hoboken, NJ: Bloomberg Press, 2011, pp. 33–55.

29 'European Union: Consolidated Versions of the Treaty on European Union and the Treaty Establishing the European Community', *Official Journal of the European Union*, 29 December 2006. Available at: http://eur-lex.europa.eu/LexUriServ/site/en/oj/2006/ce321/ce32120061229en00010331.pdf (accessed 2 April 2012).

30 E.H. Brown, *The Public Bank Solution: From Austerity to Prosperity*, Baton Rouge, LA: Third Millennium Press, 2013, p. 278.

31 In Brown, *The Web of Debt*, p. 255.

32 Scheller, *The European Central Bank*, p. 12.

33 In Brown, *The Web of Debt*, p. 255.

34 Ibid., pp. 255–256.

35 G.G. Chang, *The Coming Collapse of China*, London: Arrow, 2002, p. 122.

36 Brown, *The Web of Debt*, p. 256.

37 Greco, *The End of Money*, p. 100.

38 Brown, *The Public Bank Solution*, p. 16.

39 Ibid., pp. 81–92.

40 Ibid., pp. 98–103.

41 Ibid., p. 124.

42 In Zarlenga, *The Lost Science of Money*, p. 372.

43 A. Smith, 'An Inquiry into the Nature and Causes of the Wealth of Nations', in R.M. Hutchins (ed.), *Great Books of the Western World*, vol. 39, Chicago: Encyclopedia Britannica, 1952, pp. 359 and 141 respectively.

44 Brown, *The Public Bank Solution*, p. 17.

45 Ibid., p. 34.

46 'Mutually Assured Existence: Public and Private Banks Have Reached a Modus Vivendi', *Economist*, 13 May 2010.

47 Ibid.

48 In Brown, *The Public Bank Solution*, p. 34.

49 Ibid., pp. 40–42 and 46–51 respectively.

50 Ibid., pp. 34–35.

8 Moral confusion over debt

"If one looks at the history of debt, . . . what one discovers first of all is profound moral confusion."[1] This view of Graeber evidently suggests the need for moral evaluation of the whole notion of debt. What this study has demonstrated to this point is that through gradual historical shifts, the functioning of modern economy has become largely dependent on money created as debt. The innovations in monetary and financial systems combined with technological advancements have not only made money operations more complex, but also caused debt burdens to be ever more placed on the individual consumer and the public at large. At the same time, debts have become increasingly impersonal and thus much more easily transferrable.[2] Yet the fact that lending/borrowing relationships have gradually taken on cold, impersonal institutional form and that the burdens of debts can be more easily spread throughout the financial system does not make them morally less relevant. Our depersonalized, technocratic system of debt money calls for a renewed moral scrutiny. An evaluation of the debt money system from the perspective of justice will be taken up in the next chapter. First, however, we shall look at some moral questions implicated in a broader category of indebtedness. This chapter in particular addresses the issues of indebtedness as found in two distinct categories of "gift economy" and "commercial economy," the question of moral and legal debts, and how these affect human relationships as well as the obligation to pay one's debts.

Indebtedness and "gift economy"

In the theory of gift there exists a seemingly widespread perception that the good received creates in the recipient a sense of being indebted, which can be obliterated by an act aimed at reciprocation for what one has received. Receiving, then, can be burdensome, as it also entails the pressure to reciprocate. Thus it becomes a moral duty to receive the gift offered and to allow a certain indebtedness to take place, because it is the very act of receiving that creates the possibility of establishing or strengthening a relationship. As such, indebtedness is an important factor that sets or keeps the relationship in motion, and acceptance of gifts is a sign of openness to make relationships possible. On the other hand, indebtedness can also become a tool of control.

Relational function of gift and indebtedness

Throughout human history, gifts have had viable religious functions (e.g., offerings, sacrifices, oblations), and yet have also played an important role in human interactions, such as establishing and maintaining relationships, recognizing one's status, appeasing enemies, restoring bonds that have been broken, expressing support or love, and so forth. Although the modern theory of gift has taken many diverse approaches to better place the role of gifts in the lives of individuals and entire societies,[3] the discipline has been dominated by anthropological, sociological, and moral perspectives. Economic aspects of the lives of communities have often been considered as interwoven with the social function of gifts.[4] This is why in anthropological-sociological literature the economic impact of the gift is at times referred to as "gift economy."

It has been widely recognized that the prime contributor to the notion of gift economy was Marcel Mauss (1872–1950). In *The Gift* (1925), his work on gift exchange in archaic societies, Mauss argues that across diverse cultures there can be found a moral rule that drives gift dynamics, namely that gifts are obligatory. His work led him to the conclusion that the gift is one of the most basic factors in human interactions and social systems as it draws members of a given society, and even entire societies, into three interlocking obligations: to give, to receive, and to reciprocate. A constant and widespread appearance of such reciprocal obligations prompted Mauss to call them "*total* social facts," as they were "at the same time juridical, economic, religious, and even aesthetic and morphological, etc."[5] In other words, the moral obligations induced by circulation of gifts engage not only individuals but entire societies together with their various institutions.

It was the conviction of Mauss that in every economic exchange, in addition to the value of what is being exchanged, something more is created, something that goes beyond individual interactions – a kind of "social glue," which no society could deem unimportant.[6] This is also why, for him, the separation of the social functions of exchanges into economic and noneconomic (religious, moral, aesthetic, etc.) ultimately becomes trivial because in reality they are intrinsically interconnected, forming a complex yet unified social fabric. According to Mauss, in such a cultural context persons and things intermingle, and "souls are mixed with things; things with souls." At the same time, those participating in exchanges, are primarily moral persons, who are role oriented and status bound, and not isolated individuals as seen in some modern contexts where "a cold, calculating mentality" prevails.[7]

Mauss tends to put equal weight on each of the phases in the tripartite obligation system.[8] Thus the obligation to give means that gifts are at the heart of encounters between individuals to initiate a totally new relationship or to continue the gift cycle in the existing relationships. The obligation to accept a gift, on the other hand, has an important linking function. As Mauss points out, "one has no right to refuse a gift" because "to act in this way is to show that one is afraid of having to reciprocate." Moreover, Mauss also demonstrates that across various cultures, the receiving side is considered inferior.[9] In other words, it becomes a moral duty to allow a certain indebtedness to take place, as this creates the possibility of establishing or strengthening relationship. This is why the obligation to receive a gift expresses one's willingness to be indebted in order to keep the gift dynamic in motion. Finally, the obligation to reciprocate the gift received basically means responding with a gift of at least equal value.

Over the decades following the work of Mauss, it was the principle of reciprocity that stood out in anthropological-sociological literature. Bronislaw Malinowski (1884–1942) was among the first to point out that reciprocity played the key role in the gift phenomenon. Among important tasks undertaken by him was to classify various gift phenomena during his field trips. To achieve this, Malinowski decided to place gifts on the scale from pure gift (disinterested) to pure barter (self-interested). What quite surprised him was the fact that he did not find cases of pure gift, which led him to the conclusion that reciprocity, in diverse forms and degrees, was omnipresent. But there was something equally important that Malinowski discovered with regard to the meaning of reciprocity. He noticed that reciprocity could be "associated with definite social ties or coupled mutuality in non-economic matters." Yet he also acknowledged that at times reciprocity could take on the meaning of equivalence, or, put simply, of material exchange. As a result, he took the stance that "most if not all economic acts are found to belong to some chain of reciprocal gifts and counter-gifts, which in the long run balance, benefiting both sides equally."[10]

Alvin Gouldner takes this balancing aspect of reciprocity proposed by Malinowski a step further. According to him, the norm of reciprocity primarily serves "a group *stabilizing* function."[11] What immensely contributes to the stability of social systems, argues Gouldner, is the fact of indebtedness inherent in the principle of reciprocity. The mechanism of indebtedness, however, is driven not only by the benefit received but also by the time lag over which one remains in the state of obligation to reciprocate for what one has received.[12] Although, in the view of Gouldner, status duties, which affect behavior because they are considered as inherently binding, already possess a social stabilizing function, the principle of reciprocity "provides a second-order of the stability of social systems" because of its potential to overcome emerging aberrations and to arouse additional stimuli for "conformity with existent status demands."[13]

In addition to the social stabilizing function, the norm of reciprocity engenders also what Gouldner calls a "starting mechanism." This is so because while the obligation to reciprocate solidifies existing relationships, by driving the exchange to a relative equivalence, it also "helps to initiate social interaction," mainly by "preventing" the parties from viewing each other with suspicion, or by "enabling" the parties to break out of the suspicion impasse. As a result, the "starting" function of the norm of reciprocity becomes particularly important in the nascent development phases of certain groups before they have established "a differentiated and customary set of status duties."[14]

Also for Marshall Sahlins, reciprocity forms the bedrock of exchange, economy, and indeed society. For him, what is peculiar about reciprocity in exchange relationships is that the spirit accompanying exchanges sways from disinterestedness through mutual interests to self-interest.[15] On the basis of these modes, which he ultimately considers as comprising a continuum of reciprocities, he distinguishes three types of reciprocity. At one end, Sahlins places "generalized reciprocity" (also called by him "the solidarity extreme"), which is prevalent in family relationships, and in which the obligation to "repay" the good received may be postponed for some time or even indefinitely. The other end of the continuum he calls "negative reciprocity" (or also "the unsociable extreme"), which is common in interactions among strangers as it is characterized by mutual suspicion, maximization of personal interests, and even exploitation. At the midpoint, according to Sahlins, is "balanced reciprocity," which is a dominant form in exchange phenomena, and which tends toward equivalence.[16]

"Free gift" versus corrupting potential of reciprocal obligations

The sense of indebtedness interwoven into the social function of gifts found across diverse cultures has encountered its great challenge in the notion of "free gift." As a matter of fact, the idea of gift as something that is given without any expectation of reciprocation has time and again appeared in various literary works throughout history.

One of the earlier definitions of "gift" can be found in the works of Aristotle. In his *Topics*, Aristotle states that "*dorea dosis estin anapodotos*," or that gift is "a grant given without recompense."[17] Although this definition has been repeatedly used in one form or another, including in the *Summa Theologiae* of Thomas Aquinas,[18] it must be put into a proper context. First of all, Aristotle uses this definition in a very specific context while discussing in general how things relate to one another. One of the questions that he attempts to answer touches the relation between a conceptual "genus" and its "species." He is particularly interested whether the species and the genus are used alike, and whether they occur in equal number. Aristotle claims that a general perception is that this indeed is the case and, in order to prove it, he uses the example of two Greek terms "gift" (*dorea*) and "grant" (*dosis*), where grant is the genus and gift is one of its species. And because both gift and grant represent "of something and to someone," therefore grant (the genus) and gift (the species) bear a like relation and are used in equal number. It is in the context of such argument that Aristotle concludes that a gift is "a grant given without recompense."

Second, in Greek, in addition to the term *dorea*, there is another term carrying the meaning of gift, and which has a much wider use, namely *doron*. As a matter of fact, these two terms denote different categories of gifts. *Dorea* normally is used in the context of top-down giving, where a "gift" means an act of benevolence on the part of the one superior in the giving–receiving relationship, and to which no obligation to reciprocate is attached. *Doron*, on the other hand, carries the meaning of a gift in bottom-up or horizontal types of giving–receiving situations. This distinction can already be found in Philostratus (c. 172–250), who points out that *dorea* means freely given grants by the one who is in a position of authority to provide them, and *doron* is an expression of one's wealth.[19] The biblical tradition also confirms the understanding of *dorea* as the only type of gift that can be considered as a truly free gift. According to Kittel, in the New Testament, *dorea* always indicates the grace of God,[20] or a top-down freely given gift.

As mentioned above, the definition of gift found in Aristotle was later repeated by Thomas Aquinas in *Summa Theologiae*. There Aquinas states that gift "is literally a giving that can have no return" (*donum proprie est datio irreddibilis*). For him the gift "is not given with repayment in mind" but "denotes a giving out of good will."[21] The difficulty with the argument of Aquinas is that in Latin the term *donum* covers a very broad spectrum of gifts – free grants (top-down relationships), what a person can offer to God (bottom-up relationships)[22] and acts of benevolence in human interactions (horizontal relationships).[23] As a result, by equating the Greek *dorea* with the Latin *donum*, Aquinas broadens enormously the scope of what is supposed to be freely given, and the *dorea* type of gift was, at least theoretically, imposed on other forms of giving.

Apparently, what influenced Aquinas's definition of gift as something freely given is the biblical treatment of gift. However, it should be immediately stated that such influence cannot be reduced to certain biblical quotations, such as "You received without payment; give without payment."[24] Otherwise, in the teachings of Jesus one can equally find a counterargument that Jesus also stressed the importance of reciprocity, for example, "give, and it will be given to you."[25] Instead, the understanding of gift as something freely given appears to be anchored in the model of God as "the ultimate Giver," as found in the entire biblical tradition, and particularly in the New Testament. The biblical message stresses that it is the irrevocable self-giving on the part of God in Christ that makes God's gift free and perfect. This is what makes the gift of God unique and beyond any reciprocal cycle.

It was this ideal of free gift promoted by the church that fell on the fertile soil of the developments that took place from the sixteenth century onward. First, it matched the core doctrine of the Protestant movement claiming that a person can be saved only by the grace of God (*sola gratia*), or, in other words, by God's gift, which no one in any way can reciprocate. Second, the ideal of free gift also resonated well with liberalism in the sense that its program of liberating individuals from all kinds of constraints, including social constraints, could easily embrace the notion of gift that does not have to be reciprocated, or, in other words, the concept of gift that helped individuals to be free from entanglements of obligations (indebtedness) obviously present in the gift function in traditional societies. For very different reasons, then, the ideal of free gift suited both Protestantism and liberalism, which gradually enhanced and continued to promote it.

Examples of how the ideal of free gift began to infiltrate Western societies can be found in various literary as well as anthropological and sociological works. For instance, Derrida contends that reciprocity has no place in the gift event. What is however quite unique about his argument is that he pushes the idea of free gift much further by insisting that "*the gift as gift* ought *not to appear as gift: either to the donee or to the donor.*" According to Derrida, gift should be placed outside of any form of obligation on the part of any participant in the gift event, because once the gift turns into duty or expectation of reciprocation, it loses its meaning of gift.[26] Based on this, he concludes that the gift in reality becomes the impossible. Yet it is likely that the view of Noonan represents best the understanding of the gift prevailing among Westerners. For him, a gift "is meant as an expression of personal affection, of some degree of love . . . *Freely given, the gift leaves the donee free.*"[27]

What is noteworthy here, however, is that the concept of "free gift" spread roots in individualistically oriented Western societies. According to Belk, it is Westerners who tend to hold the view of gift as something that is voluntarily given without expectation of return or compensation.[28] Similarly, David Cheal contends that the understanding that gifts have to be spontaneous and disinterested is very much part of Western societies' culture of love.[29] Yan goes even as far as stating that the notion of gift as "a pure, disinterested, unconstrained 'present', which is nothing more than a voluntary, spontaneous expression of the real inner self and inner feeling" is simply part of "contemporary Euro-American ideology."[30]

Interestingly, it was already Mauss in his work undertaken together with Hubert who claimed that, while normally in the gift phenomenon, even in sacrifices offered to deities, disinterestedness and self-interest intermingle, there is one exception to this widespread norm, namely the sacrifice in which a god is sacrificed. In such a sacrifice "all selfish calculation is absent" because "the god who sacrifices himself gives himself irrevocably."[31] However, despite the fact that some societies might have had a notion of gifts freely given, or gifts of irrevocable self-giving, it was only in the Christian context that such a form of giving has become a dominant paradigm.[32]

The realization that the gift phenomenon can enhance such diverse notions as freedom and obligation led Godbout to venture a theoretical framework for what he calls a modern gift. For him, what is quintessentially distinct about the modern gift is that it is not limited to one's family, friends, relatives, and so forth, but is inclusive in terms of strangers and enables one to reach out across cultures.[33] As such, a gift is possible only on a voluntary basis, or, in other words, a gift is something freely given.[34] On the other hand, he recognizes that "freedom thrives on social bonds"[35] and social bonding is sustained in a state of indebtedness. In order to clarify this, Godbout points out that "a successful family relationship is one where everyone thinks they receive more than they give, where everyone considers themselves indebted vis-à-vis the other, rather than feeling that the other is indebted to them." Based on this he further argues that in such a state of indebtedness, "to put off the debt is to put an end to the relationship."[36] This is why if both individual freedom and human interconnectedness are to be preserved, indebtedness has to primarily take the form of one's free commitment to be in relationship.[37] As a result, voluntary indebtedness is the prime ingredient of Godbout's model of modern social bonding.

In the context where social bonding thrives on indebtedness inherent in cycles of reciprocities, there exists however a possibility that the exploitative potential of reciprocal obligations can feed corruption. Noonan in his work *Bribes* (1984), which covers the issue of bribery in human society over millennia, comes to the conclusion that "bribes are a species of reciprocity."[38] His broad study of the problem clearly demonstrates that bribes exploit obligations embedded in human reciprocal behavior. Perhaps this is also why in some cultural contexts even the terminology has been blurred, and as a result, one of the meanings sometimes ascribed to "gift" is "something given to corrupt," or simply "a bribe."³⁹

Although corruption has been universally condemned on social, moral, or legal grounds, nevertheless corruption has never really been disavowed. The main reason appears to be that, in addition to serving one's own interests, corruption tends to exploit obligations embedded in the reciprocities of the gift, and thus breeds on indebtedness embedded in the social function of the gift. Undoubtedly, self-interest, as often expressed in anthropological-sociological literature, is also inherent in the gift phenomenon.⁴⁰ Where the gift, however, fundamentally differs from corruption is that the gift thrives on the paradox of an intermingling self-interest with disinterestedness, while corruption exploits the force of indebtedness only for self-interested ends. This is why gift giving that aims at the mere showing off of the giver's status – described by Schwartz in terms of "gift giving as an unfriendly act"⁴¹ – also represents a form of corruption of the gift dynamics. An extreme example of hostility in the gift phenomenon is the potlatch found among the Kwakiutl, where the aim of giving was to shame the receiver by offering (or destroying) so much of one's own property that the opponent could not reciprocate, or match the amount destroyed.

All in all, while the function of indebtedness in the "gift economy" turned out to be quite complex, having both positive social contributions and potential negative implications, it became even more complicated when mingled with debts in the "commercial economy."

Debt and "commercial economy"

The work of Mauss epitomized the drive toward the reciprocal view of the gift function as a reaction to the perception of many authors in Western societies, such as Machiavelli, Hobbes, Mill, or Bentham, that human beings were "inherently self-interested, rational maximizers of economic or personal utility."⁴² Such an atomistic concept of person and the exaltation of individual freedom gradually taking root in Western societies caused in some circles nostalgia for deeper human relationality and social cohesion. Nevertheless, as the impact of capitalism on Western societies intensified, the categories formed in a commercial economy over hundreds of years also grew stronger.

Commercial debts and early property rights

Already two millennia (or more) before the Enlightenment, when money had been introduced in some societies and commercial markets were gradually established, the problem of debts accompanying those developments also emerged. At an early stage of commercial economy diverse societies began to experience debt crises.⁴³ Apparently, the advent of money and commercial economy brought into play new forces. One of them was what Graeber calls "a democratization of desire," as everyone began to desire money and, ultimately, "everyone, high and low, was pursuing the same promiscuous substance." But then, as Graeber observes, "increasingly they did not just want money. They needed it."[44]

Perhaps even more importantly, debts from commercial economy intermingled with indebtedness driving the cycles of reciprocities, and ultimately with moral categories such as honor and justice (for example, in Plato's *Republic*, justice basically consists of two things: speaking the truth and settling one's debts).[45] As a result, debt became a powerful moral force, allowing some to take control over others, including their very freedom. Greek philosophers were quick to notice such a destructive potential of exacerbating debts. At the heart of the problem they identified the charging of interest on lending, or usury. This is why they became so critical of it. However, the traditional way in the gift phenomenon had always been that one should return a slightly more valuable gift than the one received. Why could not a similar dynamics be applied to a loan? But then another parallel conviction was that "friends do not charge one another interest, and any suggestion that they might was sure to rankle."[46] (As presented in this study, only much later did the medieval scholastics begin to address these tensions.)

Roman law further strengthened the power of debt. At the heart of that development was the concept of private property, which equipped owners with absolute power over their possessions. Apparently the idea of private property, in the sense of an arrangement in which the owner can exercise his absolute power over whatever is regarded as belonging to him, was taking shape in the context of the victories of the Roman army and a huge influx of slaves. Soon, owning slaves became a common practice in Roman society, and in turn, changes in Roman law also followed. The term used to express such absolute power over one's private possessions was "*dominium*," a word derived from "*dominus*," meaning "master" or "slave-owner." At the same time, slaves began to be defined as "people who were also a *res*, thing."[47]

An important aspect of the developments that took place in the legal systems was the possibility of enslavement for debts. The power to enslave somebody due to incurred debts had been a widespread phenomenon in many ancient societies, from Melanesia to Mesopotamia to Africa. According to Graeber, in those societies "husbands were not able to sell their wives to some third party." What they were allowed at most was to "send them home and demand back their bridewealth." But, as Graeber adds,

> everything changed the moment he took out a loan. Since if he did, it was perfectly legal . . . to use his wife and children as surety, and if he was unable to pay, they could then be taken as debt pawns in exactly the same way that he could lose his slaves, sheep, and goats.[48]

Debts appear to have changed even the most basic assumptions concerning human beings, including their close relationships.

In Rome, already in the middle of the fifth century BC, the Law of the Twelve Tables (451–450 BC) embraced the practice of slavery, which gradually sank deep into social consciousness. Rome became "not simply a slaveholding but a slave society." There, the treatment of debtors was particularly harsh. Once somebody defaulted on debts, he could easily be turned into a slave.[49] Perhaps the most obvious expression of the connection between debts and slavery is in Table III.1, which at the beginning states that "one who has confessed a debt, or against whom judgment has been pronounced, shall have thirty days to pay it in," after which "forcible seizure of his person is allowed." As a result, the Law of the Twelve Tables equipped some people with a formidable power over other human beings. Although the institution of slavery had existed in many parts of the ancient world, it was in Rome that to be "free" began to primarily mean not to be a slave. No wonder that in such a context, as Patterson points out, "the mass of lower-class plebs would have developed a strong feeling for, and commitment to, the value of personal freedom out of their anxiety about the very real risk of its loss."[50] In 326 BC, *Lex Poetelia Papiria* did what Solon in 594 BC had done in Athens, namely forbade enslavement for debt. Nevertheless, the value of personal freedom (*libertas*) was by then strongly perceived as meaning something opposite to slavery. With the Roman conquests, this notion of liberty spread throughout the empire and later throughout the Western world.

Utilization of the private property rights by banks

The libertarian tradition already in the thought of John Locke placed the right to own property among the basic natural rights, on par with the right to preserve and defend one's own life and the right to personal freedom. Since then these so-called natural rights have been taken for granted. Yet the moment one looks at the work of Locke, one quickly realizes that while he does not seem to put much effort in defending the rights to life and personal freedom, he deals extensively with the right to property to show that it is indeed a natural right. Some contend that by putting a strong emphasis on the right to private property, "Locke was expressing the mentality of the Whig landowners who were his patrons."[51] Regardless of what prompted Locke to put so much emphasis on the right to own property, in practical terms the result was that, as with the right to life and the right to personal freedom, the right to property had an absolute value inherent in it. How did Locke reach this conclusion?

Similarly to Hobbes (1588–1679), Locke departs from the idea of the state of nature. But he diametrically differs from Hobbes in understanding it. For Hobbes, the state of nature was principally about a war of all against all, where only the absolute power of the sovereign could provide some stability. To Locke, on the other hand, the state of nature is "a state of perfect freedom" to order actions of individuals, and "dispose of their possessions and persons as they think fit, within the bounds of the law of Nature, without asking leave or depending upon the will of any other man."[52] What governs Locke's state of nature, then, is a universally obligatory moral law established by God and discovered by human reason, which also sets limits on human liberty. This is why Locke argues that to preserve such a law, "all men may be restrained from invading others' rights, and from doing hurt to one another."[53]

Yet if Locke wanted to anchor the right to private property in such a sense of natural law, he had to show what entitled human beings to such a right. The answer Locke found in human labor. According to him, in the state of nature, the most basic "property" (in the words of Locke, "the unquestionable property") that one can claim his own is labor, and by mixing one's labor with conditions existing in the surroundings, whatever one gains becomes his own.[54] The limit to what one could claim as his property was rooted in the original condition of how much land one could till. Thus whatever one could remove from common property through labor could become private property. Moreover, because for Locke the family is also a natural society, an individual has a natural right to inherit property.

Locke's argument about the natural right to private property in a way continued what Roman law had already established. Yet while in Roman law the treatment of private property had in its shadow the system of slavery, Locke's right to property builds on the notion of perfect freedom claimed as the original condition of human beings in the state of nature. In other words, Locke tried to demonstrate that private property is one of the most basic natural rights of each human being. As such, the theory of a natural right to own property that Locke had helped to shape profoundly influenced later social, economic, and political developments. Among those who drew from this tradition was Adam Smith. One of his legacies was applying Locke's right of property to commercial economy. According to Graeber, it is this tradition that "assumes that liberty is essentially the right to do what one likes with one's own property." Moreover, he contends that this tradition not only makes owning property a right, but "treats rights themselves as a form of property."[55]

In the Western world, it was around the time Locke's ideas started to spread that the foundations of the modern banking system were also laid down and private interests began to take control over monetary systems. As one can imagine, these developments had a huge merging potential, and merge they eventually did. What helped that merger was Locke's insistence on the need of written law to protect private interests in the real world. According to him, "though the law of Nature be plain and intelligible to all rational creatures, yet men, being biased by their interest, as well as ignorant for want of study of it, are not apt to allow of it as a law binding to them in the application of it to their particular cases."[56] This is why he argued for an established and commonly accepted judicial system equipped with a written law to set the standard of right and wrong and to settle controversies. Locke considered an establishment of such a legal system as a prerequisite of society. Interestingly, an important function of the society he envisioned was to protect private property. In his view, "the great and chief end . . . of men uniting into commonwealths, and putting themselves under government, is the preservation of their property." Among the main obligations of government, then, was "to secure every one's property."[57]

With the spread of the absolutist idea of the right of property and the obligation of society and its legislative powers to safeguard every one's property, bankers needed only to gain legally protected control over the process of money creation through debt, which they had already exercised in secret. The establishment of the Bank of England in 1694, often hailed as a leap forward in the development of the modern banking system, was nothing more than an attempt to legalize the privately controlled creation of money. According to Zarlenga, "in a manner that would later set the pattern for the enactment of monetary laws in the English speaking world, the Bank of England's authorizing legislation was quietly passed, as a rider to a tax bill on shipping tonnage!"[58] It was a turning point, however, not in the sense often presented in economic literature, but in the sense that the secretive practice of private banks to create money finally became legalized. Private banks gained a legal right to monetize even the debts of the state itself. As one can imagine, in the course of time some people realized the consequences of equipping private banks with such powers. Yet their legislative challenges often turned out to be but weak attempts to regain state control over money.

Throughout the nineteenth and the beginning of the twentieth centuries, the struggle over the control of money was particularly vivid in the case of the United States. By then the bankers there were well aware of the huge potential benefits from having the power to create money, and they were very keen to gain legislative approval to keep this power in their hands. Of course, some strongly opposed giving such a formidable power to private bankers. In 1833, William Gouge, himself editor and publisher of the *Journal of Banking*, published *A Short History of Paper Money and Banking*, which was very critical of the developments taking place among American bankers, of how banks got their money, and particularly of their attempt to gain legal control over the privilege of creating money. According to Gouge, "if the superior credit the Banks enjoy, grew out of the natural order of things, it would not be a subject of complaint. But the Banks owe their credit to the charters – to special acts of legislation in their favor, and to their notes being made receivable in payment of dues to Government."[59]

The culmination of the struggle over the control of money in the United States was the establishment of the Federal Reserve System in 1913. Although the Federal Reserve Act passed all the needed legislative stages, to many it became yet another example of machinations on the part of bankers. The bill passed the Senate on December 19, the House on December 22, and was signed into law by President Wilson on December 23 – all only days before Christmas, "when Congress was preoccupied with departure for holidays."[60] The Federal Reserve System is perhaps the best example of how through legislation, money issued by a private bank became the money of the entire country (and gradually also the dominant money of the entire world). Yet it is even more important to restate that far more money is now legally created by private commercial banks.

The growing popularity of the libertarian view of private property rights, combined with the legal powers banks gained with regard to creating money, had a huge impact on the issue of debt. Because the money created by banks was considered private property, the debtors were legally bound to honor these debts. The outcome of such gradual shifts is that the public inherited the system by which the legally obtained rights of a few to create money through debt resulted in others assuming legal obligations to pay those debts, including the interest on them. Moreover, the right to create money itself became the property of banks. The financial crisis of 2007–2009 was perhaps the most obvious example of the destructive potential of the merger of libertarian ideas of private property rights and expanded legal powers over debt money creation held by banks.

Interestingly, over the past few decades, it was the notion of "free gift" that became one of the tools occasionally used to critique the growing grip of commercial economy over individuals and societies. In the face of accelerating commodification of all possible spheres of human reality and the glorification of individual gain, so characteristic of commercial economy, the concept of free gift was turned into a useful theoretical construct to critique these developments. This has been particularly true about postmodernism, for which free gift has offered "one possible way out" in the face of a widespread sense "that capitalism threatens to seep into every existing pore of the worldwide social skin."[61] Philip Mirowski, for example, notes "the importance of something for nothing" in the world of today. In his view, it is "the possibility of something outside the value sphere, namely, the gift" that helps to initiate a new exchange and uphold the functioning of the system of exchanges.[62]

In the same vein, Stephen Gudeman points out that free gift has been practically excluded from such important spheres as economics and anthropology, expressed in the view that "for economists, there are no free lunches; for anthropologists, there are no free gifts." Based on this, Gudeman contends that "anthropologists are caught in a dialectic with neoclassical economists" because each of these factions views human reality from a specific perspective, one relational, the other atomistic.[63] It is not difficult to notice that in the dialectic pointed out by Gudeman, the relational narrative is built around the principle of reciprocity and moral indebtedness, while at the heart of the atomistic narrative is the private property right, in which debt either does not exist or has an absolute legal obligation attached to it.

In *Debt: The First 5,000 Years*, Graeber apparently uses this tool of free gift, albeit without mentioning it, to demonstrate how the moral category of debt gradually expanded its grip over human interactions as well as over cultural, economic, and sociopolitical developments. His work is an expression of a growing concern over how our perception of the surrounding realities has been overwhelmed by "the logic of the marketplace" and the language of commercial economy, partly due to the fact that modern economics, with its core idea of human beings as calculating self-interested actors, holds an "extraordinary place" in the social sciences. Yet Graeber also takes a critical stance toward the contribution of anthropological-sociological literature dealing with the concept of gift in archaic societies, and claims that it too has been infiltrated by the "the logic of the marketplace." In his words, "almost all this literature concentrates on the exchanges of gifts, assuming that whenever one gives a gift, this act incurs a debt, and the recipient must eventually reciprocate in kind."[64] As a result, Graeber opts for a negative and, apparently, one-sided view of the moral function of indebtedness. He sums it up in the concept of "primordial debts."[65]

Doubtless to say, the concept of free gift in the form used by Mirowski, Gudeman, and the like can serve as a theoretical construct to critique both the atomistic exchangist market metaphor and the relationalist metaphor that has dominated anthropology. However, as pointed out earlier, to establish what is really meant by free gift is itself rather problematic and open to criticism. Of course, this is not to deny that modern societies have been caught in the dialectic of maximizing personal freedom and preserving social ties. According to Godbout, the striving for freedom "exerts a great deal of fascination," but at the same time "we are always trying to implant this marvel within social ties themselves, and to apply it to these ties." For him, freedom itself "thrives on social bonds."[66] Freedom, then, cannot be detached from social ties. Equally, social bonding cannot thrive without human interconnectedness anchored in a voluntary state of indebtedness and one's free commitment to be in relationship.[67] This is why what ultimately matters is how we utilize the concept of debt, and not whether we can eradicate its impact.

Aristotelian tradition on debt

The questions of moral ambiguity of debts and indebtedness have also found their place in the debates of the Aristotelian tradition. As a matter of fact, this tradition made a great deal of effort to balance the value of a free individual with social ties built upon personal virtue and the common good. It was these concerns that helped first Aristotle and then others to distinguish between moral and legal debt. Unfortunately, the developments that took place after the seventeenth century have increasingly shifted the focus solely to legal debt.

Moral debt versus legal debt

While discussing disputes in friendships between equals, Aristotle in *Nicomachean Ethics* states that there are two ways of being just: one unwritten, which carries an obligation in a moral sense, and the other explicit, as expressed in rules of law, when an obligation exists in a legal sense.[68] Thomas Aquinas takes up the issue of legal and moral debt in the context of the relationship of justice to other virtues. For Aquinas, "the essence of justice" is in "fully rendering to another the debt owed him." He then notes that in some relationships, such as with God or one's parents, it is not really possible to fully pay what one owes them. Moreover, even in relationships with others, no one "can adequately reward virtue." Such indebtedness means that justice cannot be fully fulfilled. This impossibility of fully "paying back" the debt one owes to others Aquinas calls a moral debt, because for him "rendering what is morally due" has still a justice aspect attached to it. As such, moral debt is only "annexed to justice." The legal debt, on the other hand, is about what one is "obliged to render because the law demands it." Paying back what is legally due "is the concern of justice as a principal virtue."[69] Aquinas chose the virtue of justice to place at the heart of his understanding of legal debt. In the next chapter, legal debt will be the prime focus of evaluating the demands of justice in the modern banking and monetary systems.

For Aquinas the distinction between legal debt and moral debt becomes crucial to a discussion of virtues connected to justice, grouped around religion (devotion, sacrifices, tithes, etc.), piety, and observance (obedience, gratitude, truthfulness, friendliness, etc.).[70] There, the meaning of legal debt remains constant: it is "a debt determined by positive law or private contract to the acquittal of which the debtor is bound by law."[71] As such, it is enforceable by written law. With regard to moral debt, however, although its meaning tends to vary, Aquinas in principle presents it as being natural, in accordance with rule of reason, and as unwritten but endowed upon human reason.[72] In other words, for Aquinas justice is a form of debt toward the source of good. Yet while legal debt is about rendering to another what originally belonged to that person, and now is due by virtue of having been stolen, or having been received as a loan or deposit, moral debt arises from giving to another what is one's own (as for example in the case of conferring benefits to one's parents without being able to really give back what one received from them). The former obliges the debtor to repay in order to fulfill the legal requirements, while in the latter, repayment is not a matter of justice proper, but rather of human fairness, or a certain fittingness. So the moral debt due does not have the meaning of debt in the strict sense, but in the sense of the demands one is expected to meet in order to live a virtuous life.[73]

Undoubtedly, Aquinas considered moral debt as an important aspect not only for living a virtuous life, but also for driving relationships forward. This is why for him the response from a recipient of good should reflect the giver–receiver relationship.[74] In the case of a legal debt, where the focal link in the relationship is the debt, repayment must take place as soon as possible (or at least in accordance with the contract or agreement). On the other hand, a moral debt should be repaid in the time most adequate to the demands of virtue.[75] Only then can it have a bonding function.

What appears to be rather crucial in moral debt is sentiment. Already Seneca argued that a favor lies not in what is done or given, but in the sentiment of the doer or giver.[76] In a similar vein, Aquinas claims that repayment should consider the sentiment of the giver more than the single question of what that person has given.[77] This is why the timing of reciprocating the favor should primarily weigh this aspect of sentiment. Another important dynamic of sentiment is repaying more than one has received. Giving back less or an equivalent could diminish the sentiment dimension of the favor and shift the focus to the material aspect of what one has received, and thus to the equality of things. So only by giving something more, or "gratis," as Aquinas calls it, can one avoid damaging the sentiment and stress the equality of wills.[78] The notion of this moral obligation to bestow something more in return seems to follow Seneca when he says:

> I ought to be more careful in the choice of my creditor for a benefit than for money; for I have only to pay the latter as much as I received of him,

and when I have paid it, I am free from all obligation; but to the other I must both repay more, and even when I have repaid his kindness we remain connected, for when I have paid my debt I ought again to renew it, while our friendship endures unbroken.[79]

It is such understanding of indebtedness and reciprocal obligations in human relationships as the factors consolidating relationships that has driven the tradition claiming that human beings are naturally relational and interconnected. Moral debt has been at the heart of this tradition. What this tradition has meant by indebtedness, however, is not something that only obliges and causes constraints, but rather a natural condition in which a human being lives. As such, the sense of indebtedness helps to acknowledge that whatever one possesses ultimately comes from God (when one is a believer in God), or at least to recognize the effort and contribution of others, including previous generations. In other words, indebtedness is perceived as a state or condition that permeates one's existence. Awareness of such indebtedness places human beings right at the heart of relationships, and helps individuals to enhance and balance both freedom and interconnectedness in giving-receiving-reciprocating relationships.

This model, despite its focus on human beings as interrelated and interdependent social beings, is not negligent of the value of personal freedom. The concept of freedom it promotes, however, is not "freedom from" (socially alienating) but "freedom within" sociopolitical structures (socially integrating).[80] Freedom within is the type of freedom that is socially unifying. It is about a free dedication to new relationships and a just response to one's "natural state of indebtedness." Such a response, then, contains a personal commitment to diverse relationships, which of course includes acceptance of the obligations that these relationships place upon the individual. And so freedom within is freedom in the sense of providing one with a personal identity and a sense of belonging, but which also requires participation, and which ultimately places some constraints on the agent's exercise of freedom. As such, freedom within actually flourishes in social bonds and, despite its intrinsic constraints, can be personally liberating.

The Aristotelian tradition has had no doubts that moral debt is an important factor not only in cultivating one's sense of virtue, but also in helping individuals to be socially integrated. This tradition gradually reached a clear stance that to fulfill the requirements of justice proper (legal debt), one was, for example, obliged to repair damages caused, to return things borrowed, or to pay back one's debts, including compensation to the lender for direct or indirect costs incurred due to lending (*damnum emergens*), or for the forgone opportunity of gain by the means of money lent (*lucrum cessans*), or, in short, whatever represented loss to the lender. Whatever fell under the category of unjustified gain from a loan, or of taking unfair advantage in money lending, was considered usury. It was such understanding of lending-borrowing relationships that helped the proponents of this tradition to see clearly the enslaving potential of debt. Yet at the same time, it was obvious to them that indebtedness in a moral sense – as an obligation toward the source of good – was also essential to human relationships and to leading a virtuous life.

Challenges of the post-Enlightenment model

The Aristotelian model emphasizing interrelatedness and interdependence of human beings has over time and trial become marginalized, and the liberal-capitalist model of the post-Enlightenment individual has become dominant in the modern world. Undoubtedly, this new model turned out to be capable of providing the conditions in which individuals could utilize their creativity and entrepreneurship and increase their wealth, as well as help the state to maintain basic safety and the protection of civil and legal rights (particularly when dealing with strangers, or in the face of abuse or external aggression), and to work toward a just distribution of goods and burdens within a political community. Yet the model's basic theoretical assumptions give particular importance to the atomistic concept of the person, where individuals are treated as totally independent self-interested beings, and where *homo economicus* plays such a dominant role. Unfortunately, these assumptions put great emphasis on liberating persons from all possible constraints ("freedom from") and, as a result, eventually make people socially alienated. In such a context, moral debt tends to lose its viability, or even be belittled, and legal debt tends to take precedence in human interactions.

The understanding of the human person, then, is what ultimately affects the ways that human relations, exchanges, money, debts, and so forth are treated. The formation of the commercial economy definitely helped individuals to gradually free themselves from various external domination and control by others characteristic of hierarchical feudal societies. Yet while this "liberation" process indeed gave rise to the modern individual, who is now "well provided with rights and goods," this individual is left "without ties."[81] Doubtless to say, a relationally disconnected person becomes much more vulnerable to manipulation. Debt has become one of the formidable tools with which the modern individual can be manipulated or even controlled. At the same time, banks have managed to gain strong legal protection of the mind-boggling system of creating money through debt. So by now all debts owed to banks have legal stamps attached to them, meaning they have to be paid back or debtors unable to pay will face legal consequences.

Of course, in order to make them look more humane, legal debts have been dressed with an image that suggests that, under some circumstances, they can be forgiven. Bankruptcy laws are a clear example. Nevertheless, apparently few can obtain their protection. For example, in the United States after the 2007–2009 crisis, many people were imprisoned because of debts, sometimes very trivial, of a mere several hundred dollars. For Graeber, this represented a move "toward a restoration of something much like debtors' prisons."[82] Historically speaking, bailouts have been a form of debt forgiveness. Yet while in ancient societies the rulers tended to bail out the poor, mostly peasants, now bailouts are given exclusively to the rich, particularly to the corporations that managed to gain the status of the "too-big-to-fail." This became particularly clear in the aftermath of the last crisis, when the big banks were rescued, while many small-scale debtors (including smaller banks) even today struggle with the consequences of the crisis. The way the crisis was handled left no illusion: now only those banks that matter to the functioning of the economic system, meaning big players, can count on being saved.

The past several hundred years saw immense changes in the ways the economic, and in particular monetary and banking systems work. Looking at all those shifts, Greco makes the following conclusion:

> Over time financial dealings have become ever more impersonal, economics has been separated from religion, and ethics has been separated from economics. Moral arguments have failed to hold sway, legal prohibitions have (rightly or wrongly) been totally obliterated, and usurious lending (even in its most oppressive form) has come to be part of the financial landscape. The "train of civilization" needs to be decoupled from the engine of destruction that is our present politicized system of money, banking, and finance. But if that is to be achieved, the problem needs to be framed not only in moral or ethical terms, but especially in practical terms.[83]

Undoubtedly, Greco's remarks, and indeed the arguments made throughout this study, point out that something has been inherently wrong with the present monetary and banking systems for a long period of time, and they are in need of thorough rethinking.

In Chapter 10, some practical solutions will be proposed. Before that, however, a further moral evaluation of the modern monetary and banking systems is needed, because practical solutions will be ineffective without a sound moral grounding. The issue of justice lies at the heart of such evaluation, and is the focus of the next chapter.

Notes

1 D. Graeber, *Debt: The First 5,000 Years*, Brooklyn, NY: Melville House, 2011, p. 8.
2 Ibid., p. 13.
3 E.g., A.E. Komter (ed.), *The Gift: An Interdisciplinary Perspective*, Amsterdam: Amsterdam University Press, 1996; A.D. Schrift (ed.), *The Logic of the Gift: Toward an Ethic of Generosity*, New York: Routledge, 1997; M. Osteen (ed.), *The Question of the Gift: Essays across Disciplines*, London: Routledge, 2002.
4 Komter, *The Gift*, p. 3.
5 M. Mauss (W.D. Halls, trans.), *The Gift: The Form and Reason for Exchange in Archaic Societies*, New York: W.W. Norton, 2000[1925], pp. 78 and 79, respectively; italics his.
6 Ibid., p. 72.
7 Ibid., pp. 20 and 47–48, respectively.
8 Ibid., p. 13.
9 Ibid., pp. 41 and 65, respectively.
10 B. Malinowski, *Crime and Custom in Savage Society*, Paterson, NJ: Littlefield, Adams, 1959, p. 39.

11 A. Gouldner, 'The Norm of Reciprocity: A Preliminary Statement', in Komter, *The Gift*, p. 65; italics his.
12 See also P. Bourdieu, 'Selections from *The Logic of Practice*', in Schrift, *The Logic of the Gift*, pp. 198–199.
13 Gouldner, 'The Norm of Reciprocity', p. 64.
14 Ibid., pp. 65–66.
15 M. Sahlins, *Stone Age Economics*, Chicago: Aldine de Gruyter, 1972, p. 193.
16 Ibid., pp. 193–199.
17 E.S. Forster (trans.), *Aristotle: Posterior Analytics. Topica*, London: William Heinemann, 1960, IV, 4, 125a18.
18 Aquinas, *Summa Theologiae*, 1a. 38, 2 and 1a2ae. 68, 1.
19 W.C. Wright (trans.), *Philostratus and Eunapius: The Lives of the Sophists*, London: Heinemann, 1922; see also H.G. Liddel and R. Scott, *A Greek-English Lexicon*, 9th ed., Oxford: Clarendon Press, 1958, pp. 464–465.
20 G. Kittel (ed.), *Theological Dictionary of the New Testament*, vol. 2, Grand Rapids, MI: Eerdmans, 1964, p. 167.
21 Aquinas, *Summa Theologiae*, 1a. 38, 2.
22 Ibid., 2a2ae. 100, 1.
23 Ibid., 2a2ae. 106, 2 and 2a2ae. 134, 3.
24 Matthew 10:8.
25 Luke 6:38.
26 J. Derrida, *Given Time: I. Counterfeit Money*, Chicago: University of Chicago Press, 1992, p. 130; italics his.
27 J.T. Noonan, *Bribes*, New York: Macmillan, 1984, p. 695; italics added.
28 R. Belk, 'Gift-Giving Behavior', in J.E. Sheth (ed.), *Research in Marketing*, vol. 2, Greenwich, CT: JAI Press, 1979, pp. 95–126.
29 D. Cheal, ' "Showing Them You Love Them": Gift Giving and the Dialectic of Intimacy', *Sociological Review*, 1987, vol. 35, 150–169; D. Cheal, *The Gift Economy*, London: Routledge, 1988.
30 Y.X. Yan, *The Flow of Gifts: Reciprocity and Social Networks in a Chinese Village*, Stanford, CA: Stanford University Press, 1996, p. 220.
31 H. Hubert and M. Mauss (W.D. Halls, trans.), *Sacrifice: Its Nature and Function*, London: Cohen & West, 1964, pp. 100–101.
32 M. Godelier, *The Enigma of the Gift*, Chicago: University of Chicago Press, 1999, p. 145.
33 J.T. Godbout (D. Winkler, trans.), *The World of the Gift*, Montreal: McGill-Queen's University Press, 1998, p. 78.
34 Ibid., pp. 61–78 and 212, respectively; see also pp. 175–186.
35 Ibid., p. 192.
36 Ibid., p. 32.
37 Ibid., pp. 193 and 211.
38 Noonan, *Bribes*, p. xiii.
39 C.T. Onions (ed.), *The Shorter Oxford English Dictionary*, 3rd ed., London: Oxford University Press, 1952; see also the Greek term *doron* (Liddel and Scott, *A Greek-English Lexicon*) and the meaning of "gift" in Germanic languages (Mauss, *The Gift*, p. 63; cf. p. 152 n.122).
40 E.g., M. Douglas, 'Foreword: No Free Gifts', in Mauss, *The Gift*, pp. vii–xviii.
41 B. Schwartz, 'The Social Psychology of the Gift', in Komter, *The Gift*, p. 73.
42 Komter, *The Gift*, p. 3.
43 Graeber, *Debt*, p. 187.
44 Ibid., p. 190.
45 A. Bloom (trans.), *The Republic of Plato*, New York: Basic Books, 1991, I, 331d.
46 Graeber, *Debt*, p. 192.
47 Ibid., p. 200.

48 Ibid., p. 180.
49 O. Patterson, *Freedom: Freedom in the Making of Western Culture*, vol. 1, New York: Basic Books, 1991, p. 208.
50 Ibid.
51 F. Coplestone, *A History of Philosophy, vol. 5: Hobbes to Hume*, Westminster, MD: Newman Press, 1959, p. 130.
52 Hutchins, M. (ed.), *Great Books of the Western World, vol. 35: Locke, Berkeley, Hume*, Chicago: Encyclopedia Britannica, 1952, p. 25.
53 Ibid., p. 26.
54 Ibid., p. 30.
55 Graeber, *Debt*, p. 205.
56 Hutchins, *Locke, Berkeley, Hume*, pp. 53–54.
57 Ibid., pp. 53 and 54, respectively.
58 S. Zarlenga, *The Lost Science of Money: The Mythology of Money – the Story of Power*, Valatie, NY: American Monetary Institute, 2002, p. 281.
59 Ibid., p. 440.
60 E.H. Brown, *The Web of Debt: The Shocking Truth about Our Money System and How We Can Break Free*, 3rd ed., Baton Rouge, LA: Third Millennium Press, 2008, p. 123.
61 S. Cullenberg, J. Amariglio and D.F. Ruccio (eds.), *Postmodernism, Economics and Knowledge*, London: Routledge, 2001, p. 8.
62 P. Mirowski, 'Refusing the Gift', in S. Cullenberg et al. (eds.), *Postmodernism*, pp. 454–455.
63 S. Gudeman, 'Postmodern Gifts', in S. Cullenberg et al. (eds.), *Postmodernism*, p. 460.
64 Graeber, *Debt*, pp. 90–91.
65 Ibid.; see esp. pp. 43–71.
66 Godbout, *The World of the Gift*, pp. 191 and 192, respectively.
67 Ibid., pp. 193 and 211.
68 Aristotle (T. Irwin, trans.), *Nicomachean Ethics*, Indianapolis: Hackett, 1999, VIII, 13, 1162b21.
69 Aquinas, *Summa Theologiae*, 2a2ae, 80, 1.
70 Ibid., 2a2ae, 80–118.
71 T.C. O'Brien, 'Legal Debt, Moral Debt', in T. Aquinas, *Summa Theologiae*, vol. 41, Eyre & Spottiswoode, London, 1971, p. 316.
72 Ibid., p. 317.
73 Aquinas, *Summa Theologiae*, 2a2ae, 31, 3 and 80, 1.
74 Ibid., 2a2ae, 106, 3.
75 Ibid., 2a2ae, 106, 4.
76 L.A. Seneca (A. Stewart, trans.), *On Benefits*, Kessinger, n.d., 1, 6.
77 Aquinas, *Summa Theologiae*, 2a2ae, 106, 5.
78 Ibid., 2a2ae, 106, 6.
79 Seneca, *On Benefits*, 2, 18.
80 A.I. McFadyen, *The Call to Personhood: A Christian Theory of the Individual in Social Relationships*, Cambridge: Cambridge University Press, 1990; see esp. pp. 224–230.
81 Godbout, *The World of the Gift*, p. 191.
82 Graeber, *Debt*, p. 17.
83 T.H. Greco, *The End of Money and the Future of Civilization*, White River Junction, VT: Chelsea Green, 2009, p. 57.

9 Injustice in the debt money system

In his extensive study of debt, Graeber demonstrates how over a long history debts have become a powerful construct affecting not only our basic assumptions regarding individual interactions, but indeed the functioning of economic and sociopolitical systems. It is in this context that he raises a very valid question: "can *all* justice really be reduced to reciprocity?"[1] Although a thorough evaluation of the validity of this question is beyond the scope of this study, a very simple answer to it is that not *all* aspects of justice should be viewed in terms of reciprocity. As a matter of fact, *some* categories of justice have long been expressed in other than reciprocal language. Historically speaking, the biblical notions of the year of jubilee and sabbatical year, stressing return of ancestral property, freeing those enslaved because of debts, and cancellation of debts can serve as examples of efforts not to reduce justice to mere reciprocity. The abolishing of death penalty is a more recent example of the attempts to move beyond the concept of justice in the Hammurabian terms of an eye for an eye and a tooth for a tooth. The ideal of including in our understanding of justice values such as forgiveness of past injuries, and thus its elevation beyond reciprocity, is undoubtedly worth pursuing.

However, it is difficult to deny that the perception of *some* categories of justice in reciprocal terms has an important moral, social, economic, political, and legal function. Much of our notion of justice developed precisely around the concept of reciprocity. As will be demonstrated in this chapter, reciprocal understanding of some aspects of justice can still be helpful in solving our contemporary problems.

Aristotle's distinction of the three types of justice, all anchored in commensurability of values, and the later treatment of them by Thomas Aquinas, has had an immense impact on debates on the issue of justice. The three justice dimensions are legal or contributive justice, distributive justice, and commutative (what Aristotle called "corrective") justice. As such, they also reflect three important relationships: the individual to society as a whole (legal or contributive justice), society or state to the individual person (distributive justice), and between individuals (commutative or corrective justice). It is from the perspective of these three dimensions of justice that we shall now evaluate the modern monetary and banking systems.

Debt money and the issue of legal (contributive) justice

Legal justice is dictated by the common good of society; in its most basic form it requires individuals to follow society's just laws. Yet because in principle legal justice regards what one owes to society, it is sometimes referred to as "contributive justice" to convey one's duty to actively partake in and contribute to the common good of society. This is why legal or contributive justice does not exclusively govern the conduct of individuals in relation to the state. Rather it is about the obligation to contribute a due share to the well-being of *the community* of which one is a member, particularly through sharing responsibilities in building an equitable society. In other words, contributive justice requires participation in the creation of the common good. As such, it binds individuals and groups as well as governments.

One of the basic expressions of contributive justice on the part of individuals and diverse entities is paying taxes. Unfortunately, an increasingly large amount of money from tax receipts goes into payments of *interest rates* on government debts (it is worth stressing that by now nobody seriously thinks that the principal of these debts will be repaid; the system is considered as working fine as long as governments can pay interest rates on their debts). After the 2007–2009 financial crisis, indebtedness of many governments increased substantially, and so did payments of interest rates. At present, at least in the case of some countries, about 20 percent of tax money is spent on interest rate payments. In the not-so-distant future, it might reach the 30 percent threshold considered by many economists as dangerous to the economy.

From the perspective of government, among important aspects contributing to the well-being of the community are its economic and social policies. Most directly related to the main concern of this work are government monetary and fiscal policies due to their impact on money supply and the financial condition of the given economy.

Monetary policies and contributive justice

Banking theories now increasingly recognize that, in principle, banks do not make loans out of preexistent money. At the same time, the banking system is presented as customer-friendly and as a contributor to the economy at large, because by creating and supplying money through loans to customers, banks provide service to the borrowers, and through them to the wider economy, by increasing their economic activity. This is why concepts such as "the multiplier effect" and "fractional-reserve banking" are also seen as tools of improving economic efficiency of both the money deposited by customers and of the base money created by central banks.

One could even make a moral argument that the present banking system is designed against hoarding as very low interest on savings (often below inflation rate) force people to invest. As such, the modern banking system could be considered as engineered to free up sufficient capital to make economy grow and at the same time to be protected by central banks (lenders of last resort) as well as by a set of requirements such as the liquidity ratio and capital adequacy ratio.

One of the basic difficulties with modern theories of banking and the supply of money, however, is that "the real world is completely excluded from the conventional model of money creation."[2] Theoretically, loans and overdrafts indeed lead to the creation of deposits, repayments of which destroy those deposits. Yet what this theoretical model describes does not cover what in reality happens to the money "paid back" to the bank in the process of debt repayment. It is true that the streams of repayments cancel the debt in the overdrawn account, but the money that flows in "is *not* cancelled or destroyed." This means that the money in the form of debt repayment "*is held and accounted an asset of the bank.*" The fact that the money from repayments is normally swiftly re-loaned helps banks to disguise this aspect of modern banking. This is also the reason why lending in modern economies expands so fast, and with it the so-called supply of money. The theory, then, says one thing, but in reality, put simply, "banks create money for themselves."[3] This is what is missing on the radar of monetary policies and theoretical modeling of modern banking.

Arguments defending the present system of money creation give enormous power to larger banks. It is no secret that big banks can now shift far too much "money" to purely speculative activities in the financial markets where returns tend to be much higher than on investments in the real economy. As a result, for the benefit of the few, the stability of the overall economy is gambled, pushing toward an ever-growing financialization of entire economies. Thus while the monetary and banking systems should help create employment, stimulate economies, and reduce existing economic inequalities by providing loans that strengthen the real economy, in reality the so-called developed world experiences less and less growth, achieved with spiraling debts. In effect, the present money creation system through debt badly hurts the economy and imposes disproportionately big burdens upon ordinary consumers and small businesses – the very ones who actually form the backbone of the real economy. From this perspective, the claim that growing debts mean that people live beyond their means sounds like nonsense, as the very supply of money depends on people, businesses, and indeed governments taking on debts.

One of the arguments critical of the modern banking system is that in reality no money is created to cover payment of interest rates. According to this argument, there is never enough money in the system to repay debts and the interest. So debts have to grow, and the requirement of interest payments turns out to be an important factor in pushing the debt machine.

The interest rate on lending is not what it was when Aristotle argued against it, or when later the scholastics tried to work out the conditions under which it would be justified to charge interest. In the present banking system, interest rates can perhaps be best explained as fees for the service of creating the credit/debt pairs and servicing the process of repaying the debts. But then one can immediately ask, "why not put a price on such a service?" The difficulty, of course, is that customers would immediately see whether the price charged for such service is justifiable. So the interest rate actually is a form of disguise by creating the image that the bank lends money it has, thus keeping the uninformed in the dark. Second, the interest payment helps banks to cover costs of risky loans, meaning it is a way of transferring the costs of risky lending onto all borrowers. Unfortunately, monetary policies and banking regulations do not consider these aspects of the modern banking system as important. Indeed, they occasionally do put limits on charging interest rates (usury laws) that are too high. Yet by doing so, they reinforce the image that banks lend money they actually possess.

The criticism that the banking system does not create sufficient money to cover payment of interest rates Hummel terms "the debt virus hypothesis." Hummel argues that this hypothesis is simply false. According to him, those supporting such an hypothesis misunderstand the flow of money between the banking system and the nonbank public. The basis of his argument is that "in reality, money flows in both directions in about equal amounts." The payment of interest that causes loss of deposit somewhere in the system makes the loss in one account reappear as deposit in another account in the system. On this basis, Hummel concedes that interest payments on existing bank loans can actually free up some reserves, and then the bank with excess reserves can "(1) pay for its operating costs, (2) pay dividends, (3) buy securities as investments, (4) buy deposits at other banks, or (5) hold the excess reserves to earn whatever interest the central bank pays on them." Essentially, Hummel's stance is: "banks return nearly all of their earnings to the public one way or another, [and] thus any drain on deposits is small and limited."[4]

In reality, however, the system is not as balanced as Hummel claims, and "money" does not necessarily flow "in both directions in about equal amounts." As argued earlier, banks create money out of thin air while giving a "loan." The money from debt repayments indeed cancels the debt, but the money created in the process of making a loan is not destroyed, and becomes an asset of the bank. For the sake of argument, let us assume that a debt repayment has occurred in the form of bank notes. Of course, an equivalent amount of debt in the borrower's account is canceled. Yet, what does the bank do with these bank notes upon receiving them? Do they not become an asset of the bank? In whatever form a debt is paid, money previously brought into existence through debt is not destroyed. Once created, money belongs to the bank that created it. Perhaps the most obvious proof of this is what happens when one is not capable of paying due debts – often some sort of real property is sought by banks to cover the amount created out of thin air. Unfortunately, the "new" theory of money creation – which admits that banks create money, but says that the money created by banks is gradually extinguished in the process of loan repayment (the numbers in the debt/credit ledgers of a particular customer's account move towards zero by equal numbers) – treats the bank–customer relationship as an isolated accounting case. This isolation hides a more complex reality of how money moves throughout the banking system. Moreover, money deposited in a bank also belongs to the bank, not to the depositor. The latter only has the right to make claims on the deposited money. Additionally, all deposits have restrictions put on them. Some have time restrictions (time deposits), while others are restricted to a certain amount which can be withdrawn each day from his or her account (demand deposits).

From this perspective, payment of interest rates becomes a very secondary issue. In fact, in order to create new money (issue new debt), banks do not need money from the repayment of the previously issued debt. Neither do they need depositors' money. Banks' issuance of debt money is for all practical purposes limited only by their confidence that the borrowers will repay the loan. So Hummel is right in that the flow of money between banks and the public is far more complex than what many would assume it to be. Yet, at the same time, this flow is far from being balanced. In the present system, the creative capacity of banks enables them to make debts expand quickly, and the "flow" of money to the public often takes the form of growing debts. This is also why the rolling of debts becomes so crucial to the stability of the modern economy. Spiraling debts and occasional difficulties to cope with the excess of debts pose a real challenge to Hummel's claim of balanced flow of money in the system.

Modern banks create money in the same way that goldsmiths once did when they issued bank notes to customers needing a loan, instead of giving them gold. Goldsmiths had no doubts that money received in the process of repaying such loans belonged to them. Not much has changed since then. The process of covering up what happens in the process of money creation by banks and repayment by customers has merely become far more complex.

Moreover, interest rates have become a tool through which the banking system can actually manipulate the supply of debt (credit) money. The way to achieve this is "by first making credit abundant, then restricting its supply" through lowering and raising interest rates.[5] So, in reality, the banking system organized around central banks can first persuade people and businesses to borrow and then, by raising interest rates, hit the system with extra costs, causing bankruptcies and foreclosures. To Rowbotham, this "management device to deter other borrowers" is itself "an injustice quite lost in the almost religious conviction" dominating the "ideology" of modern interest rates.[6]

In addition to being the lifeblood of the economy, the right supply and distribution of money is also an indispensable element of a properly functioning society. It is not difficult to imagine the chaos once money suddenly stops flowing in a given society. Of course, in such circumstances people would likely immediately resort to barter and some sort of alternative money (a striking example of such a shift is the "social money" movement in Argentina between the mid-1990s and early 2000s).[7] Nevertheless, at least for a period of time, such a society would be in turmoil. Thus modern societies are very much dependent on an adequate supply of money. Yet at present, "governments rely upon the majority of people going into debt simply to create money to supply the economy."[8] As a result, from the perspective of contributive justice, the entire system of money supply puts a disproportionately heavy burden on ordinary people and small businesses, as they have to become increasingly indebted to the banking system in order to provide sufficient amounts of money that economies require for their functioning.

An interesting insight with regard to monetary policies can be gained from the so-called quantitative easing (QE) programs following the 2007–2009 financial crisis. Quantitative easing is a very recent invention, which allows a central bank to move beyond the standard policy of buying or selling government bonds to change money supply, and to inject more liquidity (money) into the economy without affecting, at least theoretically, the change in interest rates. As such, it is a form of unconventional monetary measure to stimulate the economy when conventional policies simply do not work, mainly due to already very low short-term interest rates (often close to zero). In the aftermath of the last financial crisis, central banks of the United States, the United Kingdom, and the eurozone all resorted to quantitative easing.

From the perspective of this study, the practice of quantitative easing becomes disturbing. The reason is that governments through their central banks have sharpened their appetite for sophistication and complexity to deal with the problem of "toxic assets" that financial institutions accumulate. As such, quantitative easing is about injecting money into massive debt holes that banks were allowed to dig in the financial system. Put simply, quantitative easing programs aim at reducing the debt burdens in the financial system in order to increase lending, and at the same time to encourage consumers and businesses to take on more debt, upon which economic revival is thought to rest. So in effect, the logic of these programs is to increase liquidity of financial institutions and at the same time to further burden consumers and businesses with more debts to increase the flow of "money" (debt) in the economy to boost assumed growth. This logic shows astonishingly clearly where the priorities of monetary policies lie, and how through forced debt creation, financial institutions, intentionally or not, are expanding their control over individuals, institutions, and entire nations.

Unfortunately, the logic of quantitative easing raises another problem. In reality, quantitative easing is nothing other than the cleaning up of banks' balance sheets by swapping some of their securities for cash printed by central banks. This means that liquidity injected into the banking system strengthens the reserve accounts of banks. Banks, in turn, are free to use these reserves in numerous ways, including payment of bonuses or even shifting of money to tax havens. However, they do not lend reserves to their ordinary customers. For lending to take place, the willingness of banks to lend must be matched by the willingness of the public to borrow. This is also the reason why an enormous amount of money was poured into the banking system without any substantial changes in the increase of bank lending to the private sector in the countries that resorted to quantitative easing.[9]

In sum, the first aspect of injustice built into the modern money creation system is that monetary policies do not provide sufficient monetary means for proper functioning of economies. The very nature of the present system is that it forces debts to escalate, causing "artificial scarcity" in the supply of money.[10] Furthermore, the real danger to the present financial system is not even in the amount of debt money that it creates, but rather "in the cascading of debt relations in which a single default can result in a system-wide reaction."[11]

Interconnected with this is the second issue of injustice in the present monetary system, namely the insertion of the debt imperative into the money creation process, which puts a disproportionately heavier burden upon the economically weaker members of society. Put bluntly, "modern money is *not* a neutral medium; indeed the way in which money is currently created gives it a specific nature and a serious bias."[12] Monetary policies do not deal with this "bias." What we now have is a cleverly designed system where private banks have been granted a monopolistic control over money created as debt and, ultimately, a net transfer of assets toward the wealthiest strata of societies. Unfortunately, monetary policies only scratch the surface of the modern money system and project the image that despite the evidence of some occasional disturbances, the system works, and governments have the situation under control.

Fiscal policies and contributive justice

Similar to monetary policies, fiscal policies of many countries are flawed because of injustice issues ingrained in them. And again, theory says one thing, but reality shows something quite different. In theory, for example, government debt can be rolled over and over practically indefinitely. This is so, the argument goes, because government can always obtain sufficient funds to redeem maturing debt securities by selling new securities to the public.[13] History shows, however, that the rolling over of national debts cannot go on indefinitely. At times the ability of some governments to roll their debts is put into question, which ultimately may lead to losing the theoretical indefinite potential to borrow. In August 2011, the downgrading of the US credit rating by Standard & Poor's, the first in over seventy years, sent shockwaves throughout the financial world. Although this incident did not suggest any immediate danger to the United States, it nevertheless showed that even economic giants are vulnerable to high debts. Historically speaking, government bankruptcies are not that infrequent. No government is totally immune to failure caused by extreme debts.

Occasional crises, however, tend to be real tests to ideologically charged theoretical assumptions and to the projected image that the system works. Perhaps the financial tsunami of 2007–2009 serves as the best illustration of the rupture between theory and practice. In the aftermath of the crisis, many governments began (or were forced) to introduce so-called austerity programs to show that they were still committed to balanced budgets. Looking at the ongoing struggle of Greece one can clearly see the impact of such programs. In the words of Greek economist Costas Lapavitsas (2012), "the figures for Greece are reminiscent of war damage – unemployment of 22 percent and loss of output of about 20 percent." In the three years since the implosion of the Greek debt crisis in 2009, one-third of its population lived below the poverty line.[14] To a lesser degree, countries on the eurozone periphery, such as Spain, Portugal, and Ireland, have faced similar hardships. The main tools of driving public finances closer to ideologically set balanced budgets are higher taxes and budget cuts in public spending. This is why the times of implementing austerity programs have been particularly tough on those with lower incomes and those who rely heavily on social services. In short, the most vulnerable sections of society tend to bear a disproportionately heavy burden of austerity programs.

A report released in October 2013 by the International Federation of Red Cross and Red Crescent Societies (IFRC) has confirmed the observable worsening of living conditions for millions of Europeans. These conditions are at least partly the consequences of the post-crises policies that some countries adopted or were forced to adopt. The report particularly emphasizes an important concern: "a growing number of people living below the poverty line and needing assistance, and also a rise in the intensity of poverty, whereby those who were already poor are now poorer, as well as a widening gap between the rich and the poor." Rising impoverishment has apparently hit even the wealthiest societies of Europe, such as Denmark and Luxembourg. In Germany, a country considered to be Europe's economic engine, 5.5 million people have lost their middle-class social status over the past decade. Unemployment, especially long-term unemployment, has exacerbated the problem of impoverishment. Vulnerability to poverty, in turn, is translated into weakening health conditions, increased migration, social exclusion, and growing despair.[15]

While forcing the majority of ordinary people into painful austerity programs follows theoretical assumptions, the treatment of the "too-big-to-fail" totally departs from what the theory says. Letting Lehman Brothers go bankrupt was nothing more than a false start in the wake of the 2007–2009 financial tsunami. It was rather an exception to the rule that the big corporate players have to be saved. This is why prior to the last crisis, financial companies gambled on an unprecedented scale. Because banks are now equipped with the right to create enormous amounts of money through debt, they can gamble. And gamble they did in the past, and gamble they will continue to do, as they have almost nothing to lose.

Among the unanswered questions of bank bailouts is why only some banks deserved to be saved. What now appears to guide the logic of bailouts is purely utilitarian calculation devoid of any principle of justice. Examples from recent history show unequivocally that only the chosen few tend to be saved in a time of crisis, and that smaller banks that face bankruptcy are often swallowed by the bailed-out banks, making the big banks even bigger and more eligible to be bailed out in the future. As such, the present practice of bailouts only exacerbates the vicious circle of gambling on the part of big banks. The bigger problem, however, is that the system has remained untouched, and citizens of many countries continue to be inevitably locked in the role of carrying the burden of saving banks when a crisis hits again. In effect, what we now have is a system driven by the collusion of politicians (government) power and banking interests. While the Hobbesian Leviathan had only one head, the present system has two joined together.

Looking at the outcome of the last financial tsunami, Paul Krugman has concluded that "punishing the populace for the bankers' sins is worse than a crime:

it is a mistake."[16] From the perspective of this study, Krugman's statement is very revealing. Crime is normally understood as a harmful act or omission against a public law, often punishable by fine or imprisonment. Crime occurs when laws are already in place, and various individuals or groups choose to disobey them. On the other hand, a mistake is a result of defective judgment, lack of sufficient knowledge, or careless attitude. Once realized, at least some attempts should be made to correct a mistake. While some of the most serious crimes of the last financial crisis have been punished,[17] "mistakes" so much ingrained in the present banking system are barely addressed. What is instead presented to the public is nothing more than smoke and mirrors, because correcting the real mistakes would mean giving up the extraordinary privileges that banks have gained over the past several centuries. The same is also true about the power of politicians the banking industry has often sponsored and heavily lobbied. This lack of commitment to correct the mistakes of the system is a main reason why injustices will continue and the system will remain very unstable.

In short, fiscal policies of government also pose questions of justice. Despite theoretical rationalizations, government debt cannot be rolled over indefinitely. Meanwhile, growing payments of interests on growing public debts eat up growing portions of taxes paid by the public. Yet the problem of justice becomes particularly obvious at times of crisis, when the public, especially the economically weaker members of society are disproportionately overburdened by so-called austerity programs. As such, the present system in effect privatizes rewards by channeling them to the biggest risk takers during booms, and socializes costs of busts by forcing the public to share the bill.

Debt money and the issue of commutative justice

Commutative (or corrective) justice regards dealings between individuals or entities, and is exercised on the basis of an arithmetic equality, or equality between exchanged objects. This means that the prime concern in exchange is in *what* is due without any regard to the status or wealth of the individuals or entities involved.

Modern bank loans are not contracts of *mutuum*

For Aristotle as well as for the scholastics, the focus of the discussion of money was commutative justice, and at the heart of it was usury. As seen earlier, Aristotle understood usury as the charging of *any* interest on money lent. He (and many others in the ancient world) strongly opposed usurious lending on the argument that money as a means of exchange could not "bear" (yield) more money in the same way children or animals were born or crops increased. Money at that time was principally in the form of metal, and the amount in circulation could be increased only by minting more of it. But minting could only occur at the behest of recognized authority. Thus because ordinary money users could not increase the amount of money in circulation, and justice in exchanges was about commensurability, it would have been unjust to force the borrower to make "barren money" increase by itself. This is why for Aristotle, the charging of interest on money lent – usury – was unjust by its very nature.

The scholastics shared the basic views of Aristotle in condemning usury. They agreed that in what they called a loan of *mutuum*, for which the transfer of ownership of the object or money lent to the borrower is crucial, justice can be preserved only when the value of what is borrowed equals the value of what is returned. Because the money they knew had a relatively stable fixed value, the mere passing of time was not a sufficient basis for charging over the principal in a loan of *mutuum*. However, the scholastics gradually began also to raise more arguments from the perspective of the lender. To maintain the principle of commensurability of values in such a loan, they came to the conclusion that the lender was rightfully entitled to compensation on two grounds: emergent loss (*damnum emergens*) and cessant gain (*lucrum cessans*). Put simply, for the scholastics, only the circumstances that accompanied a loan of *mutuum* provided grounds for legitimate compensation, or charging of some interest. The two forms of compensation themselves formed a part of commutative justice.

However, while the scholastics set a clear principle upon which the just moneylending system should be built, the very nature of money as created through debt gradually changed. Looking at this shift, Dempsey has come to the conclusion that with the change in the nature of money, the nature of usury also changed – it became institutionalized, meaning it became part of the entire system of money creation. According to him, the forms of money we now have, which can be produced without any significant costs, "have raised some very nasty problems about money as an object suitable for a loan under the contract of *mutuum*." The central concern of Dempsey is that "whenever money is lent that has not previously been saved, there is a gain from a loan of *mutuum* for which no moral title exists."[18] To him, such a process of money creation is usurious, but because it is not an outcome of the personal fault of anyone involved, but takes place on the systemic level, the usury is institutional.[19] More recently Greco has come to a very similar conclusion:

> The truly devastating thing about the dominant monetary system is that usury has been built into its very foundation, resulting in a *debt impera-tive* and the *growth imperative* that derives from it. This dual imperative creates a Hobbesian war of "all against all" as those in debt to the banks vie with one another in the market to capture enough money from an insufficient supply to repay their loans with interest. This not only causes gross inequities and social strife, but it also drives the destruction of our physical environment.[20]

Dempsey and Greco highlight the point that usury still continues its destruc-tive impact on economic systems. But compared with the past, usury has taken on a new, much more elaborated institutional form. The system of bank-created debt money, which allows banks to make huge gains without any proportionate danger of loss or risk, poses a moral challenge modernity cannot ignore. Most loans in modern banking systems are not contracts of *mutuum*, as there is no transfer of ownership of previously existent money. Nonetheless, banks treat loans as such, thus still projecting the image that they lend their own money or the money of their depositors. As such, lending/borrowing contracts raise serious problems in terms of discrepancies in information between consenting parties. When borrowers enter into a contract without knowing that actually it is their very act of borrowing that helps banks to create money, this clearly suggests that such contracts should be considered as tainted.

Justice problems in collateralized loans

From the perspective of the scholastic theory of usury, the basic problem regarding the lending–borrowing agreements with banks, then, is that in principle these are not contracts of *mutuum*, and thus do not fulfill the demands of commutative justice. (It may be worth stressing that this is very different from loans provided by nonbank financial institutions [NBFIs], which resemble contracts of *mutuum*). In the process of lending, normally there is no transfer of money that belongs to the bank, or any depositor, despite the fact that banks (and many others) like treating bank loans as such. Therefore, in reality present loan contracts do not provide sufficient grounds for charging interest, because there is no forgone opportunity of gain (*lucrum cessans*) – as the money in question does not exist before the issuance of loan – and no real emergent loss (*damnum emergens*) involved – as the majority of loan contracts are secured loans that include some form of collateral (an asset with which a borrower secures the repayment of the loan and that, theoretically, provides the possibility to obtain a loan on "better terms").

Taking the fact that modern lending–borrowing agreements with banks are in principle not contracts of *mutuum*, charging interest rates on such lending poses some serious questions of commensurability of values, or simply justice. Perhaps the greatest among them is the issue of what are called compound interest rates. Although known already to the ancient world, and often condemned not only on moral but also legal grounds (e.g., in Roman law), compound interest is now very much taken for granted in long-term loan contracts (e.g., mortgages) and time deposits. Compound interest is the kind of interest that is calculated on an exponential basis, meaning that interest is paid not only on the principal but also on any interest from the past. In other words, in addition to the interest paid on the principal, the interest also earns interest.

In a somewhat simplified example of a mortgage contract (as mortgage interests may differ much from country to country and within a country), compound interest could cause a house mortgaged for 30 years to induce total payments of almost the price of two such houses at the end of the agreed period. If one takes into consideration that the entire contract does not cause banks to incur any significant costs or forgo any other opportunities of gain, it is difficult to argue that such charges are justified.

Undoubtedly, one can also argue that now banks pay compound interest to depositors on their time deposits. Are such interests equally unjustified? To answer this question it is important to first realize that these deposits are nothing but loans of *cash* to banks. As such, they actually fall under the contract of *mutuum*, meaning the providers of such loans can justifiably claim compensation for any emergent loss (*damnum emergens*) or forgone opportunities of gain (*lucrum cessans*). Unfortunately, banks "forget it all the time in their dealings with their customer/creditors" and "act as if it's their money" and pretend that they are doing a favor to customers "by letting it sit in their bank earning interest."[21] Put simply, banks do not appreciate the loans of their depositors because they can create money much more cheaply and additionally charge payment on their acts of creation. They need depositors' money partly to meet the demands for sufficient capital relative to their assets, but mostly to maintain the image that they loan the money they have.

The most obvious expression of the fact that banks do not appreciate their creditors' deposits is the very low interest rate paid on savings. In many developed economies the annual rates on time deposits are notoriously kept under the rate of inflation. Taking into consideration the fact that many economies operate predominantly under the condition of permanent inflation, money put into savings accounts loses its purchasing power, and depositors suffer losses. From the perspective of the scholastic principle of the equality of values, the interest rates given by banks do not meet the requirements of justice. This is also why many depositors keep as savings in banks mainly what they need for "rainy days" or some form of emergency. The rest they "invest," which in turn exacerbates the financialization of modern economies.

Yet despite all criticism, what cannot be denied is that through lending, modern banking provides some form of benefit to the borrowers. From a moral perspective, bank's "creation" of principal at the same time provides some form of good for the borrower (e.g., he or she "buys" a house). Concerned with the principle of equality of values, the discussion of commutative justice cannot neglect this aspect. This "good" has to be reciprocated.

However, the basic problem with evaluating *what* has to be reciprocated is the fact that the entire lending–borrowing relationship in modern banking has been totally blurred. A still rather simplistic explanation that banks indeed create the principal and the interest rates charged on such agreements can be considered as service fees raises the question why banks do not call those "services" what they really are. Quite obviously interest rates and fees for services belong to different categories. Why misinform the borrowers, and indeed the general public? The only way to deal with modern loans, then, is to consider them not as contracts of *mutuum*, but as a service that requires certain payments. But this definitely needs a new way of establishing how to value such services.

Moreover, there also appears to be a need of critical evaluation of what happens to money created as the loan's principal when it is gradually repaid. As pointed out earlier, banks normally treat as their own the stream of money coming from repayment of long-term loans. How are we to value such "services" that borrowers provide to banks? For now, these issues are still taboo, and banks (and many academics) continue to keep the public ill-informed, or rather misinformed, about the realities of bank "lending." As a result, the banking system benefits from the public's ignorance and confusion.

Justice issues in unsecured loans

Credit card loans involve another set of justice questions. In contrast to the collateralized loans discussed above, these normally are unsecured loans. As such, they are almost automatically labeled as being much more risky. Yet a closer look at the practice of issuing credit cards is sufficient to see that credit card companies usually thoroughly check payment capabilities of their potential clients before providing them with credit cards. (It should be stressed here that this is what happens under normal circumstances, because in some countries, particularly at the turn of the millennium, there were instances of totally reckless issuance of credit cards, the holders of which could not honor incurred debts, and many of them were turned into "credit card slaves"). Additionally, there are also caps on overdrafts set on the basis of the regular income of the card holder. More risky borrowers might even be pressured to buy "insurance" on their loans.[22] As a result, the risk of default is actually quite minimal, which ultimately makes the emergent loss (*damnum emergens*) also very minimal.

The second crucial justice question in credit card loans regards cessant gain (*lucrum cessans*). To respond to this concern, it is important to first clarify how credit cards actually work. This is how Brown describes it:

> when you sign a merchant's credit card charge slip, you are creating a "negotiable instrument." A negotiable instrument is anything that is signed and convertible into money or that can be used as money. The merchant takes this negotiable instrument and deposits it into his merchant's checking account, a special account required of all businesses that accept credit. The account goes up by the amount on the slip, indicating that the merchant has been paid. The charge slip is forwarded to the credit card company (Visa, MasterCard, etc.), which bundles your charges and sends them to a bank. The bank then sends you a statement, which you pay with a check, causing your transaction account to be debited at your bank. At no point has a bank lent you its own money or its depositor's money. Rather, your charge slip (a negotiable instrument) has become an "asset" against which credit has been advanced. The bank has done nothing but *monetize* your own I.O.U. or promise to repay.[23]

As a matter of fact, even in the case of overdrafts, when withdrawals exceed deposits, the basic mechanism is the same. The only difference is that in such an instance, the bank provides the card holder with a loan created, just like the majority of bank loans, without transfer of any preexisting money. And without preexisting money, there can be no forgone opportunity of gain (*lucrum cessans*).

Thus, because money creation through debt does not involve the possibility of cessant gain, and the use of credit cards does not entail high risks, charging *high* interest rates on delayed payments appears to be unjustified, or simply, usurious. Such practices need a proper evaluation just as in the case of secured loans discussed earlier.

Similar to loans on credit cards, lending used in microfinance falls under the category of unsecured loans. There is, however, a crucial difference between them – in the case of microlending, the money lent (usually a very small amount) is normally in the form of cash. What this means is that as such, microloans are contracts of *mutuum*, at the heart of which lies a transfer of ownership. Although in such lending compensation could justifiably be claimed for any emergent loss (*damnum emergens*) or forgone opportunities of gain (*lucrum cessans*), this does not mean that microloans do not pose questions of justice. One of the widespread criticisms of microfinance is that interest rates charged on such loans are too high. Supporters usually claim that the interest rates are kept in the range of 20 percent or slightly above, which for unsecured loans is rather reasonable, and at the same time helps some disadvantaged people to gain access to loans and to avoid exploitation by local loan sharks, who often charge much higher interest rates.

Opponents, on the other hand, have pointed to examples of rates of 30 percent or more (in some cases even over 50 percent). For example, in the Indian province of Andhra Pradesh, before the debt crisis in microfinance broke out in 2011, it was not uncommon for microlenders to charge interest rates above 30 percent. In the midst of the crisis, the Reserve Bank of India (its central bank) issued new rules for microlenders, which limited annual interest rates to 26 percent and put the cap of 50,000 rupees on the total lending made to a single borrower.[24] Additionally, some practices accompanying both lending and recovery of debts in microfinance leave space for exploitation (for example, taking advantage of illiterate customers, making a group responsible for repayments, using physical force to secure repayment) as the sector is underregulated, especially in poor countries where such lending is most widespread.

This, of course, does not deny the fact that some poor indeed managed to improve their life conditions because of microloans they took. The prime concern here is whether the high interest rates charged in microlending are justified. Already in ancient Rome, an average annual return on investment was calculated in the range of about 5 percent. The late scholastics (the sixteenth century), who had at their disposal more data, including those from commerce, saw the charging of interest rates at 4 to 5 percent justifiable. Lesius appears to have been the most liberal among them, as he singled out 6.25 percent to be "the highest rate on loans from which risk has largely been eliminated."[25]

In the modern economy, rather conservative investments could likely provide higher returns than those mentioned by Lesius. Yet at the same time, even relatively risky investments could hardly claim returns of 20 percent or more. No wonder that microlending businesses mushroomed over the past two decades, as microfinance turned out to be highly profitable. Moreover, when one considers that well over 95 percent of microfinance debts are paid back (higher than in the case of collateralized debts), we may ask whether charging interest of over 20 percent is justifiable to compensate for any emergent loss (*damnum emergens*) or forgone opportunities of gain (*lucrum cessans*). One can have no doubt that for the scholastics, charging such high interest rates was clearly usurious. Thus the claim that so many poor take microloans misses the point, because they do so out of dire necessity, and diverse religious and secular traditions throughout history repeatedly condemned such profiteering on the plight of the poor.

A great disproportion between the interest rates in microlending and collateralized lending also points to a profound bias in modern finance. Those with deep pockets, especially institutional borrowers who can easily provide collateral, even if in name (signature) only, can borrow at interest rates that may be well below the level of inflation. Microborrowers, on the other hand, have to pay high interest for the mere fact that they are poor and cannot produce some form of "collateral." As a result, even *if* they manage to make some money on loans, much of what they earn feeds the rich providers of microloans, thus extending the distressing conditions of the poor and keeping them dependent.

Institutionalization of injustices

What should be apparent by now is that the modern banking system has cleverly institutionalized what for centuries was fought over, namely usury. From the perspective of commutative justice, the focal issue now is not the charging of interest rates as such, but rather the injustices buried in the structures of modern monetary and banking systems. It is the interplay between the two systems that blurs justice issues, misleads the public, and allows banks to take advantage of the structures they themselves "helped" to gradually establish over the past four centuries. The morality of interest rates is simply part of this complex reality. The vast majority of loans made now by most banks are not loans of *mutuum*, meaning loans that allow banks to make gains without corresponding risk or loss on their part. As such, these loans do not meet the demands of commutative justice. The risks that banks speak of have hardly anything to do with the ordinary loans they issue. Many of the risks for banks come from gambling involving so-called financial products. In the ever-expanding financialization of the economy, the banking sector is evolving into an increasingly complex financial Moloch, and "money" unjustly extracted from lending is increasingly used to feed the money mania of "trading" increasingly sophisticated "financial products."

Moreover, despite their rhetoric of personalized services, banks have gradually moved into a depersonalized mode of dealing with their customers. The most obvious example of this is debt collection. To many banks, debt collection, particularly debts incurred on credit cards, can occasionally become a horrendous problem. But they managed to find a solution by outsourcing the dirty work. As a result, their hands remain clean, while debt collectors harass and sue people.[26]

It has to be stressed, however, that the above critique is addressed toward banks as structural entities. There are undoubtedly many honest bankers as well as people working for banks, some of whom (perhaps the majority) are not even aware how the system really works, because their involvement is mostly fragmentary, reduced to merely a few operations. Some employees themselves might be very much concerned about what is happening in the banking indus-try.[27] The point here is that the issue of injustices in modern banking has been shifted to the level of the system, and thus depersonalized. This is why during crises the public is quickly presented with some guilty individuals apparently responsible for what has happened. As always, the system needs scapegoats. The assumption continues that the system in principle works.

The institutionalization of injustices has even infiltrated international monetary and financial arrangements. Perhaps the most obvious example is the role of the US dollar in international transactions. (Although here the example of the US dollar is used, the underlying principle with regard to other international cur-rencies is the same.) Intensification of globalizing tendencies has caused many countries all over the world to strive for a sufficient amount of foreign curren-cies to gain access to natural resources, goods, or services of other countries. The US dollar has by far become the most important currency for mediating international transactions.[28] But how does this affect the issue of justice?

One way of looking at the problem of justice in exchange transactions in a dollar-dominated international trade and financial system is to study what hap-pens when a country wants to acquire dollars from the United States. As one may immediately guess, this usually works on the basis of "money for goods." It means that other countries must provide the United States with real goods (to a lesser degree, services) to obtain dollars. In other words, to obtain a $100 bill, which costs the Bureau of Engraving and Printing only a few cents to produce, other countries have to provide actual goods and services worth $100. At present, the amount of dollars circulating outside the United States is estimated at about 500 billion. This means that other countries have had to supply the United States with $500 billion of goods and services.[29]

Barry Eichengreen calls the dominance of the US dollar in international markets an "exorbitant privilege." Over recent decades, this "privilege" has been "a sore point for foreigners, who see themselves as supporting American living standards and subsidizing American multinationals through the operation of this asymmetric system."[30] The issue of obtaining US dollars is, of course, totally different when countries gain them through exchanges with countries other than the United States, as each country that already possesses reserves of dollars had to previously pay for them with goods and services. On the other hand, borrowing dollars solves the problem of shortage of this currency only temporarily, because debts, including interest, normally have to be paid in dollars.

Yet the problem of "asymmetry" between nations goes even deeper by the fact that now "economic success is essentially outward-looking."[31] Examples of countries with strong export orientation show clearly that their economies tend to thrive. In a debt-based economic system, countries that can manage to export more than import, and thus obtain a bigger pool of debt-free money, appear to gain the sufficient edge to boost their economies. The issue of commutative justice in trading exchanges across borders is complicated because trade of this kind is not carried on by nations but by concrete entities or individuals, and winning export battles (so crucial to modern economies) increasingly depends on the ability to tap into systems of subsidies. Although international trade agreements have attempted to mitigate this problem, in reality they can at most address only the most obvious cases of unfair trading practices. They can hardly address the issue of subsidies buried in the monetary and financial systems, such as beggar-thy-neighbor type of devaluations of currencies[32] or generous deficit financing of a country's own economy for export purposes.[33]

Debt money and the issue of distributive justice

Distributive justice expresses the responsibility that society or the state has toward the individual. It is anchored in proportional equality in which the give-and-take is in "geometrical proportion" to one's needs and contributive abilities. Its prime focus is the well-being of each individual in relation to the common good. As such, distributive justice governs the relationship of society (represented by government) to the individual, and aims at enforcing rights of some individuals against others. Among its basic expressions are opportunities to share in the wealth of a society. The crucial question, however, is how these opportunities are allocated. From the perspective of the Aristotelian concept of justice, the present monetary and banking systems fail to meet the requirements of distributive justice.

First is the problem of privatization of profits and socialization of losses. The way in which the banking crisis of 2007–2009 was handled shows once again that what is crucial in the modern monetary-banking system is to be well connected and to gain the status of the "too-big-to-fail." Once this is achieved, protection is basically guaranteed, and one can feel entitled to gamble at the risk and cost of others. In the present system, the distribution mechanism is geared toward the wealthy. It favors the wealthy, supports the wealthy, and if necessary, saves the wealthy. In short, instead of distributing wealth, modern monetary and banking systems benefit a small number of the privileged, and thus contribute to the concentration of wealth.

One of the spillovers of the growing concentration of wealth is the decrease in the ability of many people to own a house or an apartment.[34] In the over-financialized economy, in which money is supposed to bear more money, the rich tend to invest heavily (often aided with borrowing) in real estate, thus artificially pushing up housing prices. This, in turn, hits poorer market participants, who cannot afford to join the race. Even those among them who might be considered "worthy" of a mortgage tend to become "debt slaves," as for years afterwards they have to pay debts for overpriced housing.

Another spillover of the growing concentration of wealth and power is lack of sensitivity, which became particularly visible during the recent financial crisis. In 2008, when the entire system was crumbling, banks asked for taxpayers' money to save them and at the same time distributed millions of dollars as bonuses.

Apparently, for the banking system bonuses became such an expected entitlement that even monstrous failures had to be rewarded.

Undoubtedly, the great bailout of the banking system was a difficult decision to make. What makes that decision morally questionable is that the bailout followed the precedent set in the past that big business entities should be saved. The difference was that this time "salvation" came on the biggest scale in human history. Yet if banks needed to be saved, why were smaller banks not included in the bailout? Moreover, the bailout should at least have been followed by a strict reform to ensure that earlier mistakes would not be repeated. Unfortunately, except for tough talk, not much happened in the aftermath. Big banks have become even bigger, thus insuring that they will be saved whenever needed. (In fairness, part of the problem with the implementation of some reforms has been strong resistance from banks, which shows how they gradually gain the confidence that they are untouchable.) As a result, the entire system retains a form of moral hazard, which encourages people to be less cautious in their decisions, providing their entities become large enough. This process also exposes an evident failure of the distributive system, transferring society's wealth to its richest members.

As is already well known, during the 2007–2009 financial crisis many home buyers got into trouble when they couldn't continue paying mortgages, which they often had not really understood or recklessly had agreed to. The mortgage providers, on the other hand, who were in a far better position to know the risks involved, were rewarded with bailouts. Many bankers even collected bonuses for their performance. Securitization of mortgages made a number of people in the banking sector very rich, bank bailouts made governments further indebted, and many citizens lost their homes. Robert Reich has summed it up well: "The little guys get tough love. The big guys get forgiveness."[35] This is a total reversal of the ways the forgiveness of debts was exercised in the ancient world.

Yet an even greater issue is ingrained in the system that underpins the unjust distribution, bailouts, or moral hazards in the modern banking system: the fact that banks function as limited liability companies. The medieval partnerships operated on the principle of the shareholder's *unlimited liability* set against all his personal assets. So, for example, in the case of bankruptcy the shareholder could lose not only the amount he invested, but was also liable for other losses, including repayment of the partnership debts if incurred. The invention of the limited liability corporation about four hundred years ago reduced investors' liability only to the funds invested in the corporation. As such, it contributed immensely to development of the capitalist system, and gained widespread praise.[36] But there is a deep-seated problem with the limited liability company when applied to the modern banking system.

In the limited liability corporation, because stockholders' (owners') liability is limited only to their equity capital, investors normally absorb losses, but they can lose only what they invest. While for many companies, despite growing reliance on borrowing, equity still forms a big chunk of their entire capital, this is a very different story when the limited liability company is a bank. What is characteristic about modern banks is that they have very low equity. In 2006, before the financial crises erupted, the five largest American investment banks kept their equity asset ratios in the range of about 3 to 4.5 percent. In other words, their total assets exceeded their equity over twenty or thirty times.[37] (Note that bank loans are the major component of their assets.) Undoubtedly, such a colossal leverage provides very high returns on equity. Yet at the same time, it "generates enormously high risks, initially for the bank itself, then for its creditors, and finally for the taxpayers, who must pay for the rescue packages in the end."[38] In the face of huge potential returns on the investment and legal liability limited only to equity capital, it is no wonder that so much risky, if not foolish, speculation took place in the banking sector.

But this is not all. Bank executives can either satisfy this urge of investors or look for another job. So, while blaming some bank CEOs for their reckless decisions, we must remember how the entire system that immensely limits the liability of the owners puts pressure on these executives. One can but exclaim: welcome to the world where money is forced to "bear" more money!

In 1833, William Gouge wrote *A Short History of Paper Money and Banking.* One of his arguments was that

> wealth and poverty are the result of a country's institutions. Political privi-
> leges are the common cause: but commercial privileges have the same effect:
> and when the foundation of this artificial inequality of fortune is once laid,
> whether by feudal institutions or money corporations, all the subsequent
> operations of society tend to increase this concentration of wealth.[39]

More recently, Paul Krugman made a similar observation. According to him, "the era of an ever-growing financial industry was also an era of ever-growing inequality of income and wealth."[40] Distributive justice is about widening the opportunities for all members of a given community to share in its income. Yet the present system of control over money creation in reality exacerbates inequalities. As a result, many weaker market participants are forced to share disproportionate burdens of debts.

All in all, the distribution of society's wealth, or increasing opportunities for all its members to share in its wealth, still faces a variety of serious obstacles. This is at least partly due to the fact that money, which is supposed to contribute to community abundance and to the well-being of all, has been turned into a form of scarcity (issued by banks on the basis of debt), and is thus accessible only to the fittest. The present credit (debt) money system interlocks govern-ments and banks into an inseparable monopolistic power center. On the other hand, the players who cannot tap into this power center are often – particularly during times of crisis – burdened with debts, which have been conveniently dispersed into wider and wider segments of society. Social Darwinism is well preserved in the modern distributive system. In it, what still matters most is to become a sufficiently big player to gain access to modern political-financial power centers.

To sum up, injustices ingrained in modern monetary and banking arrangements have taken on diverse forms. Despite their theoretical justifications, the present monetary and banking systems are in serious need of improvement. Among their major shortcomings is the fact that virtually all money is now created out of thin air through the issuance of debt, which not only causes lack of commensurability in exchanges but also gives too much power to banks. This, in turn, allows for excessive risk-taking, casino-type gambling, the financialization of entire economies, and the ultimate concentration of wealth in the hands of a few. At the same time, the borrowers, in particular the economically weaker members of society, as well as medium and small enterprises, are disproportionately overburdened by debt to keep supplying money for booming economies or by the need to "save" economies during crisis. A far more profound change, then, is required than just tough talk and the patching of a few holes in the system by strengthening regulatory mechanisms and regaining "consumer confidence," which is nothing more than an effort to convince people to increase consumption and thus put even more pressure on environment and increase depletion of valuable resources. In other words, the world clearly needs a system of money supply that is far more just than it is at present.

Notes

1 D. Graeber, *Debt: The First 5,000 Years*, Brooklyn, NY: Melville House, 2011, p. 91. Italics added.
2 M. Rowbotham, *The Grip of Death: A Study of Modern Money, Debt Slavery and Destructive Economics*, 4th ed., Charlbury, UK: Jon Carpenter, 2009, p. 23.
3 Ibid., pp. 29 and 28, respectively; italics his.
4 W. Hummel, 'The Interest Time Bomb', in *Money: What It Is, How It Works*, 2011.
5 T.H. Greco, *The End of Money and the Future of Civilization*, White River Junction, VT: Chelsea Green, 2009, p. 95.
6 Rowbotham, *The Grip of Death*, p. 27.
7 Greco, *The End of Money*, pp. 155–159.
8 Rowbotham, *The Grip of Death*, p. 5.
9 E.H. Brown, *The Public Bank Solution: From Austerity to Prosperity*, Baton Rouge, LA: Third Millennium Press, 2013, pp. 412–413.
10 Greco, *The End of Money*, p. 55.
11 W. Hummel, 'Money as Credit', in *Money: What It Is, How It Works*, 2004. Available at: http://www.wfhummel.net (accessed 22 March 2012).
12 Rowbotham, *The Grip of Death*, p. 4; italics his.
13 W. Hummel, 'Some Common Misconceptions', in *Money: What It Is, How It Works*, 12 March 2008.
14 J. Henley, 'Questions on Greek Crisis Get Answers', *Taipei Times*, 17 June 2012, p. 9.
15 International Federation of Red Cross and Red Crescent Societies, Think Differently: Humanitarian Impacts of the Economic Crisis in Europe, Geneva, 2013; the quotation is from p. 5.
16 P. Krugman, 'Eating the Irish', *International Herald Tribune*, 27–28 November 2010, p. 7.
17 James Howard Kunstler argues that much of the criminality present in the financial industry in the United States prior to the financial crisis has gone unpunished.

After the crisis, a massive lobbying machine pushed for diluting the boundaries between business and crime, while the main agencies overseeing the financial market, such as the Securities and Exchange Commission and the US Department of Justice, failed to act (J.H. Kunstler, *Too Much Magic: Wishful Thinking, Technology, and the Fate of the Nation*, New York: Atlantic Monthly Press, 2012, pp. 111–154).
18 B.W. Dempsey, *The Functional Economy: The Bases of Economic Organization*, Englewood Cliffs, NJ: Prentice-Hall, 1958, pp. 436 and 439.
19 Ibid., p. 441; see also B.W. Dempsey, *Interest and Usury*, London: Dennis Dobson, 1948, pp. 227–228.
20 Greco, *The End of Money*, p. 54; italics his.
21 J. Lanchester, *I.O.U.: Why Everyone Owes Everyone and No One Can Pay*, New York: Simon & Schuster, 2010, pp. 32–33.
22 E.H. Brown, *The Web of Debt: The Shocking Truth about Our Money System and How We Can Break Free*, 3rd ed., Baton Rouge, LA: Third Millennium Press, 2008, p. 279.
23 Ibid., pp. 279–280; italics hers.
24 V. Bajaj, 'New Blow to Microlenders in Asia', *International Herald Tribune*, 12 May 2011, p. 14; see also V. Bajaj, 'Microlenders Swing from Darlings to Demons', *International Herald Tribune*, 6 June 2011, pp. 1 and 17.
25 Dempsey, *Interest and Usury*, p. 180.
26 J. Nocera, 'Why People Hate the Banks', *International Herald Tribune*, 4 April 2012, p. 8.
27 E.g., J. Nocera, 'The Good Banker', *International Herald Tribune*, 1 June 2011, p. 7; N.D. Kristof, 'A Banker Speaks, with Regret', *International Herald Tribune*, 2 December 2011, p. 7.
28 B. Eichengreen, *Exorbitant Privilege: The Rise and Fall of the Dollar and the Future of the International Monetary System*, New York: Oxford University Press, 2011, p. 2.
29 Ibid., pp. 3 and 4, respectively.
30 Ibid., p. 4.
31 Rowbotham, *The Grip of Death*, p. 285.
32 James Rickards envisages that in the face of massive debts following the 2007–2009 financial crisis, the currency wars will intensify (J. Rickards, *Currency Wars: The Making of the Next Global Crisis*, New York: Portfolio/Penguin, 2011).
33 Rowbotham, *The Grip of Death*, pp. 284–285.
34 E.g., ibid., pp. 16–23.
35 R. Reich, 'Moral Hazard Is for Suckers', 23 September 2007. Available at: http://prospect.org/article/moral-hazard-suckers (accessed 12 July 2012).
36 See, for example, N. Ferguson, *The Ascent of Money: A Financial History of the World*, New York: Penguin Press, 2008, p. 174; H.W. Sinn, *Casino Capitalism: How the Financial Crisis Came about and What Needs to Be Done Now*, Oxford: Oxford University Press, 2010, p. 76.
37 Sinn, *Casino Capitalism*, p. 77.
38 Ibid.
39 In S. Zarlenga, *The Lost Science of Money: The Mythology of Money – the Story of Power*, Valatie, NY: American Monetary Institute, 2002, p. 441.
40 P. Krugman, 'Losing Their Immunity', *International Herald Tribune*, 18 October 2011, p. 7.

10 In search of solutions

Economies of many countries, particularly in the developed world, are in crisis. The 2007–2009 financial collapse and continuing widespread debt problems, concerns that in the near future some countries will find it difficult to pay pensions for their aging populations, the growing costs of environmental protection, and so on are mere symptoms of this crisis. At its roots are injustices and instability embedded in the monetary and financial systems of the past few centuries. Certain ideologies, including neoliberalism and the peculiar role of modern mainstream economics, deepen this crisis. Nevertheless, it is worth remembering that while the meaning of "crisis" carries negative connotations, the concept of crisis also entails opportunity.

Modern individuals and societies deserve more just and, by extension, more stable monetary and financial systems. Nations around the world are still relatively rich in natural resources and particularly in human talent. Educational institutions spread knowledge and train professionals on an unprecedented scale. All these, combined with immense technological advancements, have tremendously increased human productivity and creativity. The world has vast potential for a far better standard of living for all its citizens. Yet all this potential has fallen prey to the ideology of scarcity dominating our economic thinking. Even money has been turned into scarcity – as coming into existence through debt. As a result, the debt money system is now at the very heart of the ideology of scarcity.

Of course, our resources are not infinite. It is increasingly apparent that many natural resources crucial to modern economy, such as fossil fuels and some minerals, may well be used up in just a few decades. Additionally, the availability of fresh water and food is becoming increasingly constrained.[1] Scarcity exists in the finite world. This is also why the present economic model focusing on growth driven by increasing consumption is *totally* unsustainable.

This chapter looks at the aspect of opportunities in modern economic crises. Particular attention is given to the Aristotelian concept of money as a potential way out of the scarcity deadlock.

Proposals of monetary/financial reforms

The ideology of scarcity has made strong inroads into modern economic thinking. Yet it is the abundance of resources and ideas still found around the world that offers prospects for improvement in the workings of our economies. Money is perhaps the most fundamental aspect of the potential abundance of and a basis for a far more sustainable economic model. Below are several strands of prospective reforms of the present money system.

Strengthening of rules within the status quo

The first and likely the most common proposal in principle does not depart from the status quo. It simply suggests strengthening the rules controlling money production. Because banks play the dominant role in issuing money through debt, what is needed is proper regulation and oversight, assuring a more stable banking system. In other words, this stance is more about restoring confidence in the present system through loudly declared "new" regulations than the introduction of new monetary models. Perhaps its most radical variation has been the suggestion of Krugman "to make banking boring again." According to him, this would mean that regulatory efforts would have to go beyond the mere rearranging of "the boxes on the bank supervisory organization chart." Yet he immediately acknowledges that "making banking boring," and thus introducing "serious financial reforms," faces two major difficulties. First, boring banking would have to substantially reduce bankers' pay, which would be difficult to enforce because bankers still have "a lot of friends in high places." Second, many people in positions of power still hold their ideological conviction that "fancy finance" is a sign of "economic progress."[2]

In terms of international exchanges, the status quo faction acknowledges the difficulty of prolonging the "exorbitant privilege" of the US dollar.[3] Although the dollar is still used in the vast majority of foreign exchange transactions, currencies of emerging superpowers increasingly challenge its dominance. To avoid the destructive effects of potential "currency wars"[4] or the monopoly of the US dollar, there is a growing consensus of the need for some sort of global monetary and financial oversight. A proposal to strengthen the role of the G20 has been steadily reemerging in various circles of global elites. As international political and economic affairs become more multipolar, one of the potential solutions is to allow other currencies, in addition to the US dollar and the euro, to play a bigger role in international markets. However, because this solution is anchored in the present unstable and unjust money production, it would not alter much. In fact, it is quite likely that more severe and multilateral currency wars would follow.[5] The mere increase in the number of international currencies, then, would likely only exacerbate the problem.

A more radical solution of the status quo faction as to the means for foreign exchange transactions is to strengthen the role of the special drawing right (SDR) of the International Monetary Fund (IMF). For a few decades, SDR has been a form of an additional international "money," which is manufactured out of thin air through the issuance of debt by the IMF. It is valued on the basis of "a weighted basket of the five leading industrial currencies."[6] Put simply, SDR is "a credit-*facility*, just like a bank overdraft." This means that if a nation qualifies for such an overdraft, it must repay the incurred debt.[7] As such, SDR is a form of international debt money.

There are, nevertheless, strong limitations imposed on the issuance of SDRs, and member countries have their own quotas, with the United States getting the largest piece. (Not surprisingly, the quotas do not have any tangible backing.) Up to now, the IMF resorted to creating SDRs only three times. The two initial, comparatively small issuances took place in the early 1970s and 1980s to mitigate the oil price shock and global inflation. After a three-decade halt, SDR issuance was resumed in 2009 (worth $250 billion) as a response to the worldwide financial crisis.[8] In practical terms, then, SDR is a form of emergency money. Its issuance could be increased if needed. The process of issuing SDRs could also be sped up by creating "a liquid SDR bond market."[9] Yet this would only mean creating a de facto world central bank and expanding the present debt money system, the very system that in 2008 brought world finance to the brink of meltdown. Moreover, the problem of lack of trust remains an issue. At present the IMF is not an institution that can claim much trust,[10] so the prospects for SDR becoming influential and a stable global currency are untenable.

In short, the status quo faction tends to accept the principles upon which the present money system operates. Among them are both Keynesians, arguing for more debt to stir up economies and reduce unemployment, and libertarians, calling for strict austerity programs. Although all acknowledge some problems inherent in the present money system, they believe the solutions lie in more adequate regulations curbing banking excesses or government spending.

However, the biggest problem with the status quo stance is that it totally neglects injustices ingrained in the system. As such, it also undermines prospects for more stable economic system.

Returning to the gold standard

The second faction of potential monetary reformers proposes to resuscitate gold as the basis of the modern money system. In a broader sense, this faction favors commodity money, or "honest money."[11] Perhaps the strongest group promoting honest money exists under the umbrella of the Austrian School of economics. Austrians resort to several arguments to support their stance. First, they maintain that money developed in a natural process of economic exchanges, and "certain commodities came to be money quite naturally, as the result of economic relationships that were independent of the power of the state."[12] Second, because the commodity money system requires backing every bank note with gold or silver, it functions as a natural safeguard preventing government from defrauding the public through inflation. Third, Austrians are convinced that even a modest monetary inflation beyond specie results in an inequitable redistribution of income and wealth.[13] In short, for many Austrians, a 100 percent gold standard, as expressed by Rothbard, is "the soundest monetary system and the only one fully compatible with the free market and with the absence of force or fraud from any source." As such, it is also claimed to guarantee the upholding of property rights, the end of inflation, and business cycles.[14]

In the aftermath of the 2007–2009 financial crisis and looming currency wars, Rickards also proposes a return to the gold standard. His primary concern, however, is the stability of international transactions. Although the US dollar is still the dominant international currency, the present "currency wars," as Rickards puts it, gradually undermine confidence in the dollar. This is why, in his view, to avoid sliding into chaos, "a studied, expertly implemented return to the gold standard offers the best chance of stability."[15] Rickards cites several reasons to support the gold standard: (1) the growth of the gold supply is relatively stable and predictable – about 1.5 percent a year, which helps to control inflation; (2) compared to other metals, "gold has a high density," with its weight compressed into a small space; (3) gold is "of uniform grade" (high purity); (4) it is durable; (5) it is malleable, thus easily formed into coins or bars; and (6) gold has a long record as money across many civilizations and cultures.[16]

Yet a return to the gold standard also poses big challenges. Even Austrians do not deny it. This is why at least some of them tend to favor "free banking," or a totally laissez-faire trading of money.[17] Among the greatest difficulties the so-called gold standard faces, however, is the fact that attributing to gold the status of real money means giving the power of money to those who could get hold of the gold supply: the modern plutocracy.[18] Moreover, at present the quantity of gold in the world is very small, and so it would be difficult to sustain the present level of economic activity, or the price of gold would have to greatly increase. This, in turn, would put enormous pressure on the mining of gold and search for ever more ledges of gold. (Historically speaking, the Spanish plunder of American gold mines provides a good lesson in this matter.) Under such arrangements the largest producers of gold (such as China, Australia, the United States, South Africa, and Russia) would become particularly privileged, and, as in the case of oil, cartelization of gold prices would likely occur. In truth, proponents of the gold standard basically accept this argument but claim that the prices of goods and services would gradually adjust to the supply of gold. They also admit that at least in the short run, a return to the gold standard would cause economic havoc. Nonetheless, some believe that the very scarcity of gold makes it an ideal monetary base. For example, in the view of Rickards: "Gold is not a commodity. Gold is not an investment. Gold is money par excellence. It is truly scarce."[19]

The basic problem with gold as money, then, is that the proposed solution for a monetary base would only replace the present form of scarcity (debt) with a new form of scarcity (gold). And, as history shows, any attempt to base a money system in scarcity causes an appearance of some sort of power that tends to tap into it and benefit from that scarcity at cost to others.

Furthermore, while the present monetary system tends to be inflationary, making gold a monetary base would put deflationary pressures on economies. Thus the gold standard would limit economic growth. In case of strong private influence over the gold supply, the likelihood of manipulation of gold supply would exist, and result in overt restrictions or contractions in the money supply. Potential deflation, following such contractions, would in turn enrich lenders, who could additionally benefit from falling prices, and punish debtors as costs of servicing debts in real terms would increase. Under such conditions, industrialists, who in a given society are usually large debtors, would be harmed, but this harm would be quickly transferred to labor and, ultimately, harm production.[20] Moreover, as those in lower- and middle-income brackets tend to be net debtors and those in higher income brackets net creditors, the gap between the rich and the poor would continue to grow in the same way as under the present system.[21] Additionally, the gold standard system would lack sufficient flexibility to stimulate the economy, particularly during economic recessions. Attempts to use monetary policies to stimulate the economy and provide a social safety net in times of economic crisis would become essentially obsolete.

There is also an important practical reason against returning to the gold standard. Although in the past precious metals, gold in particular, formed a transparent and widely recognized monetary base, shipment of tons of gold around the world to settle international payments was costly and caused transportation safety concerns. In the present world, so influenced by information technologies and extensive acceptance of fiat currencies, such shipments appear totally unnecessary.

Local money

The third faction can be grouped under the umbrella of local money. The Local Exchange Trading System (LETS), using currencies with local names that are valued in relation to national currencies, can serve as an example of such money. Another example is so-called time banking, a form of a virtual currency functioning on the basis of one "time credit" for one hour of work; account balances are held on computers, and users contact each other through brokers.[22] In principle, local money movement seeks ways to mitigate the shortage of national currency felt in many localities.[23] As presented in this study, modern economies have been injected with a strong tendency toward financialization and, as a result, money is increasingly drawn toward financial centers. Because the present money system is built around scarcity, local communities, especially in rural areas, are particularly vulnerable to this scarcity. In the view of North, "money always tends to leach away from poorer, less well-endowed communities to their richer ones, so some communities always seem to win, and others always lose."[24] Big corporations occasionally take advantage of this by inserting themselves into disadvantaged local economies and thus further siphoning resources out of them. Moreover, with the movement of money toward financial centers, people also move to the centers where money is available, causing enormous migration and destructive impact on environment and the fabric of societies. The local money movement attempts to supplement the local shortage of national currency and stimulate localization of economic growth, and eventually make economies more sustainable and environmentally friendly.

However, while diverse local money can alleviate cash shortages of some localities, they can hardly bring long-term benefits. The idea and practice of local money has been around for well over 150 years. Nevertheless, much local money does not exist long enough and gain sufficient trust to make a real impact. As a result,

> These currencies will continue to be limited unless they can qualify as a true money form. That means taxes, at least local taxes, have to be payable in them. One would then expect them to be issued by the taxing body. At present this is not possible, except in emergencies.[25]

Yet perhaps more importantly, the local money movement does not challenge the present monetary system, but simply attempts to coexist with it and supplement its shortcomings. As such, it only mitigates the problems created by the dominant money system, but does not help to solve the main problem of injustices ingrained in it. In order to create a viable and trustworthy money system, ending injustices embedded in the present system should become a definite priority.[26]

Democratization of money through depoliticization

The fourth faction of monetary reformers proposes complete democratization of the ways money is brought into existence. Although relatively tiny, this group appears to be the most thorough critically and is likely to propose the most just and stable money system. Under this umbrella, however, some tend to favor the total depoliticization of money, while others argue for the money system to be anchored in strong democratic political institutions.

Thomas Greco's views serve as an example of those proposing a thorough depoliticization of money. Among the greatest problems with modern money, Greco sees the fact that the issuance of money has been overly politicized and centralized, and that too much power has been given to the banking regime. In short, the present money system has been too elitist. At the same time, because money is issued through essentially irredeemable debt, a form of artificially created scarcity, it has become economically dysfunctional by concentrating wealth and causing poverty, unemployment, and destruction of the environment.

In his proposal for reinventing our entire money system, Greco departs from the view that "the substance of modern money is credit and every currency is a credit instrument."[27] As pointed out earlier, mainstream economists, bankers, and other financiers also claim that modern money is "credit money," the other side of which, of course, is debt. Yet, for Greco, credit has two very distinct functions: the exchange function, which is a short-term form of credit that helps to pay for the delivery of goods to market and their sale; and the finance function, which is long-term credit that facilitates renewal or increase of productive capabilities. For Greco, long-term sources of credit are savings, because investments should have their origin in savings. In such a money creation system, money "should be matched to goods and services." This is due to the fact that "if more money is put into the economy but more goods are not, the value of a currency will be diluted. Under legal tender, that shows up as rising prices."[28] Although the present conventional money system is also based on credit, it malfunctions mainly because the two functions of credit have been mixed up, and at the same time credit has been politicized and centralized, thus providing the political and banking elite with monopolistic use of credit.[29]

For Greco, giving credit power to people is an alternative to the present system. In an Internet-based, community-oriented money system built around short-term exchanges, money creation would be tied directly to the productive (real) side of the given economy. Capital investments, or long-term credit, would have to be matched by savings rather than financed by the creation of new money through debt, as happens under the present banking system. Thus long-term capital formation would be in principle based in equity, which means that the scope of the gambling aspect of the economy would be reduced substantially while encouraging equity-sharing partnerships for long-term investments. As for short-term credit, Greco argues, only those who offer goods and services for sale in the market would be entitled to issue currency. In the system he proposes, it would then be critical that "*money should be issued on the basis of goods already in the market or on their way to market.*" The amount of currency allowed each issuer to create would be limited to what the individual or business would be able to redeem by selling.[30]

There would be two important vehicles backing Greco's proposed system: the unit of account and credit clearing. Because his stance is that the exchange and accounting functions of money are different matters, buyers and sellers could use their own credit on the basis of "an independent objective unit of account." Although an affixed weight of silver could function as such a unit, Greco believes that "a unit that is defined on the basis of a 'market basket' of commodities" would be more appropriate due to the fact that over a long period of time, the price fluctuations in such a basket would average each other out.[31] The use of exchange credit within a network of buyers and sellers would be controlled by a credit clearing system, in which debits from purchases are offset against credit gained from sales. For him, such a process of "clearing" is both the simplest and most efficient way of settling reciprocal exchanges. In contrast to the local money faction, which proposes to utilize third-party credit instruments as payment media, Greco favors the system in which buyers and sellers would rather "use their own credit within an extensive (eventually global) network of locally controlled credit clearing exchanges."[32] This form of direct credit clearing would provide basis for a future cashless society.

Undoubtedly, Greco's proposal is comparatively utopian, whereby economic exchanges would be freed from political influence and the use of the present politicized money. The foundation of the new system would be privately established clearing associations. Yet the clear separation of money and state he recommends[33] is in fact more a matter of principle than of necessity. In the end Greco admits that central governments eventually "*could* and *should*" play their role in monetary and financial matters.[34] The main role of government would be in providing a stable unit of account that could protect users of different currencies against inflation and deflation. But to achieve this, the measure of value would have to be free from pegging to the national or other currencies. The second important role of government would be to prevent any monopolistic control over credit, be it by government or private entities, and encourage a free private credit clearing system to enable more effective and efficient exchanges of goods and services. The third crucial task for government would be to balance public finance. In Greco's proposal, central as well as local governments could also issue their own currencies, but their creation should be apportioned to the amount of anticipated revenues from taxes and fees. Such currencies would have to be able to circulate on their own merits and compete with other media of exchange.[35]

Among the key concerns of Greco's monetary proposal are that the entire money system should be community based, and that the role of the government should be only supportive to this main drive. Such a system of exchange networks, Greco believes, could eventually become global. The question, however, is whether it could gain such an extensive trust. There has been a growing recognition in economic circles that human behavior in economic exchanges is far from being driven by a uniform set of values, and is more of a subtle mixture of rational and irrational decision making, competition and cooperation, trust and distrust.[36] As a result, the fear is that just as in the case of local money, despite some successful initiatives, many local exchange networks will not exist long enough and gain sufficiently wide trust to provide expected outcomes. It is therefore doubtful that on the wider national and international level the monetary model proposed by Greco would be possible without stronger political backing than he seems to be willing to accept.

One of the main problems with Greco's proposal is the strong confidence he gives to the Enlightenment idea of a minimal state. This is why he insists so much on the depoliticization of money, or a clear separation of money and state. Yet, in reality, the libertarian stance is not free of its internal difficulties. It is being challenged on different grounds. For example, in the view of Foley, market capitalism is not a stable system capable of regulating itself. It requires both "conscious political effort to foster the institutions necessary to make it function at all," and "continuing political and regulatory intervention to keep the pursuit of self-interest from running off the rails."[37] In fact, the advances in human condition and sense of stability, particularly in developed economies, have been to large extent results of strong democratic institutions and collective vigilance.[38] As such, states play an increasingly vital role in modern economies. Expectations of state actions are in particularly high demand in times of crisis, when stimulation of economic activity is needed. This is why it is hard to imagine that all this could be achieved in the depoliticized money system proposed by Greco.

Democratization of money through nomisma

The conviction that the state serves people anchors Zarlenga's proposal for monetary reforms.[39] Like Greco, he also favors democratization of the process through which money is created. In contrast to Greco, however, he praises the virtues of the money system founded upon strong democratic political institutions.

In building his argument, Zarlenga first recognizes the value of Aristotle's concept of money as *nomisma*, or as money based primarily on law. Following some monetary historians, particularly Del Mar, he argues that throughout much of our history money indeed came into existence through legal enactments, and what private banking gradually captured were both the power to create money (through credit/debt issuance) and the legal right to do so. Second, Zarlenga argues that the flourishing of the medieval Venetian and Islamic societies is proof that enrichment is possible without violating the prohibition of usury. Their success was (and still is, in the case of Islamic banking) anchored in the principle that return on investment was (and still is) tied to *actual profits* resulting from sharing of risks, which ultimately contribute to real economy. Third, examples from US history demonstrate that government has generally maintained a "good monetary management," which totally contrasts with "generally nefarious business dealings by the bankers."[40] This convinced Zarlenga that Aristotle's concept of money as *nomisma* is the right direction for the modern money system. Fourth, in contrast to Greco, for whom "the substance of modern money is credit and every currency is a credit instrument,"[41] Zarlenga takes the stance that money and credit represent two different constructs. For him, those who argue that credit "is the only form of money, should realize that they are actually defining 'money' out of existence, and substituting 'credit' for it."[42]

On the basis of such building blocks, Zarlenga proposes that the present government monetary departments "should evolve into a fourth branch of government," in addition to the executive, judicial, and legislative branches. As such, it would be responsible for democratically controlled, government-issued, debt-free money. In contrast to the current workings of monetary policies that aim only at "managing the money system," the fourth branch would gear the money creation toward "general welfare."[43] It would end the "unjust money and banking system" as we know it, and with it the extraordinary privileges of the small group of banking elite. Another group of losers, according to Zarlenga, would be the ideologues, mainly economists, who "devote careers to justifying the worst predations upon mankind," and thus "value so-called free markets above life itself." The winners, of course, would be the rest of the public.[44]

The second crucial aspect of Zarlenga's proposal is to end the present fractional reserve banking system and institute the 100 percent "reserve solution."[45] Such a "solution," nevertheless, does not mean that banks would simply be required to keep 100 percent reserves, as this would lead to "disastrous deflation, and a repudiation of all monetary and banking reform." Rather, what forms the 100 percent reserve solution is cheaply created government money, which could be loaned to banks at very low rates. Banks in turn could use these loans to fulfill the 100 percent reserve requirement. This means that banks, unlike now, would make loans only on the basis of the funds they actually had. Quite likely such a reform would not resolve all the problems involved with bank failures, particularly if banks and borrowers engaged in reckless lending/borrowing activities, but the potential bankruptcies (most likely extremely rare) would not bring down the entire banking system and with it the money system. Yet perhaps more importantly, the outcome would be that the banks would become "servants" of the public rather than continue being its "masters."

The third aspect of Zarlenga's proposal of monetary reform is to put in place programs and legislation that would back government money creation and the 100 percent reserve solution for banks.[46] One of the important tasks of the fourth branch of government would be to provide the public with all the money needed for its proper functioning and to raise the quality of infrastructure and quality of life. Definitely, some would be very much concerned that equipped with such monetary powers government could engage in irresponsible creation of money and stir up inflation. Yet it has to be admitted that in the present money system inflation is already almost a constant threat to economy. Moreover, according to the Keynesian view, injection of new money into the economy (demand) drives up prices only if its productive (supply) side of the equation remains unchanged. Along this line, Zarlenga argues that "when new money is used to create real wealth, such as goods and services, . . . there need not be inflation because real things of real value are being created at the same time as the money, and the existence of those real values for living, keeps prices down."[47]

The major task of the fourth branch of government, then, would be to strike this important balance between the needs of the real economy and the *amount* of money put into circulation. (As the case of the paper fiat money issued in China by the Southern Song shows, what is crucial for the money in circulation is not what it is made of but the right amount of it.) Additionally, while the nationalized money creation and the 100 percent reserve solution could bring more justice into the monetary system, it still would be pivotal to put in place stricter usury laws on diverse forms of lending. Yet perhaps the biggest challenge for the fourth branch of government would be not so much overcoming extraordinary privileges of the banking elite, but facing group interests and powerful ideologies that are the ultimate obstacles to monetary reform.

Amid scarcity, abundance

Ideology of scarcity causes modern economic thinking to attach the meaning of scarcity to virtually all diverse resources available for economic activity, and thus encourages fierce competition. This in turn has an immense destructive impact on the environment, community relations, and quality of life. A money system anchored in the Aristotelian concept of *nomisma* offers a way out of the scarcity deadlock.

Abundance of the *nomisma* money system

Considering all that this study has argued, Zarlenga's proposal for monetary and financial reforms appears the soundest. The money system suggested by

Greco, although anchored in deep human longings for a life of freedom from the state, is actually quite utopian. The reality is that, due to huge diversities of modern societies, we not only allow governments to play a bigger role, but actually demand their increasingly growing participation in our daily lives. In fact, we allow ourselves to be immersed in an ever-deeper contradiction. On the one hand, we expect governments to be responsible for the diverse economic, social, and cultural strata of our life. So we expect subsidies for, or at least protection of, some of the sectors of our economies, good transportation and communication infrastructures, safety of our communities, functional justice systems, efficient public services, good education, support for medical care, well-functioning pension systems, care for the unemployed and disadvantaged, well-equipped cultural centers, sports facilities and recreation areas, care for the environment, and so on. On the other hand, we are bombarded with the notion of the small state, which stays away from our lives. Along the lines of this narrative, we expect governments to function on the basis of the money they can collect from taxes and fees, but at the same time expect these taxes and fees to be low, and governments (ideally) to run no public debts.

Every election is a reenactment of this drama whereby our expectations are revived, and are often matched by promises of the candidates. Yet what often follows are disappointments as, under present arrangements, governments are simply incapable of meeting many of our expectations. The attempts to ground a money system in the Enlightenment idea of minimal state and free market are merely ideologies that ultimately hurt us. Through long historical processes we have managed to entrust execution of justice, including death penalties in the case of some countries, to the judicial branch of government. Why could we not entrust modern democratic governments with the power to create money?

Equipped with government-issued, debt-free money, which could be issued cheaply and at the same time meet the demands of justice, economies could be boosted with enormous creative potential. The present debt money system suppresses this potential. Yet perhaps even more importantly, our economies would become more stable, as the new money system would reduce substantially the gambling aspect (money for the sake of money) of modern economies and divert more resources into the real economy. The requirement that banks could only issue loans backed by the funds they actually had would reinforce one of the crucial economic tenets, as found for example in Islamic finance, that capital is the basis of credit, and not vice versa.

Once the scarcity aspect of money disappeared, grassroots communities could gain far larger empowerment than what could be achieved under the current system. At present, local economies rely heavily on outside investments, and thus have to constantly compete for them through creating conditions "attractive" to investors. The result often is that investors bully local governments to offer increasingly attractive conditions to invest (or continue investing) in their con-stituencies, or move elsewhere as soon as they find it more attractive. A stable national currency provided in sufficient amounts would substantially diminish the need for local monies, which tend to have a shorter life span. Communities endowed with all the money they *need* could immensely improve infrastructures, but perhaps more importantly could make economies much "greener" by providing a far larger quantity of locally produced and locally sold products (including an increase in organic products) and services. As such, the *nomisma* money system would naturally add far more care for the environment than any present initiative. With it, our economies would also become decentralized and freed from a destructive globalizing drive and currency wars.

Additionally, the local communities supplied with sufficient amounts of money could radically increase employment and provide far better care for the needy in our societies. Despite governments' declarations of fighting unemployment, the truth is that global unemployment has been on the rise. In many countries, it has also begun to affect educated youth.[48] According to Bernard Condon and Paul Wiseman, the situation in job markets is in fact "worse than it appears," and "most of the jobs will never return" while "millions more are likely to vanish as well." In contrast to the widespread view that jobs are being taken over by booming economies in China and other developing countries, Condon and Wiseman argue that loss of jobs is increasingly affecting "the service sector, home to two-thirds of all workers," and that "they are being obliterated by technology."[49]

For years, the dominant belief was that technological advancements help boost employment. While this might be true for those who can quickly tap into their use, there is a growing concern that technology further alienates the lower classes from the job market. It becomes increasingly apparent that now "entire employment categories are beginning to disappear faster than labor economists had believed as computer software, robots and other devices become more sophisticated and powerful – and millions of more jobs will follow suit."[50] Undeniably, an increase in labor mobility could help to mitigate the problem. The difficulty, however, is that in many parts of the world labor mobility has already become problem in itself as it increases social tensions. Additionally, many people still prefer to be rooted in communities that they nurture and by which they are nurtured. Equipped with sufficient amounts of money, local governments could relatively easily deal with the pressing problem of unemployment. As a matter of fact, unemployment would likely become more a matter of choice than of necessity. In similar vein, with sufficient monetary resources, local governments could meet many other social needs arising in their respective communities.

Moreover, government-issued, debt-free money could immensely reduce the burden of taxes. In reality, government would need taxes mainly to help circulation of money rather than as the prime source for its proper functioning. Because in the new money system taxes could actually be lowered, quite likely a reduction of tax avoidance or even tax evasion could follow, thus encouraging wealthy individuals to keep money and spend it in their respective communities instead of investing offshore.

In short, the economic, social, environmental, and even moral arguments for debt-free government-issued money are very strong. Throughout this study, the present money system has often been termed the debt money system. A cold look at the situation, however, may draw us to the conclusion that we actually do not have a money system. What we now possess is a complex system of money substitutes, which provide enormous power and financial benefit for those who know how to take advantage of the system. Restoration of the debt-free *nomisma* form of money would in fact bring money back. Such a money system would provide communities with much greater control over their economies and their own well-being.

Philosophical and moral potential of nomisma

As we consider the various advantages of the new money system, it is also worth returning to the more basic philosophical and moral questions of *what* money really is, *who* should control it, and *why*. Graeber has pointed out that within any given community, "pretty much anything could function as money, provided everyone knew there was *someone* willing to accept it to cancel out a debt."[51] This view actually reflects the stance that favors giving much more autonomy to local currencies. Yet as presented earlier, the greatest problem with the local money movement is that it does not challenge the power of banks to create money as debt found in the present monetary system, but simply attempts to coexist with the dominant form of money creation and to supplement its shortcomings. In effect, the proponents of local money look for quick solutions to the problem of how to alleviate cash shortages in local communities, but ultimately they give in to the same notion, as does the present system, that the essence of money is in debt, and thus also to the injustices associated with it. According to Zarlenga, "if society defines money as credit/debt . . . then the bankers will control the system."[52] Thus the proponents of local money find it difficult to answer the questions of *who* ultimately controls the issuance of money and *why* its local aspect is so essential. Perhaps this is also the reason why local monies, despite their relatively long practice, can hardly bring long-term benefits, and many of them do not exist long enough and gain sufficient trust to make a more apparent impact on local economies.

Still for some, the essence of money is in certain commodities, the inherent value of which can function as means of exchange, unit of account, and store of value. While this stance answers the question of *what* money is, it also faces the problem of *who* controls the issuance of money, and *why*. Money cannot be easily abstracted from law and power. The question that is particularly neglected in the view of commodity money is the question of power. It is not difficult to foresee that there would be a definite drive toward the control of the money commodities, because influence over the supply of such commodities eventually means influence over money. One of the lessons from monetary history is that "if society defines money as a commodity (wealth) then the wealthy will control the system."[53] The most likely outcome of commodity money would be a new kind of plutocracy.

The argument Greco poses, on the other hand, equates the essence of money with credit. As a matter of fact, he reduces the function of money only to exchange. In his view, "*money should serve only to facilitate the exchange of goods and services.*" However, in order to make money fulfill the exchange function, there is a need of a mutually agreed unit of account. For Greco, this is where the state enters into an otherwise stateless money system. The role of the state is to provide a stable and widely recognized unit of account "declared on the basis of a specific value standard that is defined in concrete physical terms."[54] As for the "store of value," Greco appears to equate it with the *amount* of financial assets held as savings (defined by him as "financial claims"). As such, savings are not money, because they have only a long-term finance (investment) function, which is different from the exchange function facilitated by money.[55]

In the end, then, Greco totally departs from the view that money should serve all three functions – the means of exchange, unit of account, and store of value. For him, the three functions "do not describe the *essence* of money" because "the essence of money is credit,"[56] and so he considers them as separate categories. Yet he does not really explain *why* credit should be the essence of money, despite the fact that money and credit are normally considered as denoting two different constructs.[57] At the same time it is also rather perplexing why Greco has to theoretically separate the three functions of money to improve exchanges that remain suppressed by the present dysfunctional form of money. Why, for example, could savings not function as means of exchange, or simply money? Why can't the store of value be viewed as the *capability* to facilitate future exchanges, or again, money? Aristotle already argued that the store of value was a sort of guarantee for future exchanges when the necessity was not immediate.[58] Furthermore, why can the state only decide the unit of account, and why must it be defined in commodity terms?

It is also important to note that Greco stresses his interest in working out "a good theory" of money that would promote "social justice, economic equity, and personal freedom."[59] Over 2300 years ago, Aristotle already came up with a theory of money rooted precisely in the values in which Greco is interested. However, Greco has somehow missed Aristotle. Interestingly, while Greco separates the three functions of money in what he assumes to be a just and equitable theory, Aristotle, in order to achieve the same end, actually connects all three functions. The reason is that Aristotle brought into his theory an overarching concept of *nomisma*, or a social/legal power linking the three functions of money. Greco, on the other hand, in order to preserve his conviction that freedom can be increased by separation of money and state, comes to the conclusion that the three functions of money cannot coexist.

Greco's concern for "personal freedom," however, appears to neglect the fact that enfranchisements of many societies were actually accomplished with the aid of state-issued forms of money. Del Mar, a monetary economist and historian, provides a list of at least the most obvious examples. According to him,

> The Spartans won their liberties with the iron disc of Lycurgus; the Athenians, before the Alexandrian period, rehabilitated the republic with "nomisma," a highly overvalued copper issue; the Romans overthrew their kings

with the aid of overvalued "nummi," whose emissions were controlled and regulated by the State, *ex senatus consulto*. The earliest republic in Europe which had the courage to defy the moribund hierarchy of Caesar was that of Novgorod whose money was impressed upon leather and, doubtless, issued by the State; the money of the Scandinavian revolution was the "klippings" of Gustavus Vasa, which were issued by the State; the money by the aid of which Gustavus Adolphus saved the Protestant religion from being stamped out by Ferdinand the Catholic was overvalued copper "rundstyks," issued by the State; the money of the Dutch revolution was the pasteboard "dollars" issued by the city of Leyden; of American revolution, the paper notes issued by the colonial governments; of the French revolution, the "assignats" and "mandats" issued by the National Assembly; and of the anti-slavery war in the United States, "greenbacks." All these moneys were issued and the emissions were controlled by the State.[60]

Undoubtedly, Greco's argument for personal freedom reflects utopian long-ings that freedom increases only with a decrease of the role of the state in our lives. The above examples show that the concepts of state and freedom are not necessarily antagonistic in content. This is why the proposal of separating money from the state would be a move in the wrong direction. As argued earlier, the problem is not so much in depoliticizing money power, but in democratizing it. Apparently for Greco, democratization of money could only mean a clear separation of money and state.

In contrast to Greco's view that the essence of money is credit, Zarlenga comes to a very Aristotelian conclusion, that "money's essence (apart from whatever is used to signify it) is an *abstract social power embodied in law*, as an unconditional means of payment." According to him, only by understanding money as "an abstract legal power" can "control over money and society" be under a "constitutional system of checks and balances to potentially *promote welfare*."[61] This view most clearly expresses *what* money really is, *who* controls its issuance, and for what purpose (*why*). As such, this "*abstract social power embodied in law*" entitles its holders to put claims on diverse forms of wealth exercised within its legal confines. (Unfortunately, we have equated money with wealth, and forgotten that money is merely a claim on wealth.)

Even if money now increasingly takes on the form of "an information sys-tem,"[62] the "abstract social power embodied in law" can still form the backbone of the system. Greco in his theorizing avoids precisely this question of power. This is also why he ultimately has to separate the three functions of money. In fairness to Greco, he is absolutely right: one of the main problems with the present money system is the control of money as scarcity, and that the secret to money ultimately lies in trust (credit). But is the separation of three functions of money necessary to overcome the scarcity and gain trust? Could we not trust government-issued debt-free money that could easily resolve the present problem of scarcity? As argued throughout this study, and as histori-cal data show, creation of a sufficient amount of government-issued debt-free money is indeed possible and can bring about diverse economic and social advancements. But it has to be immediately added that only a money system that is democratic, transparent, and based on commensurability of values (just) can gain sufficient long-term trust.

By anchoring the theory of money in the Aristotelian concept of *nomisma*, we could expand a far more stable form of equity financing of partnerships, examples of which are present Islamic and Christian initiatives of usury avoidance and ethically charged investments.[63] At the same time, we could also make more clear distinctions between money, currency, and credit. In the view of such a stance, money would be a general term defined as a government-issued representation of the public power that has both transaction and justice functions, and that simultaneously is means of exchange, unit of account, and store of value for future exchanges. As for currency, it would stand for money of a given legal entity: a country or a zone. Credit, on the other hand, would denote a form of capital backed by the funds the lender actually possesses, which has a financial function.

Furthermore, the Aristotelian concept of money as *nomisma* could also sharpen our perception of wealth. The traditional/classical meaning of wealth was of broadly understood human well-being, which could be achieved only in the right social context, and thus had intrinsic social connotations. From an economic perspective, the concept of wealth was correlated with an abundance of land and natural resources in our environment, as well as an adequate production of goods and services (Adam Smith still kept such an understanding of wealth). Neoclassical economics not only privatized the meaning of wealth, but also defined it in contrast to scarcity. In the view of Clark, "the switch to 'scarcity' as a fundamental concept in economic theory greatly changed the theoretical handling of wealth. It now became directly linked to issues of scarcity and transferability, qualities normally associated with financial assets."[64]

While modern individuals increasingly indulge themselves with virtual wealth (in the form of digital and paper abstractions), which gradually takes over our grossly overfinancialized economies, genuine wealth lies primarily in what the environment can provide us and in the quality of life of our communities. The *nomisma* money system could tremendously definancialize our notion of wealth and strengthen the creation of more wealthy communities.

In the discussion of money, Aristotle, the scholastics, and many others were primarily driven by moral concerns, justice being one of them. More than a century ago, Del Mar described the money system as society's greatest dispenser of justice or injustice:

> money is, perhaps, the mightiest engine to which man can lend his guidance. Unheard, unfelt, almost unseen, it has the power to so distribute the burdens, gratifications, and opportunities of life, that each individual shall enjoy that share of them to which his merits entitle them, or to dispense them with so partial a hand as to violate every principle of justice, and perpetuate a succession of social slaveries to the end of time.[65]

Later, Irving Fisher concurred:

> It is no exaggeration to say that stable money will, directly and indirectly, accomplish much social justice and go far toward the solution of our industrial, commercial and financial problems. There are, I believe, a few other reforms more important. But, among strictly economic reforms, it stands, in my opinion, supreme. When we really get stable units of money we shall have the greatest economic boon of all time.[66]

Over the past several centuries, money as "dispenser of justice" has been hijacked by private interests, which managed to bury injustices associated with usury in the entire system, thus effectively institutionalizing and legalizing usury. As a result, the system we have now "obstructs the creation of values; gives special privileges to some and disadvantage to others; causes unfair concentration of wealth and power; leads to social strife and eventually warfare and a thousand unforeseen bad consequences."[67]

In contrast to the current debt money system, the debt-free *nomisma* money system could result in a much more thorough fulfillment of the principles of justice. Equipped with such money, governments could far better meet the demands of contributive justice by substantially reducing the present practice of "forcing" ordinary people to go into debt to provide economies with a sufficient amount of money for their proper functioning. At the same time, something called public debt would become basically irrelevant, and with it also such notions as budget cuts and austerity programs, themselves very controversial from the perspective of justice. Moreover, the requirement that banks could issue loans only when they could back them by the funds they actually had, or in other words, requiring banks to meet the demands of commensurability in loan contracts, would bring the banking system closer to fulfillment of the dictates of commutative justice. As such, the banking system would also be built upon a sounder foundation than the present one based upon institutional usury. Additionally, the *nomisma* money system could supply local governments with sufficient amounts of money to offer far more adequate care for the needs of their respective communities. As a result, the "abundance" of money could make the entire system fulfill more effectively the demands of distributive justice.

True, as pointed out by Lanchester, "capitalism is not inherently fair: it does not, in and of itself, distribute the rewards of economic growth equitably. Instead it runs on the bases of winner take all and to them that hath shall be given."[68] Moreover, throughout history, justice often struggled against individual or clannish money interests, and unfortunately was often on the losing side. These facts, however, should not be reasons for inaction. We should never stop searching for more just arrangements of *all* systems that so thoroughly affect and shape our society.

By refocusing the money system, and ultimately our economies, on abundance, we could reinforce the age-old conviction that as human beings, we should direct our efforts to subverting greed, not extolling it. Religious and wisdom traditions have always claimed that greed is not an admirable trait of the human person, and therefore have always tried to keep greed at bay.[69] Control of desires also means restraining the insatiability of possessing, which, if given free rein, eventually enslaves. "To possess enslaves, says the wisdom of all ages."[70] Greed is not good, no matter how many modern gurus claim the contrary. Money and the obsession for it cannot be the sole purpose of a worthy human life. Promoting the common good is the purpose of life. Only money issued with the goal of facilitating just exchanges and the common good can gain sufficient moral force to change our economies, our communities, and perhaps even the ways we perceive our world. The present debt money system, which contributes so immensely to a small number of private interests, will only deepen decadence.

Notes

1 See, for example, R. Heinberg, *The End of Growth: Adapting to Our New Economic Reality*, Gabriola Island, BC, Canada: New Society, 2011.
2 P. Krugman, 'Making Banking Boring', *International Herald Tribune*, 11–12 April 2009, p. 7.
3 B. Eichengreen, *Exorbitant Privilege: The Rise and Fall of the Dollar and the Future of the International Monetary System*, New York: Oxford University Press, 2011.
4 J. Rickards, *Currency Wars: The Making of the Next Global Crisis*, New York: Portfolio/Penguin, 2011.
5 Ibid., see esp. pp. 98–124.
6 S. Zarlenga, *The Lost Science of Money: The Mythology of Money – the Story of Power*, Valatie, NY: American Monetary Institute, 2002, p. 616.
7 M. Rowbotham, *The Grip of Death: A Study of Modern Money, Debt Slavery and Destructive Economics*, 4th ed., Charlbury, UK: Jon Carpenter, 2009, p. 140.
8 Rickards, *Currency Wars*, p. 85.
9 Ibid., p. 232.
10 E.g., J.E. Stiglitz, *Globalization and Its Discontents*, London: Penguin Books, 2002; J.E. Stiglitz, *The Roaring Nineties: Why We Are Paying the Price for the Greediest Decade in History*, London: Penguin Books, 2003; E.H. Brown, *The Web of Debt: The Shocking Truth about Our Money System and How We Can Break Free*, 3rd ed., Baton Rouge, LA: Third Millennium Press, 2008; Rowbotham, *The Grip of Death*, esp. pp. 131–149; Zarlenga, *The Lost Science of Money*, pp. 612–619.
11 M. Skousen, *Vienna and Chicago: Friends or Foes?* Washington, DC: Capital Press, 2005, pp. 141–145.
12 C. Menger, *Principles of Economics*, Auburn, AL: Ludwig von Mises Institute, 2007, p. 262.
13 Skousen, *Vienna and Chicago*, pp. 141–144.
14 M.N. Rothbard, *The Case For a 100 Percent Gold Dollar*, Auburn, AL: Ludwig von Mises Institute, 2005[1974], p. 27.
15 Rickards, *Currency Wars*, p. 255.
16 Ibid., pp. 234–235.
17 In Skousen, *Vienna and Chicago*, p. 151.
18 Zarlenga, *The Lost Science of Money*, p. 568.
19 Rickards, *Currency Wars*, p. 235.

20 Zarlenga, *The Lost Science of Money*, p. 659.
21 Cf. T.H. Greco, *The End of Money and the Future of Civilization*, White River Junction, VT: Chelsea Green, 2009, p. 56.
22 P. North, *Local Money: How to Make It Happen in Your Community*, Totnes, Devon: Transition Books, 2010, pp. 20–21.
23 Zarlenga, *The Lost Science of Money*, p. 660.
24 North, *Local Money*, p. 47.
25 Zarlenga, *The Lost Science of Money*, p. 660.
26 Cf. ibid.
27 Greco, *The End of Money*, p. 208.
28 Ibid., see esp. pp. 58–60 and 214–227; the quotations are from p. 58.
29 Ibid., p. 100.
30 Ibid., pp. 162 and 146, respectively; italics his.
31 Ibid., pp. 121–122.
32 Ibid., pp. 104 and 121, respectively.
33 Ibid., see esp. pp. 76–86.
34 Ibid., p. 205; italics his.
35 Ibid., pp. 207–213.
36 E.g., D. Kahneman, P. Slovic and A. Tversky (eds.), *Judgment Under Uncertainty: Heuristics and Biases*, Cambridge: Cambridge University Press, 1982; J. Schlefer, *The Assumptions Economists Make*, Cambridge, MA: Belknap Press of Harvard University Press, 2012; P.A. Ubel, *Free Market Madness: Why Human Nature Is at Odds with Economics – and Why It Matters*, Boston, MA: Harvard Business Press, 2009; D. Ariely, *Predictably Irrational*, New York: HarperCollins, 2008.
37 D.K. Foley, *Adam's Fallacy: A Guide to Economic Theology*, Cambridge, MA: Belknap Press of Harvard University Press, 2008, p. 224.
38 M.A. Martinez, *The Myth of the Free Market: The Role of the State in a Capitalist Economy*, Sterling, VA: Kumarian Press, 2009, pp. 286–287.
39 Zarlenga, *The Lost Science of Money*, see esp. pp. 650ff.
40 Ibid., p. 450.
41 Greco, *The End of Money*, p. 208.
42 Zarlenga, *The Lost Science of Money*, p. 661.
43 Ibid., p. 667.
44 Ibid., pp. 667–668.
45 Ibid., pp. 669–674.
46 Ibid., pp. 674–682.
47 Ibid., p. 743.
48 International Labor Organization. Available at: http://www.ilo.org/global/about-the-ilo/newsroom/news/WCMS_202320/lang--en/index.htm (accessed 28 January 2013).
49 B. Condon and P. Wiseman, 'Recession and Technology Killing Off Middle Class Jobs', *Taipei Times*, 27 January 2013, p. 9.
50 Ibid.
51 D. Graeber, *Debt: The First 5,000 Years*, Brooklyn, NY: Melville House, 2011, p. 74; italics his.
52 Zarlenga, *The Lost Science of Money*, p. 728.
53 Ibid.
54 Greco, *The End of Money*, pp. 115 and 207; italics his.
55 Ibid., p. 214ff.
56 Ibid., p. 114; italics his.
57 Zarlenga, *The Lost Science of Money*, p. 661.
58 Aristotle (T. Irwin, trans.), *Nicomachean Ethics*, Indianapolis: Hackett, 1999, V, 1133b.

59 Greco, *The End of Money*, p. 114.
60 A. Del Mar, *History of Monetary System*, Honolulu, HI: University Press of the Pacific, 2000[1896], pp. 279–280; italics his.
61 Zarlenga, *The Lost Science of Money*, p. 728; italics added.
62 Greco, *The End of Money*, p. 1.
63 C.J. Mews and I. Abraham, 'Usury and Just Compensation: Religious and Financial Ethics in Historical Perspective', *Journal of Business Ethics*, 2007, vol. 72, p. 11.
64 C.M.A. Clark, 'Wealth as Abundance and Scarcity: Perspectives from Catholic Social Thought and Economic Theory', in H. Alford, C.M.A. Clark and M.J. Naughton (eds.), *Rediscovering Abundance: Interdisciplinary Essays on Wealth, Income, and Their Distribution in the Catholic Social Tradition*, Notre Dame, IN: University of Notre Dame Press, 2006, p. 42.
65 A. Del Mar, *A History of Money in Ancient Countries: From the Earliest Times to the Present*, London: George Bell and Sons, 1885, p. 345.
66 I. Fisher, *The Money Illusion*, New York: Adelphi, 1928, p. 182.
67 Zarlenga, *The Lost Science of Money*, p. 727.
68 J. Lanchester, *I.O.U.: Why Everyone Owes Everyone and No One Can Pay*, New York: Simon & Schuster, 2010, p. 23.
69 P.F. Knitter and C. Muzaffar (eds.), *Subverting Greed: Religious Perspectives on the Global Economy*, Maryknoll, NY: Orbis Books, 2002.
70 J.T. Godbout (D. Winkler, trans.), *The World of the Gift*, Montreal: McGill-Queen's University Press, 1998, p. 215.

Conclusions

"Until we change the way money works, we change nothing."[1]

The aim of this study has not been to design new monetary or banking systems, but to show that stability of our money, and indeed, economic systems, cannot be devoid of principles of justice. The main purpose of this work has been to demonstrate *why* a change is needed. Clearly, Noonan's statement that "usury today is a dead issue"[2] has been at least very misleading. A long time ago, Aristotle, and later the scholastics, inserted the idea of justice into our economic thinking. Considering their perspective, it becomes more obvious how our modern money system has become a power mechanism that is truly destructive to our real economies. Perhaps it is worth it to look back and see that their ideas are actually still relevant. At the same time, historical analysis of the control over the issuance of money shows obvious paradigm shifts. This, in turn, suggests that a new money paradigm is as realistic as shifts of the past. It appears that such a new paradigm is necessary if we are to overcome a progressive financialization of entire economies, the growth of money manias, and the inherent instability of the modern economic system.

At present, the world has more than sufficient intellectual expertise, as well as technological ability, to design a far better system than the current one. We have the potential to design money and banking systems that are more just (in all the dimensions of justice discussed here), and stable as well. We have the capability to create a more harmonious economic and financial world order, if only we can convince centers of power to change directions.

Undoubtedly, any such attempt will face very strong opposition. The most likely counter-faction is a relatively small, extremely privileged group of financial fat cats supported by a (perhaps) small number of politicians – the modern world plutocracy. Only by curbing their exorbitant privileges, particularly the power of banks to create money out of thin air (through issuance of debt), can we extend democratic and more just processes into the spheres of money and finance.

Yet perhaps an even more challenging task that humanity faces now is to distance itself from ideologies that at present influence us far more that we are willing to admit. One of those ideologies is the idea of the minimal state, allowing the free market to play an almost sacred role in our world. According to this ideology, the laws of the market exceed the laws that our institutions attempt to put in place to make the market work better for the common benefit (thus ascribing to the market a sort of omnipotence). The market knows better than any regulator (thus ascribing it omniscience). The market is best at distributing rewards, expressed for example in the famous cliché that the rising tide lifts all boats (thus ascribing it benevolence).[3] The sheer truth, however, is that such a market is a pure myth.[4] Yet apparently in order to preserve an idealized notion of freedom, many of us prefer to stick to such myths.

The second strand of ideologizing we have to face is in economics itself. Perhaps the biggest problem with modern mainstream economics is that it has turned human and public well-being as well as the protection of environment into "externalities." In practical terms this means that certain costs, such as pollution's impact on the environment, wildlife, and human health have been left out of the main concerns of economics. Yet in the long term, such an exclusion of significant costs is at best hazardous if not dangerous.

In fact, the present form of mainstream economics has created its own universe, virtually disconnected from the real world, which is ruled by laws assumed to exist in that universe. As a result, the issues that should actually be among our core concerns in economic thought have been pushed to the margins. Some (more courageous) economic theorists prefer to focus research on those margins. It is such moves that have gradually become a fertile ground for the growth of so-called behavioral economics, ecological economics, and so on. This development, however, does not mean that economics as a social science is becoming more pluralistic. It simply means the margins of modern standard economics are broadening. The vast majority of economic theorists remain faithful to their self-aggrandizing, detached from economic realities, preferring models through which they talk with themselves. Unless the welfare of the human person and care for the environment become the core of economic theorizing, economics will not fulfill its task of being a true social science, and we will not see the profound changes we so desperately need. One could only wish that the world-wide financial crisis that broke out in 2007 would force more openness among a much broader number of economists to face the ideological dogmatism so deeply rooted in modern mainstream economics.

In the process of creating their own universe, both classical and neoclassical economics turned money into a neutral medium facilitating the exchange of goods and services. In reality, however, the influence of money is much broader and deeper than what the mainstream economics assumes. At the turn of the twentieth century, Simmel described money as "most important in illustrating the senselessness and the consequences of the *teleological dislocation*, partly because of the passion with which it is craved for, and partly because of its own emptiness and merely transitional character."[5] Almost a century later, Gay concurred: "it is the dislocation of human purposes by monetary values that is perhaps the most serious of the unanticipated and largely unintended side-effects of capitalist rationality."[6] The symbolism of money suggests that we also need "to focus on the *social relationships* that monetary transaction involves," not merely on the tokens that "mediate those relationships."[7]

One of the great contributions of Aristotelian thought has been its stress on the importance of an objectively set *telos*. For Aristotle, money was not only a means of exchange. Money primarily had a justice function anchored in commensurability of values. The *telos* of money was the good and stability of the community that used it. This teleological thought reminds us that money plays a far more important social role than the simplistic function ascribed to it by the modern mainstream economics. "The teleological dislocation" in the ways modern economics presents the purpose of money needs a thorough reevaluation.

No matter what form it takes, money will remain a strong formative force in modern societies, and information technologies will be increasingly important in this role. What is urgently needed, however, is to build money systems on far more just foundations to truly contribute to the betterment of more people in various societies. The present money system, due to its unjust basis and inherent scarcity, can drag on, causing much unnecessary destruction and suffering. But one cannot build something lasting on an unjust basis; it will eventually break down. Democracies, of which government is an essential part, deserve a far more humane money system. The current plutocratic control of money sooner or later must end. Ultimately, as Abraham Lincoln has said, "the people can and will be furnished with a currency as safe as their own government. Money will cease to be the master and become the servant of humanity. Democracy will rise superior to the money power."[8] One could only add: the sooner, the better – for individuals, communities . . . and the world at large.

Notes

1 M.C. Ruppert, *Confronting Collapse: The Crisis of Energy and Money in a Post Peak Oil World*, White River Junction, VT: Chelsea Green, 2009, p. 222.
2 J.T. Noonan, *The Scholastic Analysis of Usury*, Cambridge, MA: Harvard University Press, 1957, p. 1.
3 Cf. S. Zarlenga, *The Lost Science of Money: The Mythology of Money – the Story of Power*, Valatie, NY: American Monetary Institute, 2002, p. 726.
4 See, for example, M.A. Martinez, *The Myth of the Free Market: The Role of the State in a Capitalist Economy*, Sterling, VA: Kumarian Press, 2009.
5 G. Simmel, *The Philosophy of Money*, 3rd ed., London: Routledge, 2004, p. 490; italics added.
6 C.M. Gay, *Cash Values: Money and the Erosion of Meaning in Today's Society*, Grand Rapids, MI: William B. Eerdmans, 2004, p. 71.
7 C. Cowley, *The Value of Money: Ethics and the World of Finance*, London: Bloomsbury, 2006, p. 93.
8 In M. Rowbotham, *The Grip of Death: A Study of Modern Money, Debt Slavery and Destructive Economics*, 4th ed., Charlbury, UK: Jon Carpenter, 2009, p. 221.

Bibliography

Abbott, E., *Francis Bacon: An Account of His Life and Works*, London: Macmillan, 1885.
Ali, A., 'Globalization and Greed: A Muslim Perspective', in P.F. Knitter and C. Muzaffar (eds.), *Subverting Greed: Religious Perspectives on the Global Economy*, Maryknoll, NY: Orbis Books, 2002, pp. 137–153.
Ali, M.A., *Prohibition of Usury: Islamic and Jewish Practices*, Denver, CO: Outskirts Press, 2009.
Aquinas, T., *Summa Theologiae*. Available at: www.newadvent.org/summa (accessed 11 March 2010).
Ariely, D., *Predictably Irrational*, New York: HarperCollins, 2008.
Aristotle (T. Irwin, trans.), *Nicomachean Ethics*, Indianapolis: Hackett, 1999.
Aristotle (P.L. Phillips Simpson, trans.), *The Politics of Aristotle*, Chapel Hill, NC: University of North Carolina Press, 1997.
Aschheim, J. and Tavlas, G.S., 'Academic Exclusion: The Case of Alexander del Mar', *European Journal of Political Economy*, 2004, vol. 20, 31–60.
Bacon, F. (B. Vickers, ed.), *The Essays or Counsels, Civil and Moral*, Oxford: Oxford University Press, 1999.
Bajaj, V., 'New Blow to Microlenders in Asia', *International Herald Tribune*, 12 May 2011.
———. 'Microlenders Swing from Darlings to Demons', *International Herald Tribune*, 6 June 2011.
Barber, M. and Bate, K., *The Templars*, Manchester: Manchester University Press, 2002.
Barofsky, N.M., 'Where the Bailout Went Wrong', *International Herald Tribune*, 31 March 2011.
Beekun, R.I., *Islamic Business Ethics*, Herndon, VA: International Institute of Islamic Thought, 1997.
Belk, R., 'Gift-Giving Behavior', in J.E. Sheth (ed.), *Research in Marketing*, vol. 2, Greenwich, CT: JAI Press, 1979, pp. 95–126.
Benedict XIV, '*Vix Pervenit* (On Usury and Other Dishonest Profits)', 1745. Available at: www.papalencyclicals.net/Ben14/b14vixpe.htm (accessed 12 November 2011).
Bentham, J., *Defence of Usury*, La Vergne, TN: Dodo Press, 2009.
Berkeley, G., *The Querist*, Rockville, MD: Serenity, 2008.
Bloom, A. (trans.), *The Republic of Plato*, New York: Basic Books, 1991.
Bourdieu, P. 'Selections from *The Logic of Practice*', in A.D. Schrift (ed.), *The Logic of the Gift: Toward an Ethic of Generosity*, New York: Routledge, 1997, pp. 190–230.
———. 'Utopia of Endless Exploitation', *Le Monde Diplomatique*, 8 December 1998. Available at: http://mondediplo.com/1998/12/08bourdieu (accessed 18 October 2008).
Brooks, D., 'America's Culture of Debt', *International Herald Tribune*, 23 July 2008.

————. 'Greed and Stupidity', *International Herald Tribune*, 4–5 April 2009.

————. 'The Great Unwinding', *International Herald Tribune*, 13–14 June 2009.

Brown, E.H., *The Web of Debt: The Shocking Truth about Our Money System and How We Can Break Free*, 3rd ed., Baton Rouge, LA: Third Millennium Press, 2008.

————. *The Public Bank Solution: From Austerity to Prosperity*, Baton Rouge, LA: Third Millennium Press, 2013.

Callahan, G., *Economics for Real People: An Introduction to the Austrian School*, 2nd ed., Auburn, AL: Ludwig von Mises Institute, 2004.

Calomiris, C.W., 'Another Deregulation Myth', American Enterprise Institute, 18 October 2008.

Cato, M.P. and Varro, M.T. (Hooper, W.D., trans.), *On Agriculture*, Cambridge, MA: Harvard University Press; W. Heinemann, Ltd., 1934.

Chang, G.G., *The Coming Collapse of China*, London: Arrow, 2002.

Chang, H.J., *Joseph Stiglitz and the World Bank: The Rebel Within*, London: Anthem Press, 2001.

Cheal, D., ' "Showing Them You Love Them:" Gift Giving and the Dialectic of Intimacy', *Sociological Review*, 1987, vol. 35, 150–169.

————. *The Gift Economy*, London: Routledge, 1988.

Chilton, B., 'Debts', in *The Anchor Bible Dictionary*, New York: Doubleday, 1992, vol. 2, pp. 114–116.

Chown, J.F., *A History of Money: From AD 800*, London: Routledge, 1994.

Cicero, M.T. (A.P. McKinlay, trans.), *Letters of a Roman Gentleman*, Boston: Houghton Mifflin, 1926.

————. (W. Miller, trans.), *De Officiis*, London: Heinemann, 1928.

Clark, C.M.A., 'Wealth as Abundance and Scarcity: Perspectives from Catholic Social Thought and Economic Theory', in H. Alford, C.M.A. Clark and M.J. Naughton (eds.), *Rediscovering Abundance: Interdisciplinary Essays on Wealth, Income, and Their Distribution in the Catholic Social Tradition*, Notre Dame, IN: University of Notre Dame Press, 2006, pp. 28–56.

Clarke, S., 'The Neoliberal Theory of Society', in A. Saad-Filho and D. Johnston (eds.), *Neoliberalism: A Critical Reader*, London: Pluto Press, 2005, pp. 50–59.

Condon, B. and Wiseman, P. 'Recession and Technology Killing Off Middle Class Jobs', *Taipei Times*, 27 January 2013.

Coplestone, F., *A History of Philosophy, vol. 5: Hobbes to Hume*, Westminster, MD: Newman Press, 1959.

Cowley, C., *The Value of Money: Ethics and the World of Finance*, London: Bloomsbury, 2006.

Cullenberg, S., Amariglio, J. and Ruccio, D.F. (eds.), *Postmodernism, Economics and Knowledge*, London: Routledge, 2001.

Curran, C.E., *Catholic Social Teaching 1891–Present: A Historical, Theological, and Ethical Analysis*, Washington, DC: Georgetown University Press, 2002.

Davies, G., *A History of Money: From Ancient Times to the Present Day*, Cardiff, Wales: University of Wales Press, 2002.

Dawood, N.J. (trans.), *The Koran*, London: Penguin Books, 1974.

Del Mar, A., *History of Monetary System*, Honolulu, HI: University Press of the Pacific, 2000[1896].

————. *A History of Money in Ancient Countries: From the Earliest Times to the Present*, London: George Bell and Sons, 1885.

Dempsey, B.W., *Interest and Usury*, London: Dennis Dobson, 1948.

———. *The Functional Economy: The Bases of Economic Organization*, Englewood Cliffs, NJ: Prentice-Hall, 1958.

Derrida, J., *Given Time: I. Counterfeit Money*, Chicago: University of Chicago Press, 1992.

Dickerson, M.A., 'Over-Indebtedness, the Subprime Mortgage Crisis and the Effect on U.S. Cities', *Fordham Urban Law Journal*, 2009, vol. 36:3, 395–425.

Divine, T.F., *Interest: An Historical & Analytical Study in Economics and Modern Ethics*, Milwaukee, WI: Marquette University Press, 1959.

———. 'Usury', in *New Catholic Encyclopedia*, vol. 14, New York: McGraw-Hill, 1967, pp. 498–500.

Douglas, M., 'Foreword: No Free Gifts', in M. Mauss, *The Gift: The Form and Reason for Exchange In Archaic Societies*, New York: W.W. Norton, 2000, pp. vii-xviii.

Doyle, P. (2012) 'Resignation Letter'. Available at: http://cnnibusiness.files.wordpress.com/2012/07/doyle.pdf (accessed 24 July 2012).

Duménil, G. and Lévy, D. (D. Jeffers, trans.), *Capital Resurgent: Roots of the Neoliberal Revolution*, Cambridge, MA: Harvard University Press, 2004.

Eichengreen, B., 'Is Anything Being Done to Prevent Another Crisis?', *Taipei Times*, 25 May 2009.

———. *Exorbitant Privilege: The Rise and Fall of the Dollar and the Future of the International Monetary System*, New York: Oxford University Press, 2011.

Elliott, A.L. and Schroth, R.J., *How Companies Lie: Why Enron Is Just the Tip of the Iceberg*, London: Nicholas Brealey, 2002.

Elliott, C., *Usury: A Scriptural, Ethical and Economic View*, Millersburg, OH: Anti-Usury League, 1902.

Elliot, M. and Gumbel, P., 'The Great Fall', *Time*, 16 February 2009.

Ellis, D., 'The Effect of Consumer Interest Rate Deregulation on Credit Card Volumes, Charge-Offs, and the Personal Bankruptcy Rate', *FDIC: Bank Trends*, no. 98–05, March 1998. Available at: www.fdic.gov/bank/analytical/bank/bt_9805.html (accessed 11 November 2011).

Etzioni, A., *The Moral Dimension: Toward a New Economics*, New York: Free Press, 1990.

Farrell, J.P., *Financial Vipers of Venice: Alchemical Money, Magical Physics, and Banking in the Middle Ages and Renaissance*, Port Townsend, WA: Feral House, 2010.

Ferguson, N., *The Ascent of Money: A Financial History of the World*, New York: Penguin Press, 2008.

Fisher, I., *The Money Illusion*, New York: Adelphi, 1928.

Foley, D.K., *Adam's Fallacy: A Guide to Economic Theology*, Cambridge, MA: Belknap Press of Harvard University Press, 2008.

Forster, E.S. (trans.), *Aristotle: Posterior Analytics. Topica*, London: William Heinemann, 1960.

Foster, J.B. and Magdoff, F., *The Great Financial Crisis: Causes and Consequences*, New York, NY: Monthly Review Press, 2009.

Frier, B.W., 'Interest and Usury in the Greco-Roman Period', in *The Anchor Bible Dictionary*, New York: Doubleday, 1992, vol. 3, pp. 423–424.

Fullbrook, E. (ed.), *A Guide to What's Wrong with Economics*, London: Anthem Press, 2005.

Gaukroger, S., *Francis Bacon and the Transformation of Early-Modern Philosophy*, Cambridge: Cambridge University Press, 2001.

Gay, C.M., *Cash Values: Money and the Erosion of Meaning in Today's Society*, Grand Rapids, MI: William B. Eerdmans, 2004.

Glahn, R. von, *Fountain of Fortune: Money and Monetary Policy in China, 1000–1700*, Taipei: SMC, 1997.

Godbout, J.T. (D. Winkler, trans.), *The World of the Gift*, Montreal: McGill-Queen's University Press, 1998.

Godelier, M., *The Enigma of the Gift*, Chicago: University of Chicago Press, 1999.

Gouldner, A., 'The Norm of Reciprocity: A Preliminary Statement', in A.E. Komter (ed.), *The Gift: An Interdisciplinary Perspective*, Amsterdam: Amsterdam University Press, 1996, pp. 49–66.

Graeber, D., *Debt: The First 5,000 Years*, Brooklyn, NY: Melville House, 2011.

Greco, T.H., *The End of Money and the Future of Civilization*, White River Junction, VT: Chelsea Green, 2009.

Greer, M.J., *The Wealth of Nature: Economics as if Survival Mattered*, Gabriola Island, Canada: New Society, 2011.

Gudeman, S., 'Postmodern Gifts', in S. Cullenberg, J. Amariglio and D.F. Ruccio (eds.), *Postmodernism, Economics and Knowledge*, London: Routledge, 2001, pp. 459–474.

Harvey, D., *A Brief History of Neoliberalism*, Oxford: Oxford University Press, 2005.

Heinberg, R., *The End of Growth: Adapting to Our New Economic Reality*, Gabriola Island, BC, Canada: New Society, 2011.

Henley, J., 'Questions on Greek Crisis Get Answers', *Taipei Times*, 17 June 2012.

Huang, T.L. 'Like "Go West," Credit Debt's a Threat', *Taipei Times*, 27 December 2005.

Hubert, H. and Mauss, M. (W.D. Halls, trans.), *Sacrifice: Its Nature and Function*, London: Cohen & West, 1964.

Hülsman, J.G., *The Ethics of Money Production*, Auburn, AL: Ludwig von Mises Institute, 2008.

Hummel, W., 'Money as Credit', in *Money: What It Is, How It Works*, 2004. Available at: www.wfhummel.net (accessed 22 March 2012).

———. 'Understanding Money: The Monetary Base', in *Money: What It Is, How It Works*, 2005.

———. 'The Banking System: The Federal Reserve System', in *Money: What It Is, How It Works*, 2006.

———. 'Some Common Misconceptions', in *Money: What It Is, How It Works*, 12 March 2008.

———. 'Understanding Money: Money Basics', in *Money: What It Is, How It Works*, 2008.

———. 'Government Finance: Seigniorage', in *Money: What It Is, How It Works*, 2010.

———. 'The Interest Time Bomb', in *Money: What It Is, How It Works*, 2011.

Hutchins, M. (ed.), *Great Books of the Western World, vol. 7, Plato: The Seventh Letter*, Chicago: Encyclopedia Britannica, 1952.

———. (ed.), *Great Books of the Western World, vol. 35: Locke, Berkeley, Hume*, Chicago: Encyclopedia Britannica, 1952.

Jasnow, R., 'Pre-Demotic Pharaonic Sources', in R. Westbrook and R. Jasnow (eds.), *Security for Debt in Ancient Near Eastern Law*, Boston: Brill, 2001, pp. 35–45.

John Paul II, 'Apostolic Letter *Tertio Millennio Adveniente* (On Preparation for the Jubilee of the Year 2000)', 1994. Available at: www.vatican.va/holy_father/john_paul_ii/apost_letters/documents/hf_jp-ii_apl_10111994_tertio-millennio-adveniente_en.html (accessed 20 November 2011).

Johnson, S. 'Rise of the Financial Leviathan – Megabanks Fight Off Reform', *Taipei Times*, 23 July 2012.

Kahneman, D., Slovic, P. and Tversky, A. (eds.), *Judgment Under Uncertainty: Heuristics and Biases*, Cambridge: Cambridge University Press, 1982.

Kervick, D., 'An Open Letter to Harvard Economics Students', 10 November 2011. Available at: http://econintersect.com/b2evolution/blog2.php/2011/11/10/an-open-letter-to-harvard-economics-students (accessed 5 January 2012).

Keynes, J.M., *General Theory of Employment, Interest and Money*, San Diego, CA: Harcourt Brace, 1964.

Kim, J. and Bhangananda, K., 'Money for Nothing, Your Crises for Free? A Comparative Analysis of Consumer Credit Policies in Post-1997 South Korea and Thailand', *Pacific Rim Law & Policy Journal*, 2008, vol. 17:1, 1–40.

Kindleberger, C.P., *A Financial History of Western Europe*, London: Routledge, 2006.

Kindleberger, C.P. and Aliber, R.Z., *Manias, Panics, and Crashes: A History of Financial Crises*, 5th ed., Hoboken, NJ: John Wiley & Sons, 2005.

Kittel, G. (ed.), *Theological Dictionary of the New Testament*, vol. 2, Grand Rapids, MI: Eerdmans, 1964.

Knitter, P.F. and Muzaffar, C. (eds.), *Subverting Greed: Religious Perspectives on the Global Economy*, Maryknoll, NY: Orbis Books, 2002.

Komter, A.E. (ed.), *The Gift: An Interdisciplinary Perspective*, Amsterdam: Amsterdam University Press, 1996.

Kristof, N.D., 'A Banker Speaks, with Regret', *International Herald Tribune*, 2 December 2011.

Krugman, P., 'Making Banking Boring', *International Herald Tribune*, 11–12 April 2009.

———. *The Return of Depression Economics and the Crisis of 2008*, New York: W.W. Norton, 2009.

———. 'Eating the Irish', *International Herald Tribune*, 27–28 November 2010.

———. 'Losing Their Immunity', *International Herald Tribune*, 18 October 2011.

Kunstler, J.H., *The Long Emergency: Surviving the Converging Catastrophies of the Twenty-First Century*, London: Atlantic Books, 2005.

———. *Too Much Magic: Wishful Thinking, Technology, and the Fate of the Nation*, New York: Atlantic Monthly Press, 2012.

Lactantius (M.F. McDonald, trans.), *The Divine Institutes, Books I – VII*, Washington, DC: Catholic University of America Press, 1964.

Lanchester, J., *I.O.U.: Why Everyone Owes Everyone and No One Can Pay*, New York: Simon & Schuster, 2010.

Lawson, N., 'Back to reality', *Time*, 13 October 2008.

Lewis, M., *The Big Short: Inside the Doomsday Machine*, New York, NY: W.W. Norton, 2010.

Liddel, H.G. and Scott, R., *A Greek-English Lexicon*, 9th ed., Oxford: Clarendon Press, 1958.

Lindsey, R.R. and Schachter, B., *How I Became a Quant: Insights from 25 of Wall Street's Elite*, Hoboken, NJ: John Wiley & Sons, 2007.

Luther, M., *Three Treatises*, Philadelphia: Fortress Press, 1960.

Lynn, M., *Bust: Greece, the Euro, and the Sovereign Debt Crisis*, Hoboken, NJ: Bloomberg Press, 2011.

MacIntyre, A., *After Virtue*, 3rd ed., Notre Dame, IN: University of Notre Dame Press, 2008.

Malinowski, B., *Crime and Custom in Savage Society*, Paterson, NJ: Littlefield, Adams, 1959.

Maloney, R.P., 'The Teaching of the Fathers on Usury: An Historical Study on the Development of Christian Thinking', *Vigiliae Christianae*, 1973, vol. 27:4, 241–265.

Martenson, C., *The Crash Course: The Unsustainable Future of Our Economy, Energy, and Environment*, Hoboken, NJ: John Wiley & Sons, 2011.

Martinez, M.A., *The Myth of the Free Market: The Role of the State in a Capitalist Economy*, Sterling, VA: Kumarian Press, 2009.

Marx, K., 'Capital', in M. Hutchins (ed.), *Great Books of the Western World, vol. 50: Marx*, Chicago: Encyclopedia Britannica, 1952.

Mauss, M. (W.D. Halls, trans.), *The Gift: The Form and Reason for Exchange in Archaic Societies*, New York: W.W. Norton, 2000[1925].

McCall, B.M., 'Unprofitable Lending: Modern Credit Regulation and the Lost Theory of Usury', *Cardozo Law Review*, 2008, vol. 30:2, 549–615.

McCambley, C., 'Against Those Who Practice Usury by Gregory of Nyssa', *Greek Orthodox Theological Review*, 1991, vol. 36:3–4, 287–302.

McFadyen, A.I., *The Call to Personhood: A Christian Theory of the Individual in Social Relationships*, Cambridge: Cambridge University Press, 1990.

Menger, C., *Principles of Economics*, Auburn, AL: Ludwig von Mises Institute, 2007.

Mews, C.J. and Abraham, I., 'Usury and Just Compensation: Religious and Financial Ethics in Historical Perspective', *Journal of Business Ethics*, 2007, vol. 72, 1–15.

Minsky, H.P., *Can 'It' Happen Again? Essays on Instability and Finance*, Armonk, NY: M.E. Sharpe, 1984.

———. *Stabilizing an Unstable Economy*, New York: McGraw-Hill, 2008[1986].

Mirowski, P., 'Refusing the Gift', in S. Cullenberg, J. Amariglio and D.F. Ruccio (eds.), *Postmodernism, Economics and Knowledge*, London: Routledge, 2001, pp. 431–458.

Mises, L. von, *Human Action: A Treatise on Economics*, 4th ed., San Francisco, CA: Fox & Wilkes, 1996.

———. *The Theory of Money and Credit*, Lexington, KY: Pacific Publishing Studio, 2010.

Mochrie, R.I., 'Justice in Exchange: The Economic Philosophy of John Duns Scotus', *Journal of Markets & Morality*, 2006, vol. 9:1, 35–56.

Mofid, K. and Braybrooke, M., *Promoting the Common Good: Bringing Economics and Theology Together Again*, London: Shepheard-Walwyn, 2005.

Monbiot, G., 'Neoliberals Stole the Wealth of Nations', *Guardian Weekly*, 31 August 2007.

Montesquieu, C., 'The Spirit of Laws', in R.M. Hutchins (ed.), *Great Books of the Western World*, vol. 38, Chicago: Encyclopedia Britannica, 1952, pp. 1–315.

Morgenson, G. and Rosner, J., *Reckless Endangerment: How Outsized Ambition, Greed and Corruption Led to Economic Armageddon*, New York: Times Books, 2011.

Muller, J.Z., *Capitalism and the Jews*, Princeton, NJ: Princeton University Press, 2010.

Munck, R., 'Neoliberalism and Politics, and the Politics of Neoliberalism', in A. Saad-Filho and D. Johnston (eds.), *Neoliberalism: A Critical Reader*, London: Pluto Press, 2005, pp. 60–69.

Nocera, J., 'Bonus Rules Lack Smart Incentives', *International Herald Tribune*, 21–22 February 2009.

———. 'The Good Banker', *International Herald Tribune*, 1 June 2011.

———. 'Why People Hate the Banks', *International Herald Tribune*, 4 April 2012.

Noonan, J.T., *The Scholastic Analysis of Usury*, Cambridge, MA: Harvard University Press, 1957.

———. *Bribes*, New York: Macmillan, 1984.

North, P., *Local Money: How to Make It Happen in Your Community*, Totnes, Devon: Transition Books, 2010.

O'Brien, T.C., 'Legal Debt, Moral Debt', in T. Aquinas, *Summa Theologiae*, vol. 41, Eyre & Spottiswoode, London, 1971, pp. 316–320.

Onions, C.T. (ed.), *The Shorter Oxford English Dictionary*, 3rd ed., London: Oxford University Press, 1952.

Oresme, N., 'A Treatise on the Origin, Nature, Law, and Alterations of Money', in C. Johnson (ed.), *The De Moneta of Nicholas Oresme and English Mint Documents*, London: Thomas Nelson and Sons, 1956.

Osteen, M. (ed.), *The Question of the Gift: Essays across Disciplines*, London: Routledge, 2002.

Owen, R., 'Bank of England Nominees', 2000. Available at: http://forumnews. wordpress.com/about/bank-of-england-nominees (accessed 2 April 2012).

Pangle, T.L. (trans.), *The Laws of Plato*, New York: Basic Books, 1980.

Patterson, O., *Freedom: Freedom in the Making of Western Culture*, vol. 1, New York: Basic Books, 1991.

Patterson, S., *The Quants: How a New Breed of Math Whizzes Conquered Wall Street and Nearly Destroyed It*, New York: Crown Business, 2010.

Petronius (W. Burnaby, trans.), *The Satyricon of Petronius Arbiter*, New York: Modern Library, 1929.

Plutarch (J. Dryden, trans.), *The Lives of the Noble Grecians and Romans*, New York: Modern Library, 1932.

Porter, E., 'On the Origin of Giant Bonuses', *International Herald Tribune*, 10 March 2009.

Pressman, A., 'Community Reinvestment Act Had Nothing to Do with Subprime Crisis', 29 September 2008. Available at: www.businessweek.com/investing/insights/ blog/archives/2008/09/community_reinv.html (accessed 28 November 2011).

Prins, N., *Other People's Money: The Corporate Mugging of America*, New York: New Press, 2004.

Quigley, C., *Tragedy and Hope: A History of the World in Our Time*, New York: Macmillan, 1998[1966].

Reich, R., 'Moral Hazard Is for Suckers', 23 September 2007. Available at: http:// prospect.org/article/moral-hazard-suckers (accessed 12 July 2012).

Reinhart, C.M. and Rogoff, K.S., *This Time Is Different: Eight Centuries of Financial Folly*, Princeton, NJ: Princeton University Press, 2009.

Richey, C.D., *Whom Shall We Trust?* Baltimore: PublishAmerica, 2004.

Rickards, J., *Currency Wars: The Making of the Next Global Crisis*, New York: Portfolio/Penguin, 2011.

Rodrik, D., *The Globalization Paradox: Democracy and the Future of the World Economy*, New York: W.W. Norton, 2011.

Rothbard, M.N., *The Case for a 100 Percent Gold Dollar*, Auburn, AL: Ludwig von Mises Institute, 2005[1974].

———. *A History of Money and Banking in the United States: The Colonial Era to World War II*, Auburn, AL: Ludwig von Mises Institute, 2005.

———. *The Mystery of Banking*, 2nd ed., Auburn, AL: Ludwig von Mises Institute, 2008.

———. *Man, Economy, and State with Power and Market*, 2nd ed., Auburn, AL: Ludwig von Mises Institute, 2009.

Rowbotham, M., *The Grip of Death: A Study of Modern Money, Debt Slavery and Destructive Economics*, 4th ed., Charlbury, UK: Jon Carpenter, 2009.

Rubin, J., *Why Your World Is About to Get a Whole Lot Smaller: Oil and the End of Globalization*, New York: Random House, 2009.

———. *The Big Flatline: Oil and the No-Growth Economy*, New York: Palgrave Macmillan, 2012.

Ruppert, M.C., *Confronting Collapse: The Crisis of Energy and Money in a Post Peak Oil World*, White River Junction, VT: Chelsea Green, 2009.

Ryan-Collins, J., Greenham, T., Werner, R. and Jackson, A., *Where Does Money Come From: A Guide to the UK Monetary and Banking System*, London: New Economics Foundation, 2011.

Sachs, J., 'The Roots of the US Financial Crisis Lie with the Fed', *Taipei Times*, 27 March 2008.

Saft, J., 'Big Winners in Crises: The Banks', *International Herald Tribune*, 13 April 2011.

Sahlins, M., *Stone Age Economics*, Chicago: Aldine de Gruyter, 1972.

Saint Augustine (P. Schaff, ed.), 'Expositions on the Book of Psalms', in *A Select Library of Nicene and Post-Nicene Fathers of the Christian Church*, vol. 8, Edinburgh: T & T Clark, 1996.

Saint Basil (A.C. Way, trans.), *Exegetic Homilies*, Washington, DC: Catholic University of America Press, 1963.

Saint Cyprian (M. Bevenot, trans.), *The Lapsed. The Unity of the Catholic Church*, Westminster, MD: Newman Press, 1957.

Saint Leo the Great (J.P. Freeland and A.J. Conway, trans.), 'Sermons', in *The Fathers of the Church*, vol. 93, Washington, DC: Catholic University of America Press, 1996.

Samuelson, P.A., 'Heed the Hopeful Science', *International Herald Tribune*, 24–25 October 2009.

Sandel, M., *Justice: What's the Right Thing To Do?*, New York, NY: Farrar, Straus and Giroux, 2009.

Scheller, H. K., *The European Central Bank: History, Role and Functions*, Frankfurt am Main, Germany: European Central Bank, 2004.

Schlefer, J., *The Assumptions Economists Make*, Cambridge, MA: Belknap Press of Harvard University Press, 2012.

Schrift, A.D. (ed.), *The Logic of the Gift: Toward an Ethic of Generosity*, New York: Routledge, 1997.

Schumpeter, J., *History of Economic Analysis*, London: Routledge, 1997[1954].

Schwartz, B., 'The Social Psychology of the Gift', in A.E. Komter (ed.), *The Gift: An Interdisciplinary Perspective*, Amsterdam: Amsterdam University Press, 1996, pp. 69–80.

Schwartz, N.D. and Bennhold, K., 'A Suspicion in France "That This Was Inevitable" ', *International Herald Tribune*, 6 February 2008.

Sen, A., *On Ethics and Economics*, Oxford: Blackwell, 2004[1987].

Seneca, L.A. (A. Stewart, trans.), *On Benefits*, Kessinger, n.d.

Simmel, G., *The Philosophy of Money*, 3rd ed., London: Routledge, 2004.

Simpson, R., 'Foreword', in E. Brown, *The Web of Debt: The Shocking Truth about Our Money System and How We Can Break Free*, 3rd ed., Baton Rouge, LA: Third Millennium Press, 2008, pp. xi–xiv.

Singleton, J.D., ' "Money Is a Sterile Thing": Martin Luther on the Immorality of Usury Reconsidered', 2009. Available at: www.econ.ucdenver.edu/home/workingpapers/zinke.pdf (accessed 7 January 2012).

Sinn, H.W., *Casino Capitalism: How the Financial Crisis Came About and What Needs to Be Done Now*, Oxford: Oxford University Press, 2010.

Skidelsky, R. and Skidelsky, E., *How Much Is Enough: Money and the Good Life*, New York: Other Press, 2012.

Skousen, M., *Vienna and Chicago: Friends or Foes?* Washington, DC: Capital Press, 2005.

Smith, A., 'An Inquiry into the Nature and Causes of the Wealth of Nations', in R.M. Hutchins (ed.), *Great Books of the Western World*, vol. 39, Chicago: Encyclopedia Britannica, 1952.

Steinkeller, P., 'The Ur III Period', in R. Westbrook and R. Jasnow (eds.), *Security for Debt in Ancient Near Eastern Law*, Boston: Brill, 2001, pp. 47–62.

Stewart, J.B., 'UBS Faces More Than Just a "Rogue" ', *International Herald Tribune*, 26 September 2011.

Stiglitz, J. and Driffill, J., *Economics*, New York: W.W. Norton, 2000.

Stiglitz, J. E., *Globalization and Its Discontents*, London: Penguin Books, 2002.

———. *The Roaring Nineties: Why We Are Paying the Price for the Greediest Decade in History*, London: Penguin Books, 2003.

Story, L., 'As Foundations Crumbled, Bonuses Rose on Wall St.', *International Herald Tribune*, 19 December 2008.

Stowell, D.P., *An Introduction to Investment Banks, Hedge Funds, and Private Equity: The New Paradigm*, Burlington, MA: Academic Press, 2010.

Ubel, P.A., *Free Market Madness: Why Human Nature Is at Odds with Economics – and Why It Matters*, Boston, MA: Harvard Business Press, 2009.

Weber, M., *The Protestant Ethic and the 'Spirit' of Capitalism*, New York: Penguin Books, 2002.

Weisheipl, J.A., 'Scholastic Method', in *New Catholic Encyclopedia*, vol. 12, New York: McGraw-Hill, 1967, pp. 1145–1146.

Westbrook, R., 'Introduction', in R. Westbrook and R. Jasnow (eds.), *Security for Debt in Ancient Near Eastern Law*, Boston: Brill, 2001, pp. 1–3.

———. 'The Old Babylonian Period', in R. Westbrook and R. Jasnow (eds.), *Security for Debt in Ancient Near Eastern Law*, Boston: Brill, 2001, pp. 63–92.

White, L.H., 'How did we get into this financial mess?', *Cato Institute Briefing Paper*, no. 110, 18 November 2008. Available at: www.cato.org/pubs/bp/bp110.pdf (accessed 17 November 2011).

Wicksell, K., *Interest and Prices*, New York: Sentry, 1965.

Woods, T.E., Jr., *The Church and the Market: A Catholic Defense of the Free Economy*, Oxford: Lexington Books, 2005.

———. *Meltdown: A Free-Market Look at Why the Stock Market Collapsed, the Economy Tanked, and Government Bailouts Will Make Things Worse*, Washington, DC: Regnery, 2009.

Wright, W.C. (trans.), *Philostratus and Eunapius: The Lives of the Sophists*, London: Heinemann, 1922.

Yan, Y.X., *The Flow of Gifts: Reciprocity and Social Networks in a Chinese Village*, Stanford, CA: Stanford University Press, 1996.

Yang, L.S., *Money and Credit in China: A Short History*, Cambridge, MA: Harvard University Press, 1971.

Zarlenga, S., *The Lost Science of Money: The Mythology of Money – the Story of Power*, Valatie, NY: American Monetary Institute, 2002.

Zucker, L.M., 'S. Ambrosii: De Tobia. A commentary, with an introduction and translation', *The Catholic University of America Patristic Studies*, vol. 35. Washington, DC: Catholic University of America, 1933.

Other references

BBC Radio 4, 'Current Affairs Analysis: The Undeadly Sin', 28 November 2002. Available at: http://news.bbc.co.uk/nol/shared/spl/hi/programmes/analysis/transcripts/02_11_28.txt (accessed 5 January 2012).

'Companies Act 2006'. Available at: www.legislation.gov.uk/ukpga/2006/46/section/796 (accessed 2 April 2012).

'Default Settings', *Economist*, 3 April 2010.

'Dismal Ethics', *Economist*, 8 January 2011.

'European Union: Consolidated Versions of the Treaty on European Union and the Treaty Establishing the European Community', *Official Journal of the European Union*, 29 December 2006. Available at: http://eur-lex.europa.eu/LexUriServ/site/en/oj/2006/ce321/ce32120061229en00010331.pdf (accessed 2 April 2012).

'Eurostat Table, 2003–2010: General Government Gross Debt'. Available at: http://epp.eurostat.ec.europa.eu/tgm/table.do?tab=table&plugin=0&language=en&pcode=tsieb090 (accessed 16 November 2011).

'Federal Reserve Pays $77 Billion to Treasury'. Available at: http://money.cnn.com/2012/01/10/news/economy/federal_reserve_pays_treasury/index.htm (accessed 2 April 2012).

'Housing and Community Development Act of 1977/Title VIII'. Available at: http://en.wikisource.org/wiki/Housing_and_Community_Development_Act_of_1977/Title_VIII (accessed 25 November 2011).

International Federation of Red Cross and Red Crescent Societies, Think Differently: Humanitarian Impacts of the Economic Crisis in Europe, Geneva, 2013.

International Labor Organization. Available at: www.ilo.org/global/about-the-ilo/newsroom/news/WCMS_202320/lang--en/index.htm (accessed 28 January 2013).

'Mutually Assured Existence: Public and Private Banks Have Reached a Modus Vivendi', *Economist*, 13 May 2010.

'Open Letter from Economic Students to Professors and Others Responsible for the Teaching of This Discipline'. Available at: www.autisme-economie.org/article142.html (accessed 15 January 2012).

'Repent at Leisure: A Special Report on Debt', *Economist*, 26 June 2010.

'Talking Point: The Euro Debt Crisis – Similarities and Differences', 25 November 2010. Available at: www.dws-investments.com/EN/docs/research/euro_debt_crisis_article.pdf (accessed 12 November 2011).

'Taming Leviathan: A Special Report on the Future of the State', *Economist*, 19 March 2011.

'The Code of Hammurabi'. Available at: www.sacred-texts.com/ane/ham/index.htm (accessed 25 June 2012).

'The Post-Autistic Economics (PAECON)'. Available at: www.paecon.net (accessed 15 January 2012).

'Total Debt to GDP'. Available at: www.gfmag.com/tools/global-database/economic-data/10403-total-debt-to-gdp.html#axzz1bZ41xQQm (accessed 23 October 2011).

'Tulipmania'. Available at: www.investopedia.com/terms/t/tulipmania.asp (accessed 5 January 2012).

UN Conference on Trade and Development (UNCTAD), 'The Least Developed Countries Report 2010: Towards a New International Development Architecture for LDCs', 25 November 2010. Available at: www.ldc2010_embargo_en.pdf (accessed 2 November 2011).

'Usury', *Jewish Encyclopedia*. Available at: www.jewishencyclopedia.com (accessed 10 September 2010).

'What Went Wrong with Economics', *Economist*, 18 July 2011.

Index

148; gift economy 133–134, 139;
human economies 98; local economies 9, 177, 183, 185
education 20, 173, 183
Egypt 34–36, 46
Eichengreen, Barry 101, 119, 167
elite 21, 174; *see also* plutocracy;
financial (banking) elite 128, 179,
181–182
Elliott, Calvin 82
emission 91, 129, 187
empowerment 183
Enlightenment 3–5, 99, 139, 148, 180,
183
Enron 26
enslavement 18, 36–37, 69, 140–141;
see also slavery
enterprise 49, 66, 91, 171
entitlement 169
environment 9, 9n, 34, 161, 171, 173,
177–178, 182–184, 188, 194
equality 4, 42, 49, 146, 160, 163, 168
equilibrium 2, 112
equity 14, 27, 46–47, 58–59, 62–63,
169–170, 179, 188; economic equity
46, 186; return on equity 170
equivalence 42, 59, 63, 68–69, 112,
135–136; *see also* commensurability
and value
euro 23–24, 28, 97, 116, 125, 131n,
138, 174; eurozone (euro area) 28,
115–116, 125, 157–158
Europe 11, 14, 20, 54, 69, 76, 79–81,
83–84, 159, 187; European Union/
EU 24, 27–28, 125–126
evolution 18, 83, 98–100
exchange 3, 8, 19, 41–44, 49, 55,
57, 64, 68–69, 71, 76–79, 82–83,
85–87, 98–99, 101, 107, 109,
111–112, 117–119, 123, 134–136,
144, 148, 160, 167–168, 171,
174–175, 179–180, 186, 188,
190, 194; exchange function 178,
186; exchange network 180; means
(medium) of exchange 3, 42–43, 56,
71, 78–79, 98, 100, 107, 110, 115,
160, 180, 185–186, 188, 195
export 24, 29, 167–168

failure 7, 29, 37, 46, 56, 58, 63, 68, 80,
87–88, 149, 168–169, 172n; bank
failure 27, 86–87, 169, 181; government failure 92–93, 158; too big to
fail 27, 148, 159, 168
Fathers of the church 47–48, 52n, 53, 55

Federal Reserve (Fed) 88, 93, 96n, 101,
108, 116, 118, 120, 123–124, 143;
Federal Reserve Note 118; *see also*
dollar/US dollar
fee 16, 26, 39, 62, 85, 102, 105, 120,
154, 163, 180, 183
Ferguson, Niall 43, 82–83, 86, 90,
98–99
finance 15, 17–20, 27, 29, 34, 58, 80,
82, 84–85, 87, 91, 109, 122, 127,
149, 166, 175, 179, 186, 193; fancy
(exotic) finance 17, 29, 174; finance
function 178; financialization (of
economy) 7, 14–15, 17, 154, 163,
166, 171, 177, 193; financiers 2, 9,
13, 103, 178; international finance
126–127; Islamic finance 69, 183;
microfinance 165–166; public finance
159, 180
financial crisis 5–6, 11–13, 18, 25, 28,
84, 88, 97, 130, 144, 153, 157, 160,
168–170, 171n, 172n, 175–176,
194; financial collapse 1, 6, 173;
financial disruption 9n; financial meltdown 1, 11; financial tsunami 2, 6–7,
13, 18–19, 22, 158–159
financial engineering 25
financial history 27, 85, 99, 130
financial industry (sector) 1, 6, 15, 19,
23, 84, 170, 171n
financial institution 1, 11–13, 23–24,
27, 35, 86, 106, 112, 157; *see also*
institution; nonbank financial institution (NBFI) 106, 162
financial product 16, 89, 130, 166
Fisher, Irving 109, 189
Florence 82
foreigner 81–82, 119, 167
forgiveness 36, 152, 169
France 14, 28, 77, 80–81, 125
Franklin, Benjamin 129
free choice 67
freedom 4–5, 17–18, 20, 138, 140–142,
145, 147, 183, 186–187, 194; *see also*
liberty; freedom from 147–148; freedom within 147; personal (individual)
freedom 4–5, 138–139, 141, 145,
147, 186–187
Friedman, Milton 21–22
Fuggers (the) 84, 95n
fund 13, 16, 34, 56–57, 80, 83, 88,
106, 109, 116, 158, 169, 181, 183,
188–189; International Monetary
Fund (IMF) 11, 28–29, 88, 122,
128, 174–175

212   *Index*